Dominican Series: 1

English for Theology
A Resource for Teachers and Students

Gabrielle Kelly OP

The Dominican Series, a Series of ATF Press, is a joint project of Australian Dominican women and men and offers contributions on topics of Dominican interest and various aspects of church, theology and religion in the world.

Series Editors: Mark O'Brien OP and Gabrielle Kelly OP

ENGLISH FOR SPECIAL PURPOSES

English for Theology

DEVELOPING PROFICIENCY IN ACADEMIC ENGLISH FOR THEOLOGICAL STUDIES

WITH A

SPECIAL FOCUS ON READING SKILLS

An Upper-Intermediate to Advanced English Language Resource Book
for EFL Teachers and
Asia Pacific students of theology from Language Backgrounds Other
Than English

Gabrielle Kelly OP

Copyright 2004 © Gabrielle Kelly OP

All rights reserved. Except for any fair dealing permitted under the Copyright Act, no part of this book may be reproduced by any means without prior permission. Inquiries should be made to the publisher.

First Published 2004

Reprinted 2016

Cover design: Anne Stewart OP

National Library of Australia
Cataloguing-in-Publication data

Kelly, Gabrielle
English for Theology: a resource for teachers and students

Bibliography
ISBN 1 920691 15 4

1. English language - Study and teaching - Foreign speakers.
2. Theology - Terminology. I. Australian Theological Forum
II. Title (Series: Dominican Series; 1)

428.0071

Initial pilot project funded by:
    Dominican Sisters
    11 Mullins Street
    Pasadena, South Australia, 5042

Published by
ATF Press
An Imprint of the Australian Theological Forum
PO Box 504
Hindmarsh SA 5007
Australia
ABN 68 314 074 034
www.atfpress.com Fax +61 8 8340 34 50

Printed by Openbook Print, Adelaide, Australia

To the Word Who is Life

CONTENTS

	Page
Foreword, Gustavo Gutiérrez	ix
Acknowledgments	xi
Introduction: About this book	xiii
How to use this book: Notes to Teachers and Students	xv

SECTION 1 DEVELOPING ACADEMIC READING SKILLS IN ENGLISH FOR THEOLOGY

Unit 1	Introduction to Reading Theology	1
Unit 2	Types of Publications: Theological Texts in English	7
Unit 3	Meaning in Text: Modes of Discourse	13
Unit 4	Meaning in Text: Genre and Organisation of Ideas	23
Unit 5	Prediction as an Aid to Comprehension	30
Unit 6	Reading for Specific Information: Scanning	34
Unit 7	Reading for the General Idea: Skimming	40
Unit 8	Paragraph Structure and Comprehension	44
Unit 9	Sentence and Clause Structure and Comprehension	49
Unit 10	Cohesive Devices and Comprehension	56
Unit 11	Levels of Meaning and Authorial Voice	60

SECTION 2 APPLYING READING SKILLS AND DEVELOPING SPEAKING, LISTENING AND WRITING SKILLS

Unit 12	Focus on Asia and the Pacific; grammar focus—present simple, present continuous tense	73
Unit 13	Theology and Spirituality; grammar focus—passive voice, present and continuous tense	84
Unit 14	Theology and Language; grammar focus—articles	93
Unit 15	Religion and Culture; grammar focus—simple past, past continuous tense	103
Unit 16	Revelation and Theologising; grammar focus—prepositions	113
Unit 17	Christology; grammar focus—relative clauses	122
Unit 18	The Problem of Suffering; grammar focus—nominal or noun clauses	133
Unit 19	Grace; grammar focus—modal verbs and present perfect tense	144
Unit 20	Justice, Development and Good News; grammar focus—adverbial clauses	154
Unit 21	Understanding Scripture: grammar focus—gerunds and gerund phrases	164
Unit 22	Ecological Theology; grammar focus—conditional clauses	173
Unit 23	Genes, Ethics and Theology; grammar focus—participles and participial phrases	184
Unit 24	Christianity and Religious Pluralism; grammar focus—apposition	194

Linguistic Glossary	204
Theological Glossary	205

Appendices - A	Listening Texts	208
B	Answers to Exercises	216
C	List of Sources of Theological Texts used	235
Evaluation Form		239

Foreword

Theology is a language. It tries to say a word about that mysterious reality that we believers call God. It is a *logos* about *theos*.

It is a mysterious reality indeed, in the biblical sense of the term mystery. God is mystery because God is a love that embraces all human reality. God is at once present in history and in the heart of each person, and is the totally 'Other' according to Karl Barth. God is, as Gabriel Marcel says, the mystery of 'you, whom we can only recognise and invoke'.

Within the biblical context however, it is not an ineffable mystery in the literal sense of the word. We can, and we must, speak of God. Despite all the limitations involved, God has to be communicated. To restrict our relationship with God to the private domain, or to limit the biblical message to a few initiates, is to ignore that sense of God's love. The mystery of the love of God must be proclaimed in the streets and squares. This supposes a language, a communication. It will be a God-talk, expressed as a message, conscious of the limitations of its experience and of the knowledge that it communicates.

The mystery of God must be welcomed in prayer and in human solidarity; it is both a moment of silence and of practice. In this way, and only in this way, can the language and the categories necessary to transmit the mystery to others emerge. It is communication in the etymological sense of the term: to create a bond, to enter into communion with others; this is the moment of speaking.

In a beautiful text, the book of Ecclesiastes says to us that everything in human existence has its hour and its season: 'a time to be born and a time to die . . . a time to be silent and a time to speak' (3, 2.7). They are not juxtaposed moments; one depends on the other, one nourishes the other. The present book helps us in relation to that second moment: speaking.

In our time, English is becoming more and more the international language of theology. Books from all over the world appear in English before other languages. For many in the non-English speaking world it is very useful to be able to read and, if possible, speak English in order to enter into fruitful dialogue in cross cultural contexts.

However, I would like to emphasise that this is not only a book about the use of English *in* theology, but it is also, to some extent, a book *on* theology. The well-chosen examples teach us how to express our understanding of the Christian message in appropriate English terms. Moreover, they are accompanied by copious remarks and clarifications that make this work much more than a list of words. In searching for the appropriate English expression, they invite us to reflect on what we want to say about our faith. In this sense it is a unique book.

I first became familiar with this book when I saw it in draft form and met the author in the Philippines in 2002. I discovered its benefits for those in Asia and beyond, who are studying theology in English. I am delighted that this book is now being published and distributed internationally, and I am happy to give it my full support.

I am also happy that this book, written by an Australian Dominican Sister, will be the first in a new Dominican Series published by ATF Press.

I congratulate Gabrielle Kelly on an excellent work in which she continues the best of the Dominican tradition by handing on the fruits of her study and making an important contribution to the preaching of the gospel. This is the authentic way of of doing theology and of employing theological language.

Theology, any theology, is a hermeneutic of hope; it is a way of giving a rational account of our hope (cf 1 Peter 3:15). Thank you for helping so many people to do that . . . in good English!

Gustavo Gutiérrez OP
Santa Sabina
Rome
1 December 2003

ACKNOWLEDGMENTS

The author:
I would like to thank the following persons who have been significant in the genesis and/or production of this resource book:

Fr Laurens da Costa, SVD, whose invitation to teach English to seminarians at Ledalero in Flores, Indonesia, was the catalyst for this book; my sister, Sheilagh Kelly of the University of Technology, Sydney, for initially encouraging the project and for editorial support; Fr James McEvoy of the Adelaide College of Divinity for advice on some texts; Margaret Cargill, writing teacher and consultant of many years at The University of Adelaide and active lay person in the Uniting Church of Australia, for editorial advice and ecumenical suggestions; members of the Language and Learning Service team (IBP) at The University of Adelaide, in particular, Ursula McGowan, Margaret Cargill, Kate Cadman and Dr Jo Seton in whose professional company over some years I grew in appreciation of the discipline-specific approach to tertiary language learning; Anne Stewart OP for proof-reading; Dr Helen F Bergin OP, Dr Ann L Gilroy RSJ and volunteer theology students from Oceania studying at the University of Auckland, New Zealand, for giving generously of their time to trial sections of the book; and any others who have assisted me in any way.

I acknowledge also the following references:-

Crystal, D, 1992, *The Cambridge Encyclopedia of Language*, Cambridge University Press, Cambridge.
Glendinning, E & Holstrom, B, 1992, *Study Reading*, Cambridge University Press, Cambridge.
Greenbaum, S, 1996, *The Oxford English Grammar*, Oxford University Press, Oxford.
Leech, G & Svartvik, J, 1975, *A Communicative Grammar of English*, Longman, UK.
Nuttal, C, 1982, *Teaching Reading Skills in a Foreign Language*, Heinemann, Oxford.
Oshima, A & Hogue, A, 1991, *Writing Academic English*, 2nd edition, Addison-Wesley Publishing Company, New York.
Pender, J, 1996, *English on Cue*, University of Southern Queensland, Toowoomba.
Swales, J, 1990, *Genre Analysis*, Cambridge University Press, UK.
Swales, J & Feak, C, 1994, *Academic Writing for Graduate Students*, University of Michigan Press, USA.
Wajnryb, R, 1994, *Grammar Dictation*, Oxford University Press, UK.
Weissberg, R & Buker, S, 1990, *Writing Up Research*, Prentice Hall Regents, Englewood Cliffs, New Jersey.

Sources of theological texts used in this book are listed in Appendix C.

Gabrielle Kelly OP

The publisher:
The following have made generous financial donations to the production of this book: the Aboriginal and Islander Commission of the National Council of Churches in Australia (NCCA), Australian Catholic University, the Australian Centre for Christianity and Culture, Canberra, the Australian New Zealand Association of Theological Schools (ANZATS), the Australian Research Theological Foundation, the Australian Theological Forum Literary Fund, the Christian Conference of Asia, the Federation of Dominican Sisters of Australia, the Dominican Friars of Australia, New Zealand, Papua New Guinea and the Solomon Islands, the Jesuit Fathers and Brothers of the Australian province, the Lutheran Church in Australia, the Faith and Order Commission of the National Council of Churches in Australia (NCCA), the Sisters of Mercy: Brisbane, Singleton and Perth Congregations, the Society of the Divine Word (SVD), Australian Province, the Uniting Church in Australia (Secretariat for Indonesia and East Timor), the Discalced Carmelite Nuns, Adelaide, and Australian Catholic University. To all these groups, or individuals, our heartfelt thanks for such an ecumenical contribution.

INTRODUCTION

ABOUT THIS BOOK

Welcome to *English for Theology*. This is a resource workbook for the development of English language skills in theology and related disciplines for teachers and students of the Asia-Pacific region from language backgrounds other than English. The contents presuppose a level of proficiency in English suitable for entry to tertiary-level studies using the medium of English. A sound grasp of the basic structures and grammar of English is therefore assumed, but the need for ongoing revision and practice is also recognised.

While directed towards the single goal of promoting proficiency in the use of academic English in the theological setting, the contents of this book are structured into two parts. **Section 1** provides instruction and practice in the skills of reading comprehension in English, using authentic theological texts. As well as a survey of the main types of publications, units of work include a consideration of the more common text types or *genres*, and ways of organising ideas within those texts. The role of structure in the paragraph and the sentence, cohesive devices and discourse markers as aids to comprehension, the specific reading strategies of scanning and skimming, and other textual features such as levels of meaning and authorial voice are also included.

Theological language and the religious discourse from which it comes have particular qualities which say something 'not said by other kinds of discourse—ordinary, scientific, or poetic … '.[1] Hence, Unit 1 includes a short explanation of the problems and possibilities of theological discourse, with an introduction to the concept of *modes of discourse*. Some of these modes are further examined in Unit 3.

The most fundamental principle in acquiring language proficiency—indeed in acquiring any skill—is to practise using it. **Section 2**, therefore, offers further practice in applying the reading skills outlined in Section 1. It also provides a readily accessible variety of authentic theological texts, with structured language tasks, which facilitate students' engagement with the target language (of theology) in all four macro-skills. Each unit of work is focused on a theme of theological relevance and has four parts. Part 1 introduces the theme centred around a simple reading text, where vocabulary and structure are basic. An aspect of grammar, usually exemplified in the text, is reviewed and reinforced with exercises. Parts 2, 3 and 4 in each unit contain reading passages of increasing complexity for further practice. An additional part of each unit is the opportunity to focus on pronunciation through the listening exercises, if this is important for students. (A CD is provided.)

The units of work in Section 2, as noted, are focused around reading material. This emphasis reflects the requirements of academic study in theology. However, since language proficiency progresses in a more or less integrated way in all four macro-skill areas[2], each unit provides tasks in speaking, listening, and writing, as well as in grammar, vocabulary extension, pronunciation and comprehension. It should be noted that while a range of the more common grammatical structures is revised, students will need to supplement this where necessary by reference to a comprehensive English grammar.

The discipline-specific approach to promoting language proficiency has grown during the past decade from analysis of the needs of undergraduate and postgraduate students from language backgrounds other than English (LBOTE) in Australian and other universities. On-arrival or first semester language programs have sought to integrate 'the development of academic and language skills with the content of students' study programs'.[3] This resource book, while focusing mainly on reading skills and promoting familiarity with theological language, draws on this theoretical background.

English for Theology

This is an English language resource book for theology students and their EFL teachers in the Asia-Pacific region. Because theology is and must be grounded in a cultural context—'*a theology mediates between a cultural matrix and the significance and role of a religion in that matrix*'[4]—the geo-physical and socio-cultural realities of the Asia-Pacific region are background themes in many of the units. Moreover, the scope of theology itself continues to expand as we move into the twenty-first century. Developments in ecology, cosmology, feminist thought, bioethics, and interfaith matters are just a few of the expanding horizons extending the more familiar theological landscapes. The themes in this resource book draw on many of these areas.

Gabrielle Kelly OP
Exaltation of the Holy Cross
September 14, 2003

HOW TO USE THIS BOOK:
NOTES FOR TEACHERS AND STUDENTS

As a language development resource for EFL teachers and post-school or tertiary theology students who already have at least a post-intermediate level of English, this book may be used in a number of ways according to learner needs.

It has been compiled, first of all, with the class group situation in mind, where ideally 10 to 15 students work with teacher guidance. Such a situation is necessary, of course, for the functioning of the discussion and speaking activities.

As an intensive course, the units of work may be programmed in a schedule of daily or at least thrice weekly class sessions. It is preferable to complete Section 1 on Reading Skills before undertaking the exercises in Section 2, and to work through the four-part Units of Section 2 in sequence. But this order may be varied according to student need. For example, in Section 2, students may prefer to complete Part 1 and the grammar revision exercises and then move straight on to the next unit, leaving Parts 2, 3 and 4 of the unit for later practice. Or if there is a need to work on the vocabulary and language of a particular topic (for example, grace, liberation theology), then the student may want to proceed directly to the relevant unit.

This resource book may also be used concurrently with General English language studies, and it may be used for individual or small group study. Answers are provided in Appendix B to facilitate student learning in this situation.

Since this is a *resource book* rather than a course or text book, teachers and students should adapt the contents where desirable. For example, the purpose of the Preparatory Discussion task in the units is simply to prompt student thinking in terms of the concepts, language and vocabulary of the unit topic. It is *not* a test of knowledge. If some other 'warm up' discussion better serves that purpose, then teachers and students should adapt the suggestions.

The listening exercises are constructed to give practice in listening both for specific information and for general meaning. Dictogloss exercises are included to promote general aural comprehension, and to give students opportunity to practise actively using language to express meaning.[5]

In a class situation, the teacher may choose to read the listening texts. For students using the book for individual study, a compact disk is provided. This may also assist with pronunciation.

The speaking and writing suggestions similarly provide opportunities to practise those skills, using the language and vocabulary of a given topic. Alternative exercises may be more appropriate for students in some local situations.

Students need not be concerned if some of the ideas in Section 1 or some texts in Section 2 seem too difficult for them at this stage. As a language resource, the book contains material to cover a range of proficiency levels from Upper Intermediate to more Advanced levels. Students are advised to use what is useful now, and to come back at a later time to the more difficult exercises.

As indicated elsewhere, this is not a comprehensive grammar book. Where further information on some aspect of grammar is needed, the student should consult an appropriate reference. Useful books include:

> Willis D & Wright J, 1995, *Collins Cobuild Basic Grammar*, HarperCollins, London. [Any of the Cobuild series are useful.]
> Eastwood, J, 1993, *Oxford Practice Grammar*, Oxford University Press, Oxford.

> Murphy, R, 1985, *English Grammar in Use*, Cambridge University Press, Cambridge.

---

1. Ricoeur, P, 1995, *Figuring the Sacred*, Fortress, Minneapolis, p 35.
2. Kumaravadivelu, B, 1994, 'The Postmethod Condition: (E)merging Strategies for Second/Foreign Language Teaching', in *TESOL Quarterly*, Vol 28, No 1, pp 27-45.
3. Cargill, M, 1996, 'An Integrated Bridging Program for International Postgraduate Students', in *Higher Education Research and Development*, Vol 15, No 2, pp 177-178.
4. Lonergan, B, 1971, *Method in Theology*, Darton, Longman and Todd, London, p xi.
5. Wajnryb, R, 1994, *Grammar Dictation*, Oxford University Press, UK.

SECTION 1

DEVELOPING ACADEMIC READING SKILLS IN ENGLISH FOR THEOLOGY

UNIT 1 INTRODUCTION TO READING THEOLOGY

1 THE READING PROCESS

The ability to read in any language can greatly enlarge a person's life experience. To be able to do so in a foreign language can only magnify this. It is a most valuable life skill, then, to find ways of improving your reading competence; for you as a student, especially one for whom English is a second or foreign language, it is an academic necessity.

The knowledge and skills involved in reading
What is involved in reading? Reading is a process where the *reader seeks to understand* what the *writer intends to communicate* through the written word, *the text*. It is essentially about *meaning* and how this is transferred from the writer to the reader.

From this definition it is clear that the ability to comprehend a written text requires several different kinds of knowledge and skills. Obviously, as a reader you need to have a sufficient knowledge of the *basic syntax of the English language*, as well as an adequate *vocabulary*. You also need to have some *background knowledge* of the writer's subject area (in this case, theology and spirituality), and an ability to grasp the *concepts* involved.

On this foundation, you can build a systematic working knowledge of the ways in which writers use various linguistic resources to express their meaning. At the macro level, there is the mode of discourse—mythic, symbolic, existential and so on—used by the writer. Likewise at the level of the whole text there is format or genre to consider—for example, the essay, report, reflection, critique. Within any of these genres, you as the reader further need to understand how the organisation of ideas, structure of the sentence and paragraph, cohesive devices and discourse markers or 'signpost' words are used by writers to convey meaning. Texts of whatever mode or genre come to us in a variety of publication types—for example, book, journal article, letter, news item—and these too have their conventions. The units of work in Section 1 of this resource book deal with all these topics.

Purposes for reading
Effective academic reading also depends upon selecting the particular strategies required according to your purpose for reading. You may want to read for leisure, for information or for aesthetic purposes; you may read to help you to reflect more deeply—to pray, or to proclaim the Word; you may want to read to make your activity more informed, more thoughtful; and you may read in order to study. All of these purposes for reading have their own specific skills and strategies, but it is with the last, namely, reading for study purposes, or academic reading, that this resource book is concerned.

Strategies for academic reading
Academic reading involves at different times three main purposes, each with its own particular reading strategy. You may read in order to find particular information or facts quickly, without reading the whole text. This is usually referred to as *scanning*. You may want to read to find out the general idea of a text, perhaps to assess its usefulness for more detailed reading. This is called *skimming*. Finally, you may want to read to gain a detailed understanding of the whole text. This calls for skill in recognising the writer's purpose and meaning, and this requires a range of interpretive skills. You will need to distinguish between facts and opinions, between explanation, argument and criticism, and you will need to understand the various levels of structure and other linguistic devices which the writer uses to express those meanings.

Yet further interpretive skills are called for in theological writings. As noted in the Introduction, theological language and religious discourse say something which other kinds of discourse do not say. So it is useful to include here a brief introduction to the nature of religious and theological discourse.

2 THEOLOGICAL LANGUAGE: THE PROBLEMS AND POSSIBILITIES

The problem

From ancient times, people have understood that there is a unique problem about theological language: it claims to be talking about 'something' which by definition cannot be put into words. All other uses of language are very much grounded in what is accessible to human experience or to human powers of reasoning. But as the ancient Hebrew writer said so long ago concerning God

> *[God's] knowledge is beyond my understanding*
> *a height to which my mind cannot attain.*   Psalm 139:6

Yet all the peoples of the earth, and believers in the major religious faiths, have felt impelled to try to use language about this Divine Mystery beyond our reach. How can such language communicate meaning and how are we to interpret it?

What is theological language?

First, we must look at what is meant by theological language. Theological language can be understood only within the community of religious believers. In response to divine initiative, the community comes to an *experience of living faith* which is then expressed in *primary religious language* or *discourse*. Such religious 'language' may be verbal or non-verbal. It is when the community begins to reflect in a serious way on these primary expressions of faith, bringing them into conceptual form with the help of speculative philosophy, that we have *theological language* or *discourse*. These relationships may be represented in the following diagram.

<u>The matrix – community of believers</u>

Experience of living faith
▼
expressed in
▼
Religious language/discourse

Verbal
e.g. prayers, hymns, scriptures (narratives, prophecy, laws, proverbs, wisdom sayings) liturgical formulas

Non-verbal
e.g. rites, rituals, acts of love, images, symbols, art, music, silence, dance

reflection on the above using concepts of speculative philosophy
▼
Theological language/discourse

Theological language is thus some steps removed in process from the living faith experience in which it is originally rooted. It can be no other way, yet this distance can cause serious problems for meaning. If separated entirely from its 'native soil',[1] theological language, with its propositions and statements, can be as meaningless and as lifeless as an uprooted, shrivelled and misshapen plant.

How theological language can be meaningful

Given the difficulty of using language to express the inexpressible, how do we interpret theological language? Linguists today generally agree that the meaning of words and sentences can only be understood in *the way in which they are used in specific discourse situations*.[2] That is, particular choices of language (vocabulary, syntax, text structure, etc) are made by groups of people associated with particular subject areas, for example, technology, medicine, education, the environment. Look at these two examples of discourse:

> *1 This printer is equipped with an IrDA 1.0 compatible infrared wireless communication interface **port**. The IrDA **interface** is very popular among **notebook** or laptop users because no cable is required. In order to use this interface, your computer must . . . have an IR Comm **Driver** installed.*
>
> *2 Diagnosing anaemia is not easy. Symptoms or no symptoms, people with anaemia tend to have simple iron-deficiency. The body needs iron to **manufacture** red blood cells, which are responsible for **transporting** oxygen in the blood. Anaemia causes apathy and poor **resistance** to infection.*

You will easily recognise that the subject areas of these examples are computer technology and medicine respectively.

In the first example, there are certain words which have a particular meaning within the discourse of computer technology which is different from everyday meaning, as set out below.

Word	Meaning within the discourse of computer technology	Everyday discourse meaning
Interface	1 Part of a computer system which connects one system or device to another. 2 As a verb: to actively connect one system to another. 3 Contact point between person, computer and program, e.g. keyboard.	A surface considered as a common boundary between two things.
Port	The electrical connection point of a computer through which data is sent and received.	A place where sea-going vessels load and unload. (Note: There are other meanings also.)
Notebook	A type of lap-top computer, small and portable.	A small booklet (paper) for recording notes and other information.
Driver	A software program which controls a particular part of a computer's hardware system.	A person who operates a car or other usually land-based vehicle.

There are also some special technical words in the first example, such as *wireless, infrared, cable*.

The second example likewise contains words which have a meaning within the specialist discourse area which is different from everyday meaning, as set out in the table below.

Word	Meaning within the discourse of medicine	Everyday discourse meaning
manufacture	Iron interacts in the body to cause red blood cell growth.	Making things by hand or by machinery.
transport(ing)	Red blood cells carry oxygen through the body.	To carry or move things/people from one place to another by means of a vehicle, with human involvement.
resistance	A chemical/biological process in the body which prevents infection (or fails to prevent it).	The act, with human involvement, of opposing someone/something.

Specialist medical words in the second example include *symptom, anaemia, infection, diagnosing*. Sometimes these words may be applied to everyday discourse—for example, *Watching too much TV can infect young people with consumerism*—but their primary meaning is in the field of medical discourse.

These few examples illustrate the notion of discipline-specific meanings for words. This aspect of language use—that meaning is dependent upon context or discourse situation—is especially relevant in the area of religious and theological language.

A full examination of this very complex issue, which is itself an important area of academic enquiry, may be found in the references at the end of this unit. For now it is sufficient to note two key areas of language, namely, vocabulary and syntax, which provide a path to understanding how the *discourse situation* creates and communicates meaning. Of course, the language used by theologians is, for the most part, the same as that used by everybody else. The rules of grammar work in the same way, and a great many of the words are the same for them as for others. It is in the functioning of what John Macquarrie calls *theological vocabulary* and *theological syntax* that we can gain insight into the problem of meaning. The explanation below follows this approach and draws substantially on Macquarrie's classic work.[3] There is brief reference also to the descriptions of theological language preferred by some other theologians.

Theological vocabulary

A distinctive theological vocabulary consists of those words, mainly nouns, which are characteristically used by theologians (for example, *faith, salvation, grace* and so on). Noun words in general can communicate meaning in two ways: by referring to something quite specific in human experience in a *univocal or denotative* way, and/or by the interpretive power of association which draws on shared experiences (by *connotation*). The noun *mosquito*, for example, even though it may include a variety of types, refers to a specific insect. *Mosquito* has just one meaning in the Australian Macquarie Dictionary. *Rice* denotes a specific type of food grain/plant. It has just the two meanings in the Macquarie Dictionary —that is, the grain of the plant or the plant itself.

Dream, on the other hand, has many connotations. To understand the meaning of *dream* in any given instance, we must rely upon the discourse situation in which it occurs. For example, *Last night I had a dream that I was swimming in a beautiful sea*. Here, *dream* refers to those commonly experienced images which occur in a person's mind/imagination during sleep. But when Martin Luther King said, *'I have a dream!'*, he was talking about something quite different. In that context, *dream* referred to King's very conscious great hope and desire and firm commitment for a free and racially inclusive society. In the Macquarie Dictionary, *dream* has no less than sixteen listed meanings!

In the area of theology, the noun *cross* may *denote* the specific instrument of execution used in Roman Palestine, or it may communicate a wide range of meanings (experiences, attitudes, events, beliefs) through its *connotations*. What is of key importance is to be aware that within the theological discourse situation, noun words (and their derivatives, for example, salvation, save) tend to function in a more *connotative* or *non-univocal* way than in non-theological discourse.

Theological syntax

This indirect use of language to try to speak about what is ultimately beyond the grasp of human reason extends to theological syntax, or 'the way in which theological sentences and arguments get constructed'.[4] Theologians commonly use one or more *modes of discourse* which together communicate their meaning. Macquarrie has summarised these modes as mythical, symbolic, existential, ontological, metaphysical, authority-based, empirical and paradoxical. Examples of some of these modes are studied in Unit 3.

Other theologians use related but different descriptions. McFague prefers to describe the main mode of theological language simply as metaphorical, embracing the tension of the *is/is not* character of descriptions of the transcendent, while Aquinas and Rahner write that all theological language is analogical. Both of these approaches mean that the truth of any statement about God and the things of God can be found only in both affirmation and negation (similarity-in-difference). [See excerpt from Rahner in Unit 14.] For example, God *is good*, but not in any sense of the word *good* that we understand; God is *light*, but not in any sense of the word *light* that we understand. Tracy writes that there are two major conceptual languages used for theology, namely, analogical language and dialectical language.[5] Another writer, Williams, also speaks of two kinds of theological language: in one kind, argument tends to be linear, and in the other, helical or spiral. (Williams refers to these as 'regular' and 'irregular' theology.)[6] Students interested in pursuing these other approaches to theological language may consult the references in the footnotes or at the end of this unit. An introduction to Macquarrie's modes of discourse is enough for the purposes of this resource book.

Individual theologians may have a preference for using some of these modes of discourse rather than others, or they may use different modes at different times. Sometimes there may be no clear-cut distinctions between them. Macquarrie's list of modes does not exhaust the possible ways of describing theological language but it does summarise a fair range of the options available to theologians.

Conclusion

For you as a theology student, it is important not only to gain proficiency in the general skills of reading comprehension. This is but the foundation. A deeper interpretation of theological texts also requires familiarity with the various modes of theological discourse and the particular way in which they communicate meaning. This book deals with these issues in Unit 3.

It is also important to be familiar with the conventions of the main types of theological publications (surveyed in Unit 2), and with the main *genres* and ways of organising ideas within texts (Unit 4). The role of prediction in comprehension is the subject of Unit 5. Scanning and skimming are covered in Units 6 and 7 respectively, while the roles of structure in the paragraph and the sentence, and cohesive devices are the subjects of Units 8 to 10. Unit

11 deals with some further aspects of levels of meaning in text and the notion of authorial voice.

The task of reading and studying theology is made much easier with the help of these reading comprehension skills. It may also be made more fruitful, for only if it is properly interpreted can theology achieve its chief purpose, namely, to connect or reconnect believers to the transforming potential of the primary faith experience of a religious tradition.[7]

For further reading on the topic of meaning in theological language, the student may consult the following references.

Bibliography
Braaten, CE, 1989, *Our Naming of God*, Fortress, Minneapolis.
Crystal, D, 1992, *The Cambridge Encyclopedia of Language*, Cambridge University Press, Cambridge
Johnson, E, 1984, 'The Incomprehensibility of God and the Image of God Male and Female', in *Theological Studies* 45, Marquette University, Milwaukee, pp 441-465.
Macquarrie, J, 1967, *God-Talk*, SCM Press, London.
McFague, S, 1982, *Metaphorical Theology*, SCM Press, London.
Porter, SE, (editor), 1996, *The Nature of Religious Language*, Sheffield Academic Press, Sheffield.
Rahner, K, 2000, 'Experiences of a Catholic Theologian', in *Theological Studies* 61, Marquette University, Milwaukee, pp 3-15.
Ramsey, IT, 1957, *Religious Language*, SCM Press, London.
Ricoeur, P, 1995, *Figuring the Sacred*, Fortress, Minneapolis.
Schneiders, S, 1993, 'The Bible and Feminism', in *Freeing Theology*, edited by CM LaCugna, HarperSanFrancisco, pp 31-57.
Tracy, D, 1981, *The Analogical Imagination*, SCM Press Ltd., London, especially Chapter 10.
Williams, AN, 1999, 'The Logic of Genre: Theological Method in East and West', in *Theological Studies* 60, Marquette University, Milwaukee, pp 679-707.

---

1. Braaten, 1989, p 11.
2. Crystal, 1992, p 102.
3. Macquarrie, 1967, especially Chapters 4 and 6.
4. *Ibid*, p 124.
5. Tracy, 1981, p 408.
6. Williams, 1999, pp 679-707.
7. McFague, 1982, p 120.

UNIT 2   TYPES OF PUBLICATIONS: THEOLOGICAL TEXTS IN ENGLISH

Theological text is published in English in a great variety of forms. This unit reviews the more common types of publication, with an emphasis on the features of books.

Common types of publications

The type of publication selected for a text usually depends upon the writer's purpose. A lengthy examination of a topic may be published as a book. A more limited study may be published as a journal article. Other theological texts which you are likely to encounter in your studies may be published in different forms. Some may be unpublished, as in the case of a degree thesis, or a letter written for limited circulation.

To gain the best advantage from your reading, it is helpful to be familiar with the conventions of these different types of publication, their overall organisation and their functions or purposes. In the case of sacred texts such as the scriptures, it is also useful to be familiar with the features of the various editions.

TASK 1: Some common types of publication you will use are **books, journal articles, church newspapers,** and **authoritative church statements** such as **pastoral** and **encyclical letters**. Five short extracts from each of these types of publications follow. Identify in the space provided the most likely publication type of each extract. How do you know? Discuss the distinctive features you can identify, either of language or presentation, for each type with students around you. Share your findings with the whole class.

1 ....

2   Early development of trinitarian thought

Within the first centuries after the death of Jesus, the Christian community began to give form to its reflections on the relationship between Jesus, whom they had come to know as the Christ, and the Unseen God. This gradually led to an understanding that

2 ....

Venerable Brothers
and dear Sons and Daughters,
greeting and apostolic blessing!

The social concern of the Church, directed towards an authentic development of person and society which would respect and promote all the dimensions of the human person, has always expressed itself in the most varied ways . . . The social doctrine of church . . . builds up gradually, as the church, in the fullness of the word revealed by Christ Jesus and with the assistance . . .[1]

3 ....

Observers, either within or beyond the culture, point to the strong emphasis on individuality to the detriment of community values. In this context, the ultimate reference point is considered to be the self, as if the self's best interests are not intimately tied to the common good ...

115

Review of Culture and Life   Autumn 2000

English for Theology

4 .... Dear Brothers and Sisters in Christ
Greetings in Christ Jesus!

With the ... announcement that...members of the ... Defence Force will be deployed ... against terrorism, we have arrived at a sombre moment in our history ... It is clear that...justice must be done ... However ... there is no place for revenge. That the Bible clearly teaches us (Rom 12:19). There is no place ... for animosity between Christianity and Islam. Indeed, at this time ... [2]

5 .... **Representatives promote religious collaboration for 21st century**
Around 250 representatives of the major world religions met in the capital last week. They shared visions and hopes for a new era of inter-religious cooperation in working for a more humane world. A spokesperson reported that the gathering had exceeded the expectations of the organisers.

Before continuing with the next task, how many more types of publication can you name? Write them in your notebook.

Check your answers in Appendix B.

TASK 2: Here is a more extensive list of types of publication, including the above, which you may encounter in your studies. Name an example of each of these and write its full title in the space provided. (Note: Extracts from several of these are included in the texts in Section 2 of this resource book.)

a	Books................................	g	Scriptures ....
b	Reports	h	Magazines ....
c	Journals..............................	i	Encyclicals ....
d	Authoritative church documents: Pastoral statements/Synod statements	j	Conference Papers/Proceedings ....
e	Journal articles	k	Unpublished theses ....
f	Newspapers	l	Letters ....

TASK 3: Read through the descriptions of different types of publications below. Match each one with the appropriate item from the list in Task 2 above.

Description of purposes   **Type of publication**

1   An academic presentation, unpublished, of the findings
    of an original research question or area of enquiry,
    usually between 150-250 pages   ....

2   A more personal communication addressed to
    a particular group of people   ....

3 A published account of some topic or area of enquiry of substantial length, usually organised into chapters and usually with copyright restrictions   ....

4 A presentation of teaching, guidance and/or exhortation following a meeting or major event by church leaders, bishops or other authoritative people   ....

5 A scholarly collection of articles, reviews, letters, opinions published at regular intervals   ....

6 The collected sacred writings of the Hebrew and Christian traditions, or of other religious traditions, in a particular translation and edition   ....

7 A popular collection of articles, usually with good quality illustrations, some news items and advertisements, published at regular intervals   ....

8 The collected papers presented by speakers at a meeting of people and afterwards available to participants and others   ....

9 An authoritative statement on Roman Catholic teaching, of limited length, written by the pope   ....

10 A collection of mainly news items and commentary, with pictures, on cheap paper, often published daily   ....

11 A shorter length scholarly presentation of an area of academic enquiry   ....

12 An account of progress after a meeting or series of meetings of representatives appointed to discuss a given issue, or after research on a given issue   ....

Check your answers in Appendix B.

Different parts of books

There is a saying in English that *you can't judge a book by its cover*. [Do you have an equivalent saying in your language?] This may be partly true. But before you ever read a word of the actual text, there is much you can find out about the contents of a book from its cover and from several other introductory or end parts.

TASK 4: Work with the person next to you to list as many of the parts of a book as you can. Compare with others in the class, extending your lists until you have at least ten parts. Check your list with the answers in Appendix B at the end of the book.

....

....

....

Now do Task 5.

English for Theology

TASK 5: Name the part of a book which gives the following information.

Example: 7 *Title, author and a coloured design*   Answer: *Front cover*

Information given by different parts of a book	Part of book
1 Authoritative sources/background used by the author	....
2 A list of the main sections of a book	....
3 The individual sections/units of a book	....
4 Detailed alphabetical list of topics referred to in book	....
5 Introductory comment, scope of book, often by a notable person other than the author	....
6 Publisher, place and date of publication, copyright details, ISBN	....
7 Title, author and coloured design/illustration	....
8 Source of particular data/opinion, with explanation	....
9 Acknowledgement of people who assisted with the book	....
10 Brief reviews of the book, author details	....

[Check your answers in Appendix B before continuing.]

TASK 6: Read through the following examples and decide from which part of a book each one comes.

a

....

Buechner, F, *Telling Secrets*, San Francisco: Harper and Row, 1991.

Green, L, *Let's Do Theology: A Pastoral Cycle Resource Book*, London: Mowbray, 1990.

Groome, TH, *Sharing Faith: A Comprehensive Approach to Religious Education and Pastoral Ministry*, San Francisco: Harper and Row, 1991.

Kinast, RL, *Let the Ministry Teach: A Handbook for Theological Reflection*, Madeira Beach, Fla: Center for Theological Reflection, 1992.

b

....

"Planetary Crisis" is a timely reminder to all humankind. It challenges everyone, across cultures and religions, to join in this most urgent task, intelligently, sensitively, and with great hope . . . — David Smyth, Baudin University.

"This is a brilliant, interdisciplinary account of an issue facing us all. It is destined to become obligatory reading for all academics concerned with the ecological crisis." — Amy Jacquinot, *Southern Aurora New Times*.

c

....

147. 'as far as I know': this was the qualification expressed to the writer in personal communication dated 15 August 1998. The incident is consistent with news reports of the same time.

d	This account aims to describe the history of a concept as it has evolved within the second half of the twentieth century. The work is limited to English language sources in the main, although some significant insights originally expressed in languages other than English have fortunately found their way into translation.
e	Part 2 Developments in the Twentieth Century 3 New Biblical approaches p 81 4 The contribution of archaeology p 84
f	In the lengthy process of updating this new edition, the author acknowledges with gratitude the professional and personal support of many people. Firstly, there are my colleagues at Southern Aurora University, and . . .
g	***A Brief History of the Idea of Development*** Zoe M Manchin

TASK 7: Find at least three different publications of the Hebrew and Christian Scriptures (the Bible). Complete the table below with the appropriate information for each one.

Title	....	....	....
Translation details	....	....	....
Purpose of this particular translation	....	....	....
Authorised by	....	....	....
Published by	....	....	....
Edition - if indicated (eg 2nd, 4th)	....	....	....
Date of Publication	....	....	....

English for Theology

TASK 8: Choose a book which you need to read for your current studies, but with which you are as yet unfamiliar. Without reading any of the chapters, find out as much as you can about it under the following headings.

1 Title, including sub-title ....

2 Author(s)/editor(s) ....

3 Publisher, place, date of publication ....

4 For whom is the book intended? ....

5 What is the main aim of the book? ....

6 Main topics covered ....

7 Any special emphases or features ....

8 Do you think it will be worth reading? On what basis? ....

   How did you make this decision? ....

   ....

   ....

Continue to check answers for Section 1 tasks in Appendix B.

---

1. John Paul II, 1987, 'On Social Concerns', para. 1
2. Rev Prof James Haire, Pastoral Letter to Uniting Church in Australia, October 2001.

UNIT 3 MEANING IN TEXT: MODES OF DISCOURSE

Theological meaning is communicated in part through various *modes of discourse* (see Unit 1). In this resource book we follow Macquarrie's[1] use of this term. Mode of discourse refers to the way in which writers construct sentences and arguments, and how they use language to convey the meaning they intend in the particular discourse situation. Modes are best presented through the examples which follow. A simple illustration is provided by the difference between the literal and metaphorical use of words in these two pairs of sentences:-

    a The poachers *have annihilated* nearly all the tigers in that part of the world.
    b The champion soccer players *annihilated* the opposing team.
    c The student was very keen on archaeology. She *devoured* every book on the topic she could find.
    d The starving refugees *devoured* every grain of rice they could find.

It is easy to identify the sentences where the verb is used metaphorically, and to understand the different meanings given to the same word in each pair of sentences. Understanding modes of discourse calls for extending these interpretive skills to whole texts.

Because the ultimate subject matter of theology is beyond the capacity of ordinary language, theologians are more-or-less forced to use a combination of modes of discourse—some of them quite indirect and abstract—to communicate what they want to say about human experience as it is open to the divine.

Modes of discourse may be named differently by different writers, and sometimes the distinctions between modes are not clear-cut. In this Unit we look at examples of some of the more common modes used by theologians. They can be summarised as *mythical, symbolic-analogical, metaphysical, existential* and *empirical*. Some of these modes are not common in today's theology. The mythical mode, for example, was used in ancient Hebrew times but is little used by theologians writing today. For a more detailed discussion of these modes and how they communicate theological meaning, the student may consult the references listed in Unit 1. For our purposes here, it is sufficient to study a brief description and short example of each mode.

Mythical mode

The language of myth is not commonly used by theologians today. But we can agree with Macquarrie that "it would be true to see in myth the matrix out of which the refinements of religious language, including theological language itself, have arisen."[2] Macquarrie, whose description is largely (though not exclusively) followed in this section[3], says that in spite of the most advanced thought patterns of today, the work of contemporary theologians is likely to reflect at least some traces of mythical discourse.[4] It is important, therefore, for today's *student*—and indeed the ordinary believer—to understand the features of mythical language and to realise that it communicates meaning in a way which is different from everyday language.

The language of myth is *dramatic*, portraying concrete and particular action among persons and with the involvement of *supernatural agencies*. It is *evocative*, that is, rich in words carrying multiple connotations. For those for whom the myth was originally intended, there is an *immediacy* in relation to the story that does not yet involve analytical thinking. In other words, in the mind of the listener, what is symbolised in the myth is not distinguished from the symbols. A fourth characteristic of myth is that it is *alogical*—its logic is not the same as that of everyday events. Similarly removed from everyday are the events recounted in the myth: they are *remote,* beyond the scope of historical time and place. Finally, the myth has a formative relation to the *community* which has adopted it. The myth influences the character and self-understanding of the community.

EXAMPLE: Here is part of a well-known mythical text in the Judaeo-Christian tradition. We can identify in the text some words and phrases which exemplify many of the mythical characteristics listed above. Why is it not possible to find examples *within the text* of all 7 characteristics?

Genesis 3:1-8
1 The serpent was the most subtle of all the wild beasts that Yahweh God had made. It
2 asked the woman, 'Did God really say you were not to eat from any of the trees in the
3 garden?' The woman answered the serpent, 'We may eat the fruit of the trees in the
4 garden. But of the fruit of the tree in the middle of the garden God said, "You must
5 not eat it, nor touch it, under pain of death".' Then the serpent said to the woman, 'No!
6 You will not die! God knows in fact that on the day you eat it your eyes will be
7 opened and you will be like gods, knowing good and evil.' The woman saw that the
8 tree was good to eat and pleasing to the eye, and that it was desirable for the
9 knowledge that it could give. So she took some of its fruit and ate it. She gave some
10 also to her husband who was with her, and he ate it. Then the eyes of both of them
11 were opened and they realised that they were naked . . . The man and his wife
12 heard the sound of Yahweh God walking in the garden in the cool of the day, and
13 they hid from Yahweh God among the trees of the garden . . .

Mythical features	Example in text (words/phrases)
dramatic language	Particular action—the conversation serpent/woman; the woman took some fruit, ate it, gave to husband; sudden realisation; they hid.
supernatural agencies	The serpent; God.
evocative language	Words carrying more than one level of meaning (connotations): eg eating; tree in middle of garden; dying; eyes being opened; knowledge; realisation of being naked; heard the sound of Yahweh.
immediacy	We cannot find an example of this *within* the text because immediacy refers to the inner attitude towards the story of persons within the believing community for whom the myth was originally written.
alogicality	The logic is different from that of everyday life: serpents do not speak; eating fruit gives no special knowledge, God does not walk in the garden.
remoteness	The events are described as happening in time and space far removed in the past—times not familiar to the listeners.
communal relevance	The text itself does not indicate its relevance to the community—except that it served as an explanation of the ill effects of disobeying God. The formative role of the myth for the community is to be assumed from the fact of its continued use over time.

TASK 1: Here is another well-known myth in the Judaeo-Christian tradition.
Read the text and identify some words and phrases, or elements of the text, which exemplify as many of the mythical characteristics as possible.

Genesis 32:23-32
Jacob wrestles with God

1   Before dawn Jacob arose and, taking his two wives, their serving women and his
2   eleven children, crossed the ford of Jaboc. He took them and sent them across the
3   stream and sent all his possessions over too. And Jacob was left alone.
4   And there one appeared to him who wrestled with him until dawn. At last, finding that
5   he could not get the better of Jacob, the other touched the sinew of his thigh, which
6   all at once withered; then he said, 'Let me go, for day is breaking.' But Jacob
7   answered, 'I will not let you go unless you bless me.' The other then asked, 'What is
8   your name?' 'Jacob,' he replied. The other said, 'Your name shall no longer be
9   Jacob; you shall be called Israel, one that prevails with God. If you have held your
10 own with God, you will prevail over people!' 'Tell me,' asked Jacob, 'what is your own
11 name?' But the other replied, 'Why do you ask my name?' And then and there the
12 other blessed him. So Jacob named the place Phanuel, the Face of God, 'Because I
13 have seen God face to face,' he said, 'and I have survived.' The sun rose as he left
14 Phanuel, limping because of his hip. That is the reason why to this day the Israelites
15 do not eat the sciatic nerve which is in the socket of the hip, where Jacob's strength
16 failed him, and the sinew of his thigh withered when it was touched.

Complete this table with examples of mythical features from the text.

Mythical features	Examples in text (words/phrases, elements)
dramatic language	....
supernatural agencies	....
evocative language	....
alogicality	....
remoteness	....

Check your answers in Appendix B.

As for the Genesis 3:1-8 text, we assume the original listener's inner attitude of *immediacy* towards this story, where symbol is not distinguished from what is symbolised.

Suggest what *communal relevance* this myth might have had for the believers in the listening community.

....

....

....

Symbolic-analogical mode

A symbol is something that stands for something else. For example, in some cultures, in paintings or Christmas cards or elsewhere, a *dove* often stands for *peace*. We are concerned here with linguistic symbols. In the broad sense, all language is symbolic in that letters and words stand for a sound, a thing or an idea. In the context of this resource book, a symbolic word or phrase, like a metaphor, is one which refers to something which in turn refers to something else. For example, the words *burning bush* stand for an object in the landscape which Moses encounters. In the biblical context in which it is used (Ex 3:2-4), where the bush does not burn up, it is a symbol for God. A further aspect of symbol is that while it suggests *some*thing about what God is like (for example, in this case, something alive that never dies), at the same time, we are to understand that God is *not* like a burning bush.

Think of some other symbols for God. Write them here:-

....

Symbolic language for God may be considered as ranging along a spectrum, as in the diagram. At one end are symbols which are not so easy to understand. At the other end they are easy to understand. These are called analogues.

Spectrum of symbolic language for God

Not easy to understand   Easy to understand
Symbols   Analogues

The *burning bush* symbol is probably less easy to understand than some others.
For example, when the psalmist says, speaking to God, *You are a rock of refuge*, it is relatively easy to understand a certain similarity between such a rock—shelter and protection from heat, cold, the enemy—and the safety and protection hoped for from God. But here, too, the analogue is both like and not like God. An analogue is something *similar to* but *not identical with* its referent.

The symbolic-analogical mode of discourse, then, refers to indirect uses of language, including figures of speech such as images and metaphors. What differentiates this sort of language from myth is the fact that what is symbolised is consciously understood to be different from the symbol. When this mode of discourse is employed, members of the faith community have begun to apply analytical thinking to the subject matter of their faith. The important feature of all of these symbolic-analogical uses of language is not only that they are indirect or non-literal in nature; they are essentially paradoxical, carrying the tension of both affirmation and negation, the *like/not like*, the *is/is not* relationship. That is, *God is light*, but not in any sense of the word *light* that we understand.

EXAMPLE: Read this text and then study the list below it of 'items or things' and the symbolic or analogic words used to describe them. Then decide whether you think the words are more at the symbolic or analogical end of the spectrum.

Vatican II – Constitution on the Sacred Liturgy, para. 10

1 Nevertheless, the liturgy is the summit toward which the activity of the Church is
2 directed; at the same time it is the fountain from which all her power flows. For the
3 goal of apostolic works is that all who are made [daughters and sons] of God by faith
4 and baptism should come together to praise God in the midst of [the] Church, to take
5 part in her sacrifice and to eat the Lord's supper.
6 The liturgy in its turn inspires the faithful to become "of one heart in love" when they
7 have tasted to the full of the paschal mysteries; it prays that "they may grasp by deed
8 what they hold by creed". The renewal in the Eucharist of the covenant between the

9   Lord and [humans] draws the faithful into the compelling love of Christ and sets them
10 afire. From the liturgy, therefore, and especially from the Eucharist, as from a
11 fountain, grace is channeled into us; and the sanctification of [humans] in Christ and
12 the glorification of God, to which all other activities of the Church are directed as
13 toward their goal, are most powerfully achieved.

Item or 'thing' referred to	Symbolic/analogical words used
the liturgy	[is a] summit, fountain
power [of the church]	flows
[by faith], all	[are made] daughters and sons of God
the paschal mysteries	[are] tasted
the love of Christ	sets [the faithful] on fire
the Eucharist	[as a] fountain channels grace

TASK 2: Read this text and identify as many symbolic or analogical (i.e. metaphorical) words or phrases as you can. Discuss with other students whether the words are symbolic or analogical – or somewhere in between.

The Church's mission and human destiny

1   The Church lives these realities, she lives by this truth about [humans], which enables
2   [them] to go beyond the bounds of temporariness . . . in which is expressed that
3   never-ending restlessness referred to in the words of Saint Augustine: 'You made us
4   for yourself, Lord, and our heart is restless until it rests in you'. In this creative
5   restlessness beats and pulsates what is most deeply human—the search for truth,
6   the insatiable need for the good, hunger for freedom, nostalgia for the beautiful, and
7   the voice of conscience. Seeking to see [humans] as it were with 'the eyes of Christ
8   himself', the Church becomes more and more aware that she is the guardian of a
9   great treasure, which she may not waste but must continually increase. Indeed,
10 Jesus said: 'The one who does not gather with me scatters'. This treasure of
11 humanity enriched by the inexpressible mystery of divine filiation and by the grace of
12 'adoption as sons and daughters' in the only Son of God, through whom we call God
13 'Abba', is also a powerful force unifying the Church above all inwardly and giving
14 meaning to all her activity. Through this force the Church is united with the Spirit of
15 Christ, that Holy Spirit promised and continually communicated by the Redeemer and
16 whose descent, which was revealed on the day of Pentecost, endures for ever. Thus
17 the powers of the Spirit, the gifts of the Spirit, and the fruits of the Holy Spirit are
18 revealed in [humans]. The present-day Church seems to repeat with ever greater
19 fervour and with holy insistence: 'Come, Holy Spirit!' Come! Come! 'Heal our
20 wounds, our strength renew; On our dryness pour your dew; Wash the stains of guilt
21 away; Bend the stubborn heart and will; Melt the frozen, warm the chill; Guide the
22 steps that go astray'.
23 This appeal to the Spirit . . . is the answer to all the 'materialisms' of our age . . . This
24 appeal is making itself heard on various sides and seems to be bearing fruit also in
25 different ways. Can it be said that the Church is not alone in making this appeal?
26 Yes it can, because the need for what is spiritual is expressed also by people who
27 are outside the visible confines of the Church.

[John Paul II, 1979, *Redemptor Hominis*, para. 18, pp 67-69.]

Item or 'thing' referred to	Symbolic/metaphorical words/phrases
…………………………	…………………………………..
…………………………..	…………………………………
…………………………..	…………………………………

English for Theology

....

....

Check your answers in Appendix B.

Metaphysical mode

Metaphysical discourse refers to language which relies heavily upon the words and concepts of the philosophy of being. For example, *essence* and *substance, existence* and *potency, form* and *matter, rational* and *sensible, habitual* and *actual* are terms likely to be encountered in metaphysical theology. Concepts such as the four causes are also likely to be used: the *material* and *formal causes* of things, which are said to be *intrinsic causes* because they are a constitutive part of a thing; and the *efficient* and *final causes* which are said to be *extrinsic* because they are outside of the thing. These are words referring to quite abstract concepts of being and are not usually part of everyday experience, unlike the concepts of, say, *joy, grief, anxiety, motivation* which are part of everyday experience.

The metaphysical mode was the dominant language underpinning much of the church's classic theology for many centuries, and metaphysical presuppositions continue into present-day theological discourse. Furthermore, against the view that the metaphysical age is long past is the claim that valid talk about God depends upon an understanding of the world which can be derived only from metaphysical reflection.[5] It is useful, therefore, for students to be aware of the features of this mode of discourse.

EXAMPLE: In this extract based on the writing of Thomas Aquinas, words and phrases which indicate the metaphysical mode have been identified in bold print.

How the morality of an action is judged

1 Though an action receives its **species** from the **object**, it does not receive its **species**
2 from it considered as a **material object** but according to the **rational character** of the
3 **object.** Thus, the **act of seeing** a stone is **not specified** by the stone but by the
4 coloured thing which is the **essential object** of vision. Now, every human action has
5 either the **rational character** of wrong-doing, or of a **meritorious act**, inasmuch as it
6 is voluntary. But the **object of the will**, according to its proper meaning, is the
7 **apprehended good**; and so, the human act is judged virtuous or vicious according to
8 the **apprehended good** toward which the **will is essentially attracted** and not
9 according to the **material object** of the action. For instance, if a man kills a stag,
10 believing that he is killing his father, he commits the sin of patricide. On the other
11 hand, if some hunter, thinking to kill a stag and having taken due care, kills his father
12 by chance, he is quite free from the crime of patricide.

[Bourke, editor, 1962, p 203.]

TASK 3: Now read this text from the writing of Pannenberg and identify some words and phrases which indicate the metaphysical mode. Write them in the space below. Some words in the first few lines have been identified in bold print as examples.

The distinction between God's essence and existence

1 The thesis that **God's essence** is incomprehensible did not stop the fathers from
2 maintaining that we may know **God's existence**. Thus John of Damascus argued
3 that knowledge of the **existence of God** is implanted in us by nature even though it

Unit 3 Meaning in Text: Modes of Discourse

```
4   has been obscured by sin to the point of denial of God. Gregory of Nyssa, too,
5   thought that we may rationally know both God's existence, especially by inference
6   from the order of the world to an intelligent author, and also the divine perfection.
7   On this ground he believed in addition that reason is forced to confess the unity of
8   God. The perfection of the divine being has to be admitted even by unbelievers,
9   Damascene thought. On this basis he argued for the infinity of God, and from this
10  again he deduced the unity . . .
11  In Latin Scholasticism Aquinas made the most impressive attempt to derive all his
12  statements about what God is from the proof of his mere existence as the first cause
13  of the world. His premise was that there must be a first in a sequence of causes . . .
14  This path from knowledge of the existence of a first cause to definition of its
15  distinguishing qualities seemed a much harder one to the age that followed. For
16  example, Occam agreed that God's independence and goodness follow directly from
17  his existence as a first cause but not his unity, infinity or omnipotence . . .
18  The older Protestant theologians saw clearly, however, that those who assert the
19  existence of God must have some idea of his essence, no matter how vague or
20  general. The question of the existence of a thing cannot be totally independent of
21  some idea of what the thing is. Proofs of God, as arguments that he exists,
22  presuppose that something of what he is may be known, eg, that he is the first
23  cause of the world.                                       [Pannenberg, 1991, pp 347-349.]
```

Some metaphysical words and phrases from the above text.

....	....	....
....	....	....
....	....	....
....	....	....

Check your answers in Appendix B.

Existential mode

Existential language describes the structures of human existence, and the ways we personally experience our existence here and now. For example, such language may refer to the human experiences of aspiration, dependence, hope, anxiety, success, failure, guilt, love and so on. As a philosophy, *existentialism* focuses on the importance of the individual person, on the centrality of human experience, and on the individual's personal responsibility before God.[6] This philosophy became dominant in the twentieth century when it was developed largely in reaction to the impersonal, universal and abstract categories of the classical (metaphysical) philosophical and theological tradition of the West. The language of existence is not confined to the modern era of course. As Macquarrie points out,[7] St Paul used it much in his New Testament writings, though the first century (CE) understanding of human existence differs from what we understand today.

EXAMPLE: In the following text, some words and phrases which describe human experiences (ie language in the existential mode) have been identified in bold print.

The many faces of grace

```
1   The acceptance of forgiveness of sin in Jesus opens the door to a radically new and
2   transformed existence. Grace cannot be situated in a realm that is different from
3   the one in which human projects meet success or failure. Grace confronts death,
```

English for Theology

4 **despair, fear, slavery, literalism** and **legalism**. Grace is also at the root of **beauty,**
5 **colour** and **form,** of the **loving response,** of **joy,** of **communication** and **communion**
6 of every stripe. Grace is to be celebrated in **efforts to love our children** well, in
7 physical, intellectual, spiritual accomplishments, in being **patient** with ourselves and
8 others, in facing difficulties with **courage** and **dignity**. Ultimately, even in our
9 **brokenness,** there is no human situation in which God's grace cannot reveal itself.

[Dreyer, 1990, p 238.]

TASK 4: Read the following text and identify some of the words and phrases which describe human experiences. Write the words in the space below.

Grace

1 At the heart of human life an offer is being made that can only come from God . . .
2 This gift is divine, yet it comes to us most often through the words and deeds of other
3 human beings. It is unconditional; it meets us as we are and asks only to be accepted,
4 but it arrives in our lives mediated by the very conditioned love and concern of others
5 for us . . . This gift, which is the most fundamental offer that God makes to [God's]
6 creatures, is difficult to receive and accept, because it invites a level of trust which
7 goes deeper than we are usually willing to travel. Yet the beginnings of such trust are
8 very human ones . . . The dependency of the infant on the mother is complete, and
9 the offered acceptance of the child on the part of the mother allows the young one to
10 develop trust in the mother, its environment and itself . . . gradually the child is able
11 to recognise that the world, thanks to its mother or significant other, is a basically
12 reliable world. Christians are convinced that in and through all such experiences of
13 human acceptance and trust (and indeed, even in contrast experiences of rejection
14 and distrust) God is communicating an acceptance of humankind that is more than, in
15 excess of, the human words and gestures of acceptance.

[McDermott, 1984, pp 12-13.]

Examples of existential language

....

....

....

....

Check your answers in Appendix B.

Empirical mode

Empirical language refers to facts which are in some way verifiable and observable. For example:

The disciples were cleaning their fishing nets.
The Christians developed schools and clinics in the rural areas.
The believers met in homes to study the scriptures and to pray.

Theology deals ultimately with subject matter which is not usually observable or verifiable in the scientific sense. However, theology does rely upon human experience which includes an empirical dimension, and hence empirical language, in a broad sense, can have a place in theology. Sometimes there is no clear-cut distinction between existential and empirical language.

Macquarrie identifies at least five uses of empirical language within theology.[8] These are:- 1) The arguments of natural theology based on observable facts in the world. 2) Certain empirical facts relating to the historical person of Jesus Christ who is at the centre of Christian theology. 3) Certain understandings of 'miracle' and 'prophecy' relating to God's action in the world (refer to Macquarrie for the full nuance of this use). 4) In a broader sense of empiricism, the 'facts' of religious experience as it occurs in some people's lives; 5) The observable, concrete outcomes of faith in various human lives and communities.

Think of some examples of each of these types of empirical language within the discipline of theology:-

1..
2..
3..
4..
5..

EXAMPLE: In the following text, some of the empirical statements and phrases have been identified in bold print.

The story of the crippled man

1   We have all seen him, have we not? Day after day, always at the same old pitch,
2   more or less unnoticed by people in a hurry, who still, sometimes with an air of
3   boredom or surprise, sometimes with a friendly nod, will **toss him a coin** as they
4   go on their way. There **he squats in his small corner**, alone, the familiar figure of
5   the local crock. So has it ever been. 'And **a man lame from birth was being**
6   **carried**, whom **they laid daily at that gate** of the temple which is called Beautiful to
7   ask alms of those who entered the temple' (Acts 3:2). Came the day when **Peter**, one
8   of the Nazarene's following, **noticed him sitting there**. There was **some exchange**
9   **of words between them**. The next thing **people saw** was their **neighbourhood**
10 **cripple fully restored and walking** as well as anyone. They 'recognised him as the
11 one who sat for alms at the Beautiful Gate of the temple; and **they were filled with**
12 **wonder and amazement** at what had happened to him' (Acts 3:10). Then **Peter** —
13 so Luke tells us — having first addressed the people, **said to the Jewish authorities**
14 who had afterwards chosen to concern themselves with the affair: ' . . . be it known to
15 you all, and to all the people of Israel, that by the name of Jesus Christ of Nazareth,
16 whom you crucified, whom God raised from the dead, by him this man is standing
17 before you well . . .' (Acts 4:100.

[Schillebeeckx, 1979, p. 17.]

TASK 5: Read the following text and identify some of the empirical statements and phrases used. Write them in the space below.

Ecology and theology

1   The loss of the rain forests is an ecological issue which encapsulates many others. It
2   can be seen as a symbol of the crisis confronting the whole Earth . . .
3   My argument will be that the destruction of the rain forests is an issue for the global
4   community. It has global effects and it has global causes, which include the lifestyle
5   of the middle class in affluent countries and the structure of international finance.
6   Theologically, I will argue that these rain forests are to be seen as a precious

English for Theology

```
7    expression of the exuberant fecundity of God.
8    Around the world, forests are being cleared for agriculture and grazing, burned, cut for
9    lumber, and flooded for dams and hydroelectric power. Seventeen million hectares of
10   forest are destroyed each year. In one year, an area the size of Austria is cleared of
11   forest.
12   The great rain forests of the Earth are now found mainly in the Amazon basin, in
13   Central Africa around Zaire, and in Papua New Guinea, Malaysia and Indonesia. The
14   Amazon basin, with its 2.1 million square miles of rain forest, has by far the biggest
15   part of the world's 2.9 million square miles of rain forest.
                                                                    [Edwards, 1995, pp 4-5.]
```

Examples of empirical language in this text.

……………………………	……………………………
……………………………	……………………………
……………………………	……………………………
……………………………	……………………………

Check your answers in Appendix B.

---

1. Macquarrie, J, 1967, *God-Talk*, SCM Press, London.
2. *Ibid*, p 169.
3. *Ibid*, especially Chapters 8-12, pp 168-249.
4. *Ibid*, p 169.
5. Pannenberg, W, 1990, *Metaphysics and the Idea of God*, translated by P Clayton, Eerdmans, Grand Rapids, Michigan, p 6.
6. McBrien, RP, editor, 1994, *Catholicism*, CollinsDove, North Blackburn, Vic, p 130.
7. Macquarrie, *op cit*, pp 240-241.
8. *Ibid*, pp 233 ff.

UNIT 4 MEANING IN TEXT: GENRE AND ORGANISATION OF IDEAS

In this unit we examine the role of *genre* and *patterns of organising ideas* within a text as helps to reading comprehension.

Genre and meaning

In this resource book, *genre* refers to a particular type of text with its own characteristic structure including a beginning, middle and end. The genre of a text can tell us something about the writer's purpose and can therefore help with reading comprehension. Common genres in biblical texts include narrative (story), hymns, prayers, prophecies and proverbs. Some common genres in theological texts include the essay and its many variations, the report, and the critique or critical review. Though they might be considered as variations on the essay, documents such as World Council of Churches Statements, Pastoral Letters, Encyclical Letters, Synod Statements, sermons or homilies and so on might also be considered genres in the theological field.

Common genres in theological texts

THE ESSAY

The most common genre is that of the *essay*, which has three main parts as follows.

- Introduction:- In a general opening statement, the writer introduces the topic, usually a noun phrase, and the context of the topic. The writer will also state his or her thesis, that is, point of view on the topic. The plan of the essay, or line of argument to be developed, will be outlined.
- The body of the essay:- This part sets out the writer's ideas and arguments in support of the thesis. The paragraphs in this part of the essay are likely to include analysis, description, examples, evaluation and so on. (Note: Work on paragraph structure will be undertaken in Unit 8.)
- Conclusion:- Here the writer sums up what has been said, re-stating the now well-supported claim or thesis made in the introduction and pointing to implications.

Examples of this general structure are virtually unlimited, and while an essay technically is a shorter text, as in an article, the same general structure—thesis, development, conclusion—can apply to book-length texts. An example of an essay would be Bettscheider, H, SVD, 'Truth in Interreligious Dialogue', *Verbum SVD* 40:1 (1999), Steyler Verlag, Netherlands, pp 25-40. (See Unit 24 for an extract from this article.)

TASK 1: List here some texts you have read with essay-type structure:

....

....

....

A variation on this general essay structure includes the *problem-solution* text.

PROBLEM-SOLUTION TEXTS

A *problem-solution* text usually has four main parts.

- The background situation: This part explains the context of the problem and contributing factors.

- The problem: A clear statement of the nature of the problem follows.
- Solution: Some analysis of the causes of the problem leads to proposed solutions and supporting arguments.
- Evaluation/conclusion: The desired outcome is outlined.

The papal encyclical *On Social Concerns*,[1] which examines the state of the world and the problem of inadequate human development, its causes and the direction of potential solutions, could be considered such a text.

TASK 2: Find and list some further examples of predominantly *problem-solution* texts. These may be book-length or article-length texts.

....

....

CRITICAL REVIEW

The *critical review* is another common genre used by theologians. Any of the commentaries on the encyclical referred to above, for example, "Feminist Analysis: A Missing Perspective"[2] would be such a critical review. The formal review usually includes the following parts.

- Introduction: This gives an overview of the topic or paper/book to be reviewed.
- Summary: The main points of what has been said are summarised.
- Critical evaluation: The positive and negative aspects of the position or paper/book to be reviewed are put forward, and weighed.
- Conclusion: The writer summarises her/his evaluation of the issue. This may be mainly positive or mainly negative, or sometimes balanced.

TASK 3: Find and list some critical reviews. Say, if it is possible, whether they are mainly positive or negative.

....

....

....

REPORT

Less common in the theological world, but sometimes used to give an account of dialogue or research projects, either completed or in progress, is the report. The structure of the report will usually include the following parts.

- A brief overview of the background or issue and type of research.
- The purpose of the research or dialogue project.
- An account of the methods used to gather information or the meetings held to date.
- Summary of the findings to date and their significance.
- Concluding recommendations.

Examples of reports would be:
'Jesus Christ with People in Asia': Report of a Consultation in Singapore. Singapore: Christian Conference of Asia, nd;
Kosuke Koyama, *Your Kingdom Come: Mission Perspectives*. Report on the World Conference on Mission and Evangelism. Geneva: World Council of Churches, 1980.

TASK 4: Find and list some examples of reports in the context of theology.

....

....

....

Each of these genres, then, has a predominant purpose which unifies it and shapes the structure of the whole text. In practice, texts may include variations on these main types. What is important for reading comprehension is not so much to make a black-and-white classification of every text you read, but to recognise the range of genres and how the writer uses them to communicate meaning.

Patterns of organising ideas within text

Within any of these genres, ideas are likely to be organised using a variety of patterns, which may include any of the following:-

description	*explanation*	*sequence*
example	*argument*	*exhortation*
analysis	*cause and effect*	*purpose/reason*
contrast/comparison	*order of importance*	*most significant points*
evaluation/critique	*narrative*	

Another pattern very common in academic texts is that of the definition. A *definition* is a brief explanation of the meaning of something. A *definition* may occur anywhere within a text where it is needed and is usually marked by the use of the indefinite article.

Examples: *A definition* is *a brief explanation*…
            A hermeneutics of suspicion is *a way of interpreting*…
            Conversion is **an experience** of **a change** of heart…

The role of 'signpost' words in reading comprehension

Often it is possible to identify the pattern of organisation of ideas by certain 'signpost' words (often called discourse markers) which link sentences and ideas in the text. These words, which may be adverbial conjunctions or phrases, signal to the reader the logic of the way in which ideas are organised. 'Signpost' words can operate at all levels in a text, from the whole text, through paragraphs and at sentence level. They often come at the beginning of a sentence.

Eg *However, we can be sure that the sea level will rise.*
    For example, ideas may be organised in any of the following ways.

But they may also be placed between clauses.
Eg *We can be sure, however, that the sea level…*
    Ideas may be organised, for example, in any …

Study this summary of many common 'signpost' words. Use it as a reference to help your reading comprehension. Note: It will help your writing too.

[The summary draws on a number of general sources dealing with discourse markers. The particular arrangement is based on Oshima, A, & Hogue, A, 1991, *Writing Academic English*, Addison-Wesley, New York, 2nd edition, p 262.]

SUMMARY OF COMMON 'SIGNPOST' WORDS AND PHRASES

Structural Function	Linking Sentences- Adverbials	Linking Clauses Coordinators	Subordinators
To indicate an **example**	that is that is to say namely for instance for example		
To indicate an **additional** idea	also, too besides what is more furthermore moreover in addition	and	
To indicate a **re-formulation** or **emphasis**	in other words indeed rather to put it another way in fact		
To indicate a **contrasting** or **different idea,** or to **concede** an idea	in contrast however on the other hand nonetheless nevertheless instead	but yet	though even though although while whereas
To indicate a **comparison**	similarly likewise also too	and	as just as
To indicate **an alternative**	otherwise alternatively	or	if unless
To indicate **a cause** or **reason**	for that reason	for	because since as
To indicate **purpose**			in order that so that
To indicate an **effect** or **result**	accordingly as a result as a consequence therefore thus consequently hence	so	
To indicate **chronological** order or **most significant** points	firstly (secondly, etc) next, last, finally first of all meanwhile in the year after that since then subsequently		before while until after
To indicate order of **importance**	significantly, or most significantly importantly, more/most importantly above all		
To indicate a **conclusion** or **summary**	in conclusion in summary to conclude to summarise, to sum up		

Other adverbs which indicate the writer's attitude

As well as the above table of words and phrases, there are many other adverbial words which may be used to link sentences and ideas. Such words often reveal the writer's attitude or point of view. For example, adverbs such as *significantly, clearly, obviously, manifestly, problematically, fortunately, unfortunately, sadly, tragically,* and many more tell us something about what the writer thinks, which is an important element of reading comprehension.

TASK 5: The following texts provide short examples of some of the different ways in which ideas can be organised. Read through each one and identify in the space provided the **main type of organisation used**. Choose from this list:-

a. narrative   **b. argument**   **c. cause/effect**
d. comparison/contrast   **e. explanation**

Text excerpt   Main type of organisation

1   Ecology and theology
The destruction of the rain forests contributes to global crisis not only
through increasing greenhouse gases . . . but also by changing rainfall
patterns . . . Forests themselves produce rain clouds through trans-
piration (the "perspiration" of the vegetation). In this process the sun
draws moisture up from the Earth and the trees, through the foliage
of the trees . . . condensing into an afternoon downpour . . . When forests
are destroyed, however, heavy rains continue for a while, wash away the
now unprotected, fragile topsoil, and silt up nearby rivers. Then the rains
themselves begin to bring less moisture. In Ethiopia forested land has
decreased from 50 percent of the country to 1 percent in the last forty years,
and declining rainfall has reduced much of the country to desert.[3]   ....

2   Nature of theology
Theology is faith seeking understanding. Apart from its brevity, this
definition has some distinct advantages. Firstly, it indicates that theology
is a *faith* activity. It is a discipline distinct from, say, religious studies,
which seeks to study religions from a neutral point of view. Theology
takes a faith stance. It takes place within a faith community. It is an
expression of the faith of the theologian and the community to which he
or she belongs. Secondly, it indicates the provisional nature of theology.
It is *seeking* understanding. It does not claim to possess all understanding,
but is a process which is always seeking greater understanding . . . Thirdly,
it seeks understanding. Theology involves the use of intelligence and . . .[4]   ....

3   Contemporary theology and previous theology
To write a book on contemporary theologies is to assume that contemporary
theologies differ from the theology of previous generations. Nowhere is this
more true than with Catholic theology. While Protestant theology developed
in a more "organic" manner, Catholic theology locked itself into a very defensive
position after the Reformation and the Enlightenment. Catholic theology cut itself
off from the intellectual ferment that was taking place . . . The task now at hand is to
examine what some of these differences are between contemporary Catholic
theology and the theology from which it immediately diverged. This previous
theology dominated the nineteenth century, though its roots go back much further
and unfortunately its branches reached well into the twentieth century.[5]   ....

English for Theology

4   The world of Mark's Gospel

Mark's gospel was probably the first of the four gospels and was written around 70 of the Common Era, in Rome. Its writing coincided with the catastrophic events that were unfolding in Jerusalem, where the Roman armies had laid siege to the city, and were soon to destroy both city and temple in a monumental showdown with the Jewish people . . . Meanwhile, in Rome, the Christian community in which Mark's Gospel arose had additional problems of its own. Not only were there theological differences among its members, but there was also danger from outside. It seems that there was . . . sporadic persecution of the Roman Christian community by the emperor Nero. In the wake of the great fire that had devastated the city, Nero was desperate to find someone to blame. The Christians were an obvious target. Opposed to emperor worship and suspected of engaging in bizarre rituals, they were an obvious solution to the emperor's dilemma. [6]   ....

5   Sociological, psychological and theological effects- speech about God

. . . there is an interdependent relation between a religion's symbol system . . . and . . . its concept of the general order of things. Since the symbol of God is the focal point of the whole religious system, an entire world order and…view are wrapped up with its character. . . . For example, God spoken of as a wrathful tyrant can be called upon to justify holy wars . . . Language about God as universal creator, lover and saviour of all, on the other hand, moves believers towards forgiveness, care . . . inclusive community. The effective history of patriarchal speech about God also bears directly on the religious significance and truth of what is said about divine mystery. Feminist theological analysis makes clear that the tenacity with which the patriarchal symbol of God is upheld is nothing less than violation of the first commandment . . . the worship of an idol. An idol is not necessarily a god in the shape of an animal, a golden calf or little statue . . . Rather, any representation of the divine used in such a way that its symbolic and evocative character is lost from view partakes of the nature of an idol. Whenever one image or concept of God expands to the horizon thus shutting out others . . . there an idol comes into being.[7]   ....

TASK 6: Find all the 'signpost' words in these two texts. List them in the space provided and say what logical pattern they indicate. Refer back to the summary of 'signpost' words to help you.

A   Universal problems in the world today

1   **Today**, more than in the past there is an urgent need to *foster a consciousness of*
2   *universal moral values*. We need to do this in order to face the problems of the
3   present, all of which are assuming an increasingly global dimension. For instance,
4   the promotion of peace and human rights, the settling of armed conflicts both within
5   States and across borders, and the protection of ethnic minorities and immigrants are
6   issues which face all nations. Furthermore, the safeguarding of the environment and
7   the battle against terrible diseases also call for concerted action among nations.
8   Likewise, the fight against drug and arms traffickers, and against political and
9   economic corruption require universal cooperation: these are issues which nowadays
10 no nation is in a position to face alone. They concern the entire human community,
11 and thus they must be faced and resolved through common efforts.[8]

      word/s   (logical structure)
1 Eg *today*......... (*sequence*...)   2 .... (   )
3 .... (   )   4 .... (   )
5..................... (   )

B   Human development and being part of culture

1 The need to accept one's own culture as a structuring element of one's personality,
2 especially in the initial stages of life . . . can hardly be overestimated. It is on the basis
3 of this essential relationship . . . that people acquire a *sense of their nationality* . . .
4 Love for one's country is **thus** a *value to be fostered*, without narrow-mindedness but
5 with love for the whole human family and with an effort to avoid those pathological
6 manifestations which occur when the sense of belonging turns into self-exaltation . . .
7 and other forms of nationalism, racism and xenophobia.
8 Consequently, while it is certainly important to be able to appreciate the values of
9 one's own culture, there is also a need to recognise that every culture . . . necessarily
10 has its limitations. In order to prevent the sense of belonging to one particular culture
11 from turning into isolation, an effective antidote is a serene and unprejudiced
12 knowledge of other cultures. Moreover, when cultures are carefully and rigorously
13 studied, they very often reveal beneath their outward variations significant common
14 elements. This can also be seen in the historical sequence of cultures and
15 civilisations . . . Cultural diversity should therefore be understood within the
16 broader horizon of the unity of the human race . . . In fact, only an overall vision of
17 both the elements of unity and the elements of diversity makes it possible to
18 understand and interpret the full truth of every human culture.[9]

word   (logical structure)

1 Eg thus...L4 (effect)   2.................. (   )

3.................. (   )   4.................. (   )

5.................. (   )   6.................. (   )

TASK 7: The next time you are reading for study purposes, pay special attention to the logical organisation of ideas in the text and note any 'signpost' words which indicate the type of pattern being used by the writer.

---

1. John Paul II, *On Social Concerns*, 1987.
2. Riley, 1989, pp 186-201.
3. Edwards, 1995, pp 6-7.
4. Ormerod, 1990, pp 3-4.
5. *Ibid*, p 25.
6. Kiley, 1995, pp 15-16.
7. Johnson, 1994, pp 36, 39.
8. John Paul II, Message for World Day of Peace, January 2000, para 18, amended.
9. John Paul II, World Day of Peace, January 2001, para 6-7, amended.

UNIT 5   PREDICTION AS AN AID TO COMPREHENSION

In Unit 2 we practised the skill of predicting a book's usefulness based on the information contained in its title, chapter headings, publication date and so on.

In this unit we practise predicting what might come next in a text based on two sources, namely, your own general knowledge of the context, and/or clues in the text itself.

Your own knowledge of the topic can help you to predict the general content of a text or part of a text. Clues within the text itself, as well as your own knowledge, can help you to predict the kind of idea—and the word class, ie noun, verb—which will probably occur next in the development of a text. Readers may not always be fully aware of these mental processes of predicting, which occur naturally when reading. Consciously practising both kinds of prediction can make comprehension easier.

We have already seen in Unit 4 how discourse markers ('signpost' words) can signal the kind of idea which follows, and in Unit 8 we will see how paragraph structure can also help prediction. Here we are focussing on the role of background knowledge and clues in the text itself in prediction.

Using background knowledge to predict

Consider this example.
>Book title: *To Care for the Earth: A Call to a New theology*[1]
>Section heading: Poisoning the Earth

At the level of content, your own general knowledge of ecological issues and your understanding of the word *poisoning* will enable you to predict that the following text will probably discuss the effects of fertilisers, chemical sprays and pesticides used on various food crops, and the flow-on effects to soil fertility, ground-water and river systems, not to mention the human populations involved. Being prepared in this way will enable you to read and understand the text more easily and more quickly. Now practise predicting what might follow the headings below.

TASK 1: The same book, *To Care for the Earth,* contains the following section headings:-

>i)   Air pollution
>ii) Soil erosion

Make notes of what you expect to read about under each of these headings.

Air pollution	Soil erosion
....	....
....	....
....	....
....	....

Discuss your ideas in groups of three or four students and then share your ideas with the whole class. Consult the book if it is available in your library. Otherwise, check the notes in Appendix B.

Using linguistic clues within the text to predict

Clues within the text itself can enable you to predict the kind of idea which is likely to follow.

TASK 2: Using clues within the text, complete the blank spaces.

<u>Air pollution</u>

1 Industrial era developments, particularly during the second half of the twentieth century, have
2 been critically damaging to the atmosphere. Around the world we hear numerous examples
3 of the occurrence of (**1**............... and ....), which cause ill effects to both
4 (**2**................. and ....). A number of factors have contributed to this state of
5 affairs but the interrelated developments of (**3** ....,
6 .... and ....) would have to be among the major causes of air
7 pollution.

Use this table to help you work out possible answers:-

<u>Clues in the text</u>	<u>Possible answers</u>
1 We are looking for *examples* of *damage to the atmosphere*	
'occurrence of ....*and* ....'.	....
We are looking for two nouns/noun phrases, joined by the conjunction *and*.	....
2 'cause ill effects to both ....'	....
'to' suggests noun/noun phrase; 'both' indicates two items.	....
3 We are looking for *contributing* causes of *this state of affairs*, ie pollution.	
'interrelated developments of......................., ... and ....'	....
Causes suggests a noun/noun phrase and the comma together with the conjunction *and* suggests three items.	....

Check your answers in Appendix B.

Compare the examples above with this:-

> Book title: *Contemporary Epistemology*[2]
> Chapter title: Holism and Indeterminacy
>   Section heading: The Indeterminacy of Translation
>   Atomism and Holism

English for Theology

Unless you are already advanced in the philosophy of knowledge, you would probably have some trouble predicting the text under these section headings. Consequently, comprehension would be slower and more difficult, if not impossible.

If you should need to read a book (or article) which has a title or headings difficult to understand, you might first check whether the book has a glossary of terms. You might also look up a dictionary which gives examples of word use, and perhaps even an encyclopedia to give you some understanding of terms and context.

In the tasks which follow, use your general knowledge of the context and/or clue words in the text to help you predict the sort of information which might follow. Write down your responses as brief notes in your notebook and when you have finished, compare your notes with those around you. Finally, check the answers at the end of the book.

TASK 3: In an article entitled *Revelation*, there is a section on 'Revelation outside the Bible'. What ideas, issues, questions would you expect to read about? Makes notes and discuss your ideas with the class.

Ideas	Issues	Questions
....	....	....
....	....	....
....	....	....
....	....	....

TASK 4: Read this short passage from the first chapter of a book entitled *The Way of Paradox: Spiritual life as taught by Meister Eckhart*:[3]

> . . . what are the most urgent spiritual needs of the present time, and how are they to be met? Amid the general unrest and disquiet . . . two main desires can be seen coming to the surface . . . The first is political and social . . . The second is more inward and personal.

Make brief notes on what might follow. Share your ideas with those around you and then discuss with the whole class.

Two main desires:

Political and social	Inward and personal
....	....
....	....
....	....
....	....

Which is more helpful to you in making predictions here- your own knowledge of the topic or clues within the text?

Unit 5 Prediction as an Aid to Comprehension

TASK 5: Read this first part of a chapter entitled "Problems and Opportunities for the Future" in a book with the title, *Towards Vatican III*[4]

1   From Vatican II the ecumenical movement received a strong impulse. Across the board,
2   Catholic theology began to tackle the important ecumenical issues. Catholic authorities
3   entered into wide and various contacts with other churches and ecumenical organisations,
4   and the newly founded Roman Secretariate for Church Unity developed . . . into a powerful
5   source of ecumenical expectations. Catholics got to know the Christians of other
6   denominations and learned to appreciate their heritages.
7   In recent years, however, powerful counter-forces have brought the ecumenical
8   movement both within and without the Catholic Church to a standstill.

What sort of information do you think will come next in this second paragraph? Identify clues in the last sentence to help you. Discuss with three or four students around you. Give reasons for your opinions.

Clues in the text	Probable content (in general) of next paragraph
…………………………………	………………………………………………………
…………………………………	………………………………………………………
…………………………………	………………………………………………………

TASK 6: Read this beginning of a chapter in a book with the following title.
    Title: *Asian Faces of Jesus,*[5] Chapter 3 "The Buddha and the Christ"

    Interreligious dialogue is carried out on three different, but essentially related, levels: the levels of *core-experience, collective memory*, and *interpretation* . . .

Predict what the following paragraphs of the chapter are likely to be about.

………………………………………………………………………………………………………

………………………………………………………………………………………………………

………………………………………………………………………………………………………

Which is more helpful to prediction in this text- background knowledge or words in the text?

Check your answers in Appendix B.

---

1. McDonagh, S, 1986, *To Care for the Earth: A Call to a New Theology*, Chapman, London.
2. Dancy, J, 1985, *Contemporary Epistemology*, Blackwell, Oxford.
3. Smith, C, 1987, *The Way of Paradox*, Darton, Longman and Todd, London, p 3.
4. Tracy, D, Kung, H & Metz, JB, editors, 1978, *Toward Vatican III*, Concilium, Seabury Press, New York, p 67.
5. Sugirtharajah, RS, editor, 1993, *Asian Faces of Jesus*, SCM Press, London, p 46.

UNIT 6 READING FOR SPECIFIC INFORMATION : SCANNING

Scanning refers to the skill of reading quickly in order to find particular information or facts in contrast to reading all of the written text presented. For example, we scan to find a person's telephone number, to find our own name in a long list of students, to find our own flight destination on a departure board at the airport, and so on.

In academic situations it is important to learn to scan effectively in order to save time, so try to scan as quickly as possible when doing the exercises in this unit.

What academic situations can you think of where you might want to scan for specific information? Share your ideas with the students around you.

The following tasks provide practice in scanning in academic situations which you are likely to encounter.

TASK 1: A very important book has been translated into several languages listed below. You want to read this book in your first language. Scan this list to see if your language is one of them.

English	Japanese
German	Spanish
Tagalog	Hindi
Indonesian	Farsi
Mandarin	Vietnamese
French	Korean
Russian	Dutch
Kmer	Portuguese

Now scan the above list again. How many of the languages begin with the letter F?

....

TASK 2: You are looking for articles or books by E Schillebeeckx in the reference list below. Are there any?

1   R Bultmann, *Theology of the New Testament*, London/New York 1951-55.
2   H Conzelmann, *Outline of the Theology of the New Testament*, London, 1969.
3   O Betz, *What Do We Know About Jesus?*, London, 1968.
4   Karl Barth, *Church Dogmatics*, Edinburgh, 1936-69.
5   Paul Tillich, *Systematic Theology*, London, 1968.
6   Sally McFague, *Models of God:Theology for an Ecological, Nuclear Age*, Phil., 1987.
7   L O'Donovan, editor, *A World of Grace*, NewYork, 1980.
8   G Ebeling, *The Nature of Faith*, London/Philadelphia, 1961.
9   Elizabeth Johnson, *Consider Jesus*, London, 1990.
10 HU von Balthasar, *Who Is a Christian*, London, 1968.
11 Karl Rahner, *Foundations of Christian Faith*, New York, 1978.
12 David Hollenbach, *Justice, Peace and Human Rights*, New York, 1988.
13 Rebecca Chopp, *The Praxis of Suffering*, Maryknoll, 1986.

Answer: ....YES/NO?

TASK 3: You want some references on Christology. Scan again the above bibliography and list in order of importance those books which are most likely to be useful for your purposes.

i .... ii .... etc ....

TASK 4: For some other purpose, you want to consult only those books in the above bibliography published since 1985. Which books will be useful for you? Circle the numbers of the relevant books. List them here.

....

TASK 5: Below is part of the contents of a book: Edwards D, 1995, *Jesus the Wisdom of God*, St Paul's, Homebush. You want to know whether this book's treatment of the meaning of Jesus takes into account
i)   new scientific knowledge about the universe
ii) insights of women
iii) the question of Jesus in relation to non-Christian religions.

List below some key words in relation to each question. Then scan the contents and note relevant topics and page numbers in the column opposite.

Key words	Relevant sections - topic and page number
i) New scientific knowledge about the universe	....
eg	....
ii) Insights of women	
eg	....
....	....
iii) Jesus/non-Christian religions	
eg	....
....	....

(PART OF) CONTENTS

2 Jesus the Wisdom of God
    The Wisdom of Jesus—The Preaching and Practice of Radical Compassion   45
        Wisdom's Teacher   46
        Wisdom's Banquet 47   ......
    "Wisdom Has Built Herself a Home"   50
        Jesus Identified with the Wisdom of God 50
        Retrieving Wisdom Christology   51
    Directions for a Wisdom Christology   57
        Pre-existence   57
        The Human Person and the Divine Person 59
        A Feminist Christology   61
        A Christology of Praxis   62
        Jesus the Wisdom of God and Other Religious Traditions 64
        Life in Other Solar Systems 66
    ....

4 The God of Mutual Love and Ecstatic Fecundity
    The Trinity as Mutual Love – Richard of St Victor   94
        Friendship and Mutual Love in God 94 ...
    The Universe as the Self-Expression of God—Bonaventure   101
        God as Dynamic, Ecstatic and Fecund 101 ... .

6 Human Beings and Other Creatures   133
    From Individualism to Persons-In-Mutual-Relationship   133
    Human Participation in the Community of Creatures   137
        The Sphere of Bodiliness 137

English for Theology

       Made from Stardust   139
       Two Principles for a Theological Anthropology 142
  Salvation and the Universe   145
       Science and Theology on the Future of the Universe   145
       The Salvation of the Universe   148
7 Ecological Praxis   153

TASK 6: Here is part of an index to a book on Christology. You are particularly interested in the aspects of *suffering* and the *humanity of Jesus*. First list some synonyms or alternative words that may refer to *suffering* and *humanity of Jesus*. Then identify any topics and page numbers most likely to be useful. List them below in order of importance.

cosmos, 70-71, 139-44	preaching of Jesus, 5, 51-54, 90-91
cross, 13, 58-60, 76	Rahner, K, 11-12, 19-31
Cyril of Alexandria, 46-47	reign of God, 52-56, 62, 74-79
	Resurrection, 59-61 64, 92
death of Jesus, 57-59	Reuther, RR, 103
descending christology, 69-73	
descent into hell, 59	sabbath, 142-43
divine nature, 7-9, 25-31	salvation, 4-6, 20, 53, 75
	Schillebeeckx, E, 55-56, 62-63, 122-25
ecology, 139-40	self-consciousness of Jesus, 35-47
ethics, 78-80, 126, 141	Spirit, 44, 51, 61, 74-75, 90, 106
	social justice, 62, 67-81, 84-87, 98-99
feminist christology, 97-113	story of Jesus, 49-65
	suffering, 13, 84-85, 115-127
Hilary of Poitiers, 8	
human nature, 9, 21-25, 30-32	Teilhard de Chardin, 141-42
hypostatic union, 29, 42	Tertullian, 100-101
incarnation, 19-31, 33, 69-73, 107	transcendental christology, 21-33, 38-42

[From index of Johnson, E, *Consider Jesus*, 1990.]

<u>Topics (including related topics) and page numbers</u>:-

suffering ……………………………………………………………………..

humanity of Jesus ……………………………………………………………

TASK 7: You are studying the relationship of Christianity to the other world religions. Scan below part of the contents of a book on Christianity in the world today to see if there is anything here that you should read. Note the section number/s and headings or sub-headings.

CONTENTS

1 *Approach to God*
   Transcendence
   The future of religion
   Proofs of God?
   More than pure reason
2 *The reality of God*
   The hypothesis
   Reality
   Ambiguity of the concept of God
   The task of theology

3 *Salvation outside the Church*
  Revalued religions
  Wealth of religions
4 *Bewildering consequences*
  Anonymous Christianity?
  Superior ignorance?
5 *Challenge on both sides*
  No levelling down
  Helpful diagnosis
6 *Not exclusiveness, but uniqueness*
  Christian existence as critical catalyst
  Common quest for truth

[Adapted from contents, Kung, H, 1978, *On being a Christian*.]

Section numbers/headings/subheadings relevant to relation of Christianity to world religions:

....

TASK 8: You want to read something on spirituality. Scan the contents section below of an international Catholic weekly magazine. Are there any items in this edition which may be useful for you?   List the items below.

CONTENTS

**Is Christianity dying in the
Holy Land?**
TREVOR MOSTYN
1568

A time to embrace
MATTHIAS GIERTH
1570

From ivory to celluloid
MELANIE MCDONAGH
1571

Hume's mission impossible
CLIFFORD LONGLEY
1572

My time in prison
BRUCE MCPHERSON
1574

Stop, look and listen
LIONEL BLUE
1575

Notebook
1576

English for Theology

Letters
1577

Books
RICHARD PRICE; DAVID GOODALL;
CHRISTOPHER WALTON, ISABEL QUIGLY;
JUDITH MARSHALL
1580

Arts
MARGARET HOWARD; ROY SHAW;
JOHN AMIS, LAVINIA BYRNE
1586

Cardinals look to a Reformed papacy
THE CHURCH IN THE WORLD
1589

General Synod debates
New version of the Creed
HOME NEWS
1593

The living Spirit
1596

The power of prayer
GEMMA SIMMONDS
1597

(From *THE TABLET* 20 November 1999)

Items/page numbers relevant to spirituality:-

....

....

TASK 9: Imagine that you have two essays to write, one on *liberation theology* and another dealing with the question of *Jesus Christ in relation to other world religions and peoples*.
You want to find out quickly whether the book, *Consider Jesus* will be a useful study reference for either or both of these two essays. Scan this part of the preface for any clue words in relation to your two topics. Will the book be useful or not? Give reasons for your opinion.

CONSIDER JESUS

PART OF PREFACE

1   I have chosen the metaphor of waves breaking on the beach to unify this vast body of
2   material. As a wave is created by wind at sea and then rises up, rolls in, and breaks
3   as it comes close to land, so too it seems that successive understandings of Christ have formed,
4   swelled, and broken upon Catholic consciousness since the mid- twentieth century. The first wave
5   in the 1950s consisted in remembering the genuine humanity of Jesus Christ, a memory stirred up
6   by the 1,500th anniversary of the ancient council of Chalcedon which had declared the

7   christological dogma. A decade later biblical scholarship began to flourish, triggering critical
8   discovery of the history of Jesus. Both of these waves overlapped as they arrived in a church that
9   was incorporating concern for justice into its sense of mission. Before they had time to recede, a
10 third wave formed as the voice of the poor began to be heard doing theology from the 'underside
11 of history' and so claiming Jesus Christ as liberator. Almost simultaneously the movement of
12 feminist theology stirred yet another wave to life, swelling as the majority of the church's members
13 who had long been left out of the conversation about Christ began to articulate their insights. Even
14 more recently a realisation of the vastness of the world and its peoples has arisen, and looms as a
15 question about the universal influence of Jesus the Christ. Under threat of ecological
16 disaster, global vision now grows even wider to incorporate the view that not only human
17 beings but all creatures of the earth and the universe itself are destined for final blessing in
18 Christ. Thus, pressures, needs and new scholarship both inside the church and in the wider, tightly
19 knit, anguished world have conspired together to create wave after wave of new insight into Jesus
20 Christ. As with all waves, these are not always clearly separated from one another; as waves will
21 do, they are collectively changing the shape of the landscape.

(From the preface to Johnson, 1990.]

Words in the text, with Line number reference, which may be relevant to:-

liberation theology ....

Jesus Christ in relation to world religions..

Check all your answers in Appendix B.

UNIT 7 READING FOR THE GENERAL IDEA: SKIMMING

In the previous unit you practised scanning—that is, quickly looking through an index, contents page or text to find specific information that you want.

Skimming is another strategy for quickly finding out the general idea—or the gist—of a text. For this purpose, you also read quickly. To be able to identify the writer's main message, that is, the main point she or he is trying to make, you need to be able to differentiate between that main idea and the details and examples which the writer may use.

When you study, there are likely to be many situations where you first want to find out the general idea of a text in order to decide whether you need to read it more thoroughly.

The exercises in this unit provide practice in skim reading. First you will read some short news items and then some paragraphs from books in order to identify the main idea. It is important to read as quickly as you can, and to read just enough of the text to get your answer.

TASK 1: Quickly read the following six short news passages based on a church newspaper. Identify the main point of each item and then select the <u>most suitable</u> heading for each from the list of fourteen possible headings given below.

<u>Possible headings</u>
1 *World Council of Churches acts against racism*
2 *Diocese helps impoverished farmers*
3 *Greed fuels small arms trade*
4 *Kenyan woman facilitates conference preparation*
5 *Concern over emigration of Catholics*
6 *Government-funded houses built in village*
7 *Call for Christian-Muslim harmony*
8 *Sale of body parts to repay debts*
9 *Iraq—the 'cradle of civilisation'*
10 *First visit of a Pope to Egypt*
11 *Police in search of priest*
12 *Vatican calls to control arms trade*
13 *Third UN decade against racism*
14 *Religious leader condemns Iraq sanctions*

News item	**Most suitable heading**

1 An Archbishop of the Syrian Church in Iraq was addressing a Jubilee meeting in Rome recently. Recalling that Iraq had been the 'cradle of civilisation', he lamented its present serious lack of development. Of concern too was the fact that scores of Catholics were emigrating from the country. All of this, he said, was the tragic result of the sanctions against his country, which the Archbishop called upon the international community to recognise as a grave injustice.   ....

2 As the third UN decade to counter racism goes by, many international non-government organisations (NGOs) doubt the will of national governments to tackle the problems effectively. In spite of this, the World Council of Churches (WCC) is organising a major World Conference where churches and NGOs together can work at raising consciousness and developing strategies to address this evil in their communities. A Kenyan woman, Pauline Muchina, will serve as a

consultant to the WCC in the preparatory process. She will also facilitate
regional and inter-regional consultations on the topic of racism.   ....

3 On a visit to Cairo recently, the Pope, who is the first
Roman Catholic Pontiff to visit Egypt, celebrated Mass for 20,000
members of the faithful and appealed to both Muslims and Christians
everywhere to work for harmony and peace. To strengthen this
message, the Pope held meetings with Muslim and other Christian
leaders in Egypt, urging interreligious tolerance.   ....

4 Police authorities have been looking for a priest who is said to have
destroyed some government-funded houses in the village in order to get
bricks for a church building. Local people said this was not true, and that
villagers themselves had used the old bricks for their own purposes.   ....

5 Authorities in a diocese south of the capital have established
an irrigation scheme. This follows news reports that farmers have had to
sell their own body parts as the only way to pay their debts. The project will
enable the mainly lower-caste peasants of the region to grow their crops
successfully.   ....

6 The greed of arms dealers was fuelling the 'scandal' of trafficking in
small arms trade, said Archbishop Martino in his address to the UN General
Assembly. As the Holy See's Permanent Observer at the UN, Martino was
calling on world governments to control the trade in small arms, in order to
stem the tide of armed conflict around the world.   ....

TASK 2: Skim read the short passage below and decide which of the statements best describes the main idea. Note: All of the statements are true according to what is in the text but only one encapsulates the main point of the paragraph.

In many parts of the world, forests are being cleared for agriculture, cut down for timber or burnt to make way for plantations; large areas are flooded for dams and hydroelectricity. Seventeen million hectares of forest, an area the size of Austria, are destroyed every year. This causes soil erosion, destruction of fauna and flora, pollutes the earth and inevitably causes suffering to the poor of the earth. An ethics for the third millennium will recognise that ecological integrity and justice are radically inter-related, that care of the environment is fundamentally a theological issue.*

[*Paraphrased from Edwards, 1995, pp 2, 4.]

a Huge areas of forest around the world are being destroyed each year   ❏

b Environmental damage causes suffering for the poor and loss of fauna and flora   ❏

c An adequate theology in future will take an ecological stance   ❏

d A new ethics is needed for the third millennium   ❏

English for Theology

TASK 3: Skim read the passage below and say which of the statements best expresses the writer's main point.

> This last half-century of development in christology brings into clear view the fact that the Christian community is borne by a living tradition. As a vital, creative movement in time, this tradition hands on its inherited truth enriched through living response to new experiences. The witness of generations who have believed before us has brought the church to this moment in its pilgrimage. In turn, adult believers now have the responsibility to utter their own christological word, personally and collectively as church, so that faith in Jesus Christ may be passed on to the next generation in a truly living state. These chapters have been written to that end. *
>
> [*Excerpt from preface, Johnson, 1990]

a There have been important developments in christology in the last half century ❑

b The Christian tradition hands on inherited truth about Jesus Christ ❑

c Each generation (of Christians) is responsible for passing on tradition enriched through living response to new experiences. ❑

TASK 4: Read the passage below and identify the statement which best describes its main purpose.

The present situation of the world, seen in the light of faith, calls us back to the very essence of the Christian message, creating in us a deep awareness of its true meaning and of its urgent demands. The mission of preaching the Gospel dictates at the present time that we should dedicate ourselves to the liberation of men and women in their present existence in this world. For unless the Christian message of love and justice shows its effectiveness through action in the cause of justice in the world, it will only with difficulty gain credibility with the women and men of our times.

[*Justice in the World*, Synod of Bishops, 1971, Section II.]

a The light of faith is required for preaching the Gospel ❑

b We should dedicate ourselves to human liberation ❑

c Action for justice is an essential part of preaching the Gospel credibly ❑

d The Christian message of love and justice is effective in our times ❑

TASK 5: Read this passage and select which of the statements below best describes its main purpose.

Theologians often use specialist language when talking about the mysteries of religion. The word "grace" refers to the most basic and original Christian experience. It is an experience of God, whose sympathy and love for human beings run so deep that [God] has given [Godself]. It is an experience of human beings, who are capable of letting themselves be loved by God, of opening up to love and filial dialogue. The result of this encounter is the beauty, gracefulness, and goodness that is reflected in all of creation—but especially in human beings

Unit 7 Reading for the General Idea: Skimming

and their history. Humanity is good, gracious, grateful, beautiful, cordial and merciful because it was visited by a God who is the same; and this God has made humanity what it is.

[Boff, 1984, p 3.]

a Specialist language is necessary to talk about theological mysteries ❏

b The term *grace* refers to the essential Christian experience ❏

c Human beings are capable of experiencing God's love ❏

d God visits humanity because God is merciful ❏

Check all your answers in Appendix B.

You have probably been able to identify the main points of the passages in Tasks 1-5 fairly easily. If we analyse more carefully just how you came to your correct decision, we see that, after knowledge of vocabulary, **the key to comprehension lies in understanding structure** — the structure of the paragraph and the structure of the sentence.

In the next two units of work we examine the *role of structure* in communicating meaning, first in the paragraph and then in the sentence.

UNIT 8 PARAGRAPH STRUCTURE AND COMPREHENSION

Understanding the structure of the paragraph is an important step towards gaining a detailed understanding of what the writer intends to say in her or his text. In a paragraph, sentences are grouped together to develop **one main idea**. The main idea is contained in what is called the **topic sentence**. This usually, though not always, comes at the beginning of the paragraph. Sometimes a topic sentence may come in another position or even at the end. Sometimes, it will come at both the beginning and at the end. In this last case, it acts as the concluding sentence.

The sentences following the topic sentence—the **supporting sentences**—further explain the main idea in the topic sentence. They do this by giving:-
- more detail
- an example or illustration
- a reason
- additional information
- modifying information, and so on.

[Note: The range of different sentence functions will be further examined in Unit 11.]

There will also usually be a **concluding sentence** about the topic or main idea at the end of the paragraph. This sentence often sums up or states in another way what has been said at the beginning. However, not all of the paragraphs you read in journals or in books will consist of this ideal structure.

The following text is an example of an ideal paragraph. Notice how sentences 2 to 5 give further information about the main idea indicated in the topic sentence (TS). The final sentence sums up the main idea again.

> *1 Pastoral service requires much preparation.(TS) 2 As well as knowledge and understanding, a person needs to have some experience of life, spiritual depth and interpersonal skills. 3 Several areas of knowledge are required for this formation.*
> *4 For example, a candidate may study theology, scripture, psychology, pastoral counselling and spirituality. 5 In addition, a pastoral person needs a high degree of self-awareness, a growing experience in prayer and the spiritual life, and the ability to listen carefully to others. 6 It is clear that to be effective in pastoral service, many years of dedicated prayer, study and work are needed.*

TASK 1: Study the paragraphs below. Identify the topic sentence and its position in the paragraph. Take note of the way in which the other sentences give more information or explanation about the topic. Check your answers in Appendix B.

A *1 Technology, over the last century, has given us the telegraph, the typewriter, the facsimile machine, and most recently e-mail. 2 But these are only the most recent advances. 3 In ancient times, people scratched or painted messages onto stone or wood. 4 Then they used animal skins and later again a primitive form of paper scroll on which to write. 5 After the middle ages came the printing press and then the book in more modern form. 6 In fact, some form of written communication between human beings has been used for untold centuries.*

(Topic Sentence/position)...

B *1 Destruction of rain forests is just one of the serious issues facing us. 2 There is a host of ecological and environmental concerns challenging the global community today. 3 The increasing destruction of the ozone layer, caused by chlorofluoro-carbons in certain domestic products and the use of fossil fuels, is one critical development of the late twentieth century. 4 The pollution of waterways, soil erosion and the proliferation of mega-cities with all their poisons must be added to the list. 5 Damage to the earth's 'breathing' apparatus through destroying rain forests is bad enough. 6 As a consequence there is also the irreversible loss of animal and plant species. 7 All of these critical earth developments clamour for our urgent action.*

(Topic Sentence/position)...

C *1 At the end of the twentieth century, we are beginning to see the Earth in its context of the universe. 2 Because of space travel, we have been able to stand apart from the Earth and see it, at least in photographs, as a whole. 3 We have become used to a new picture of the Earth, as a single, beautiful blue-green planet shared by all living creatures. 4 Astronauts have noted that this picture inspires a sense of our common home on Earth. 5 It gives imaginative force to the idea that we are one community and inspires the quest for global peace. 6 It is a vivid image suggesting that the Earth is one biological community and that the systems of the planet are all interconnected.*

[Edwards, 1995, p 10.]

(Topic Sentence/position)..

CONTROLLING IDEA IN A TOPIC SENTENCE

Note again the topic sentence of the example paragraph above:
Pastoral service requires much preparation.

As well as indicating the general topic of the paragraph, namely, *pastoral service*, the topic sentence also focuses on a particular aspect which is sometimes called the **controlling idea**. In this topic sentence, the controlling idea is that it (that is, pastoral service) *requires much preparation*.

The controlling idea in the topic sentence enables you to predict the information which is likely to follow. This can help you to understand how the remaining sentences in the paragraph relate to the topic.

TASK 2: Examine the following topic sentences. Identify the topic and the controlling idea. Write them in the space provided. Notice that the topic does not always have to come first.

A The study of theology today embraces many important areas.

Topic: ....

Controlling idea: ....

B Controversies around the topic of Christology are nowhere more evident than in the problem of appropriate language.

Topic: ....

Controlling idea: ....

English for Theology

C There are several reasons for planet Earth's current crisis.

Topic: ....

Controlling idea: ....

D Ethnic conflict is a problem in many parts of the world.

Topic: ....

Controlling idea: ....

E Many benefits as well as challenges flow from globalisation.

Topic: ....

Controlling idea: ....

F Different spiritual traditions in the church can be like springs of life-giving water.

Topic: ....

Controlling idea: ....

DISCUSSION

TASK 3: For each of the topic sentences above, discuss what you predict would follow in a completed paragraph. Try writing some of the paragraphs in full.

PRACTICE IN USING PARAGRAPH STRUCTURE FOR COMPREHENSION

TASK 4: Study the following groups of sentences and re-arrange them in the space provided to form a coherent paragraph. First, find the topic sentence which contains the main idea. Second, find the sentences which explain or give more information about the topic and decide on an appropriate logical order. Finish with the concluding sentence (if there is one).

Note: Some clue words which will help you to find the correct order are 'signpost' words or discourse markers. Refer back to Unit 4 to review these. Other words which will help are called *cohesive devices* and these will be studied in Unit 10.

1

a Many students nowadays are able to choose to continue study through to high school and even to senior high school years. b Elementary or primary schools provide education for children for the next six or seven years. c In most countries, education is provided at many levels. d A proportion of high school graduates may then continue with tertiary studies of one kind or another. e There are first the kindergartens where children aged between three and five years learn basic social and play skills. f In fact the comprehensive provision of education in many countries of the region has markedly improved in recent decades.

1 (Topic Sentence) ....

2 ....

3 ....

4 ....
5 ....
6 ....

2

a These solidarity rights, representing indivisible goods, belong to people precisely as a collective or group. b Human rights, as they are now understood, are usually considered to fall into three categories. c Next there are the social and cultural rights which belong to people as members of a society. d A 'third generation' of rights which has been receiving recent attention is that of peoples' rights, sometimes called solidarity rights. e First there are those rights which pertain to people as individuals. f These include such rights as the right to life, liberty, equal dignity and security of person. g All of these rights together form the basis of a just and humane society.

1 (TS) ....
2 ....
3 ....
4 ....
5 ....
6 ....
7 ....

3

a Ultimately, people also need the conditions which facilitate expression of the transcendent dimension of human life if they are to realise their full human potential. b As well as these, political freedom, gender equality and cultural inclusivity need to be safeguarded. c The conditions necessary for genuine human development have received much attention in recent decades. d Then there are the social requirements such as housing, health and education services. e All of these conditions are now widely promoted by inter-national agencies, church and religious bodies and many civic groups. f At the most basic level there are the material and physical conditions necessary for existing.

1 (TS) ....
2 ....
3 ....
4 ....
5 ....
6 ....

English for Theology

4

a *Tracing these changes both in the scriptural period and throughout subsequent history makes clear that there has been no timeless speech about God in the Jewish or Christian tradition.* ***b*** *As cultures shift, so too does the specificity of God-talk.* ***c*** *The unfathomable mystery of God is always mediated through shifting historical discourse.* ***d*** *Rather, words about God are cultural creatures, entwined with the mores and adventures of the faith community that uses them.* ***e*** *As the [story] about the baker from the fourth century makes clear, language about God has a history.*

[Johnson, 1994, p 6.]

1 (TS) ....

2 ....

3 ....

4 ....

5 ....

5

a *Some of the violence has been caused by political and economic factors.* ***b*** *An example often put forward is the religio-communal violence in Ambon and other parts of the Maluku archipelago.* ***c*** *However, the situation has changed since the mid-1990s.* ***d*** *As far as religion is concerned, Indonesia has until recently been known as a Southeast Asian country where a number of great world religions meet and develop in peaceful coexistence.* ***e*** *Since then Indonesia has been marked by social unrest and violence in various parts of the country.*
f *But the rest has been often associated with religion or at least seems to have strong religious overtones.*

[Azra, 2001, p 84, modified.]

1 (TS) ....

2 ....

3 ....

4 ....

5 ....

6 ....

Check your answers in Appendix B.

UNIT 9 SENTENCE AND CLAUSE STRUCTURE AND COMPREHENSION

At the micro-level of theological or any other written text is the sentence. This, too, has a structure which it is important to understand for accurately and quickly comprehending what the writer is saying.

An image—to use some metaphorical language!—can help in the understanding of sentence structure. Language is like people all dressed up. Many different and elegant clothes may be worn; many accessories—hats, scarves, dark glasses and so on—may be added; much jewellery may adorn the appearance of a person. But behind it all, there is essentially a human body—head, hands, arms, legs, feet and torso. Or again, language is like a building: whether the building is plain and simple or very complex and ornate, behind it all there is a recognisable structure.

A simple structure lies behind most English sentences: a subject (noun or noun phrase), a main verb, i.e. a finite verb, and usually an object (noun or noun phrase) or a complement. For example:

	Believers	*seek*	*understanding.*
	(Subject)	(main verb)	(object)
OR	*Theology*	*is*	*a faith activity.*
	(Subject)	(main verb)	(complement)

These are simple sentences, consisting of just one clause.

A complex sentence with more than one clause contains one **main or independent clause**, together with at least one dependent clause, as in this example:-

When they study theology, ***believers seek understanding***.
   (Dependent clause)   (Main/independent clause)

Most dependent clauses, too, must have a subject and a finite verb, and very often they may also have an object or complement. [Note: For more detail on the variety of English clauses, consult a comprehensive grammar such as Leech and Svartvik.]

To help with comprehension in complex sentences in a text, it is important to develop the skill of quickly identifying the main or independent clause in a sentence because this contains the main idea.

A main or independent clause is complete in itself and can stand alone, eg *believers seek understanding*—whereas a dependent clause is unfinished—it does not make sense by itself —eg *when they study theology*.
Dependent clauses may also be recognised by the connecting words—adverbs, conjunctions —or relative pronouns which introduce them.

Revise your recognition of the difference between an independent and a dependent clause in the following task.

TASK 1: Identify the subject, finite verb and object (if there is one) in these clauses and then decide whether they are independent (I) or dependent (D) clauses.

                                                                                      I/D?
1 The book was published last year   ....
2 Which he had written   ....
3 If you had already written the article   ....

English for Theology

4   When they discovered the ancient scrolls   ....

5   Who contributed greatly   ....

6   He spoke   ....

7   The villagers contributed greatly   ....

8   Although the players trained for weeks   ....

9   Words have different meanings in different contexts ....

10 Because they could not translate the documents   ....

All of the clauses above are relatively simple in structure, containing at most only an adverb or adverbial phrase in addition to the essential subject, verb, (object) structure.

Recognising independent clauses among other elements of a sentence such as participial phrases also depends upon the ability to distinguish between finite and non-finite verbs/verb phrases. A *finite verb/verb phrase* is one which has the *present* or *past tense form* of the verb either as its *first word* or *only word*, as in these examples. The verb/verb phrase is underlined.

Present tense form (first or only word)   Past tense form (first or only word)
They/she write/s very well.   They/he wrote very well.
He/they is/are kind.   She/they was/were kind.
She/they is/are coming soon.   He/they was/were working hard.
He/they is/are disappointed.   She/they was/were disappointed.
They/she have/has many books.   They/he had many books.
They/he have/has achieved success.   She/they had achieved success.
She/they arrive/s tomorrow.   They/he arrived yesterday.

TASK 2: Study this list of verbs/verb phrases. Write beside each one whether it is a completed/finite verb or non-finite verb.

Verbs	Finite (F)	Non-finite (NF)
were	....	....
is	....	....
given	....	....
was accepted	....	....
saving	....	....
recognises	....	....
helped	....	....
explaining	....	....
understood	....	....
shared	....	....
saved	....	....
were redeemed	....	....
interpret	....	....
created	....	....
liberating	....	....
accepts	....	....
broke	....	....
has been broken	....	....
had evaluated	....	....
written	....	....

For many regular verbs, the simple past tense (a finite verb) has the same form as the past participle (a non-finite verb)—both end with *-ed*. Practise distinguishing between them in the following exercise.

TASK 3: Identify the finite verbs in the following sentences by underlining. Circle the past participles.

1 Though described differently in earlier ages, grace is received in a divine-human meeting which is marked by mutual self-giving.

2 Freedom of speech is undoubtedly a most prized human value, though it has been denied to millions of people across the ages.

3 Revelation, an accepted starting point for theology, is understood in many different ways, often being dependent upon a person's inherited historical, cultural or political stance.

4 The entire world community, which has arrived at a critical point in environmental well-being, with many wilderness areas destroyed, must commit itself to comprehensive, decisive action.

5 When committed people work for justice, they are surely promoting peace, that gift desired by all people of goodwill.

TASK 4: Now identify and write below only the main clause in each of the sentences above.

1 ....
2 ....
3 ....
4 ....
5 ....

Note that even within the main clause of a sentence (or indeed within dependent clauses), some words may be less important than others. For example, adjectives and adverbs may qualify and modify words in important ways, but the essential meaning is carried by the nouns and verbs.

In the main clauses you have written above, are there any adjectives or adverbs which could be omitted without losing the essential meaning of the clause? Write them here:-

....

Brief review of main types of sentence
(For greater detail, consult a comprehensive grammar book.)

1 A **simple sentence** contains only a main/independent clause.
   eg *Theology involves the use of reason. Language filters reality by naming or ignoring it.*

2   A **compound sentence** consists of two or more independent clauses joined with a coordinating conjunction (*and, or, but, yet, for, nor, so*).

   eg *Bread or rice is essential for life, yet we do not live on bread or rice alone.*

   Religious experience already involves an interpretation, for a person always experiences a thing as something specific.

3   A **complex sentence** consists of an independent/main clause and one or more dependent clauses, linked with a subordinating conjunction. Dependent clauses may be adverbial or adjectival (relative). The main idea is in the main clause. (Main clause in bold print, dependent clause underlined in examples below.)

   eg <u>When we use fossil fuels</u>, **we pollute the atmosphere**. (Dependent Adverbial Clause)
   A culture <u>which allows its core to be changed</u> **is destined to disappear.** (Dependent Adjectival Clause)

   A dependent clause may also be a noun clause. A noun clause may be a subject or object within an independent clause. [Consult a comprehensive grammar book for detailed information.]

   eg *<u>That the rain forests are disappearing</u> concerns environmentalists and eco-theologians.*
   (Dependent Noun clause as Subject.)

   Medical researchers know <u>that gene therapy raises ethical issues</u>.
   (Dependent Noun clause Object.)

4   **A complex-compound sentence** consists of two or more independent clauses and one or more dependent clauses. Independent clauses are underlined in the example below.

   eg *In the eighth century, <u>Indian communities,</u> which had resulted from immigration, <u>flourished throughout Indonesia, and</u> around this time <u>the Sailendra rulers built Borobudur,</u> which is the great Buddhist monument.*

TASK 5: For each of the sentences below, write out the main clause.

1   The problem of suffering, whether it is physical, mental or spiritual, concerns all people.

....

2   The sun, a source of life and growth, is a religious symbol which has had meaning for people throughout the ages.

....

3   Poverty afflicts far too many of the world's people, frequently giving rise to other evils such as exploitation of the environment, corruption and war, thereby adding to the burden of suffering.

....

TASK 6: Identify the main clause in the sentences below.

1 Modern and postmodern society is characterised by cultural and ideological pluralism, which is evident in all areas of life, in the family and professions, in the media, in economic life, in civil law as well as in intercultural and interreligious encounter.

....

2 When it comes to religion, many contemporaries claim that Christianity, as a system which gives meaning to life and shows the way to salvation, has run its course.

....

3 The emergence of basic Christian communities and their praxis are of singular importance when it comes to questioning the prevailing manner of being church.

....

TASK 7: Identify the main clause in the sentences below.

1 Given what we know today about interpreting the scriptures, we must keep an open mind about the traditional presentation of the church, which may not in fact accurately reflect the gospels.

....

2 Expressing the experience of some Asian women, who bear the mark of colonised people as well as sexist discrimination, one theologian writes that the focus is not "who" is Jesus Christ but "where" is Jesus Christ for Asian women.

....

3 Whereas earlier theologies focused on salvation as future-oriented and belonging to the next world, liberation theologians hold a more present-oriented eschatology, which calls the church to be the agent of the inbreaking of the signs of God's reign in this world.

....

The Constituent Structure Tree

Another way which may help some students to understand complex sentence structure is by means of a diagram called a **constituent structure tree.** [A full account may be found in a suitable reference on grammatical/syntactical aspects of English.] Such diagrams may be useful if you have a strong 'visual' dimension to your thinking.

Use this diagram only if you find it useful.

The words in a sentence can be divided into two main groups—**a subject or noun phrase (NP) and a verb with its object, the verb phrase (VP).** Within those two major groups there may be several sub-groups of words, ordered into clauses and phrases, but each relating in some way to either the subject or the verb phrase. Each group of words occurs in a particular place within a sentence and with a particular word order, according to the rules of syntax. For example, articles must precede nouns, never follow them: *the church,* not *church the.* Adjectives normally precede nouns: ***liberation*** *theology,* not *theology liberation.*

Consider the second sentence in Task 5 above:-

English for Theology

The sun, a source of life and growth, is a religious symbol which has had meaning for people throughout the ages.

The structure of that sentence, and the relationships between its parts, can be illustrated by representing it in a structure 'tree'. The complete sentence forms the main 'trunk' which can be broken down into its natural 'branches'. At each 'branch', the word groupings form a **structural constituent** of the sentence, until all that remains are the individual words.

Example: A Constituent Structure Tree

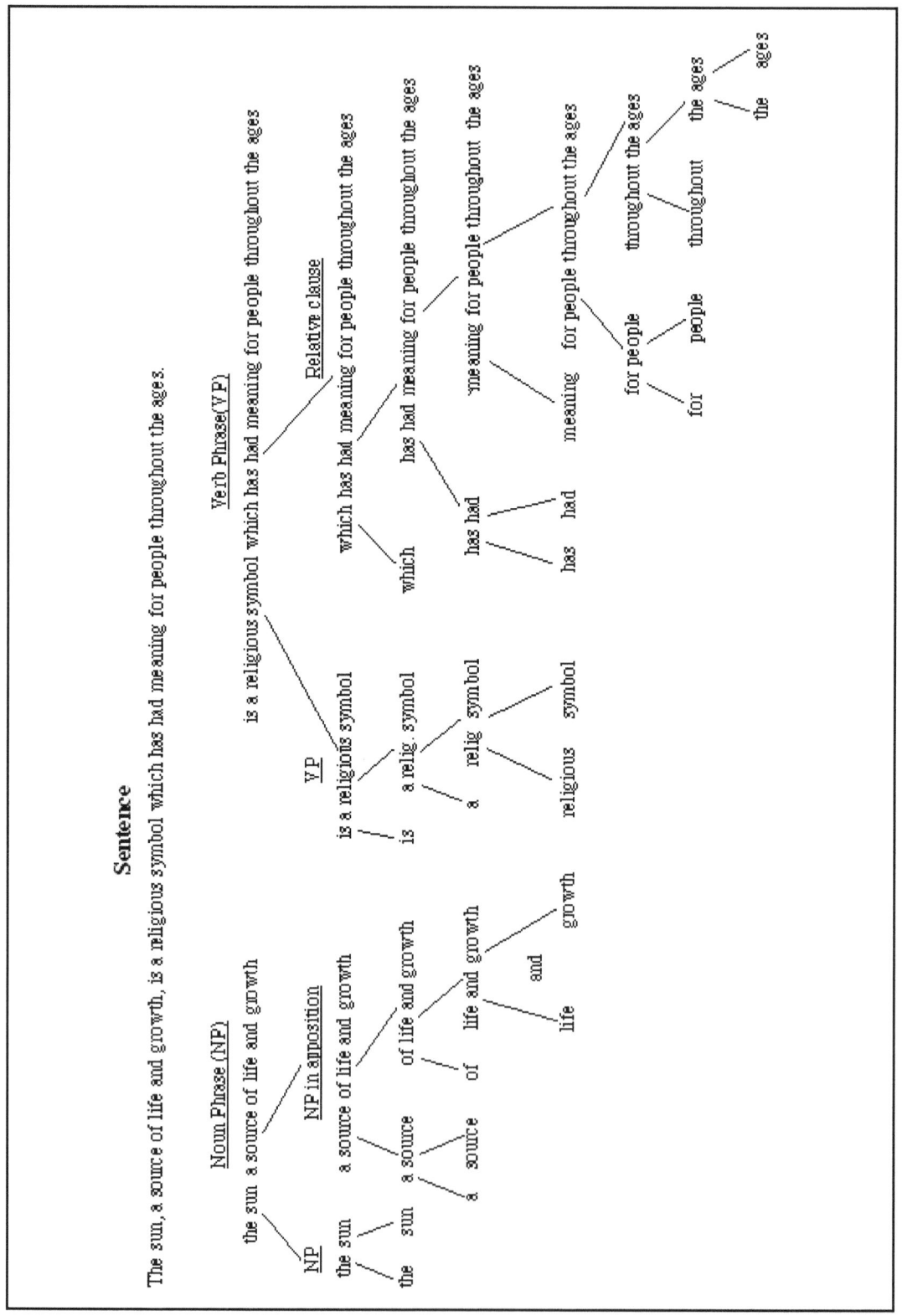

TASK 8: On a large sheet of paper, try drawing constituent structure trees to represent some of the complex sentences in Tasks 3-7 above. Do this exercise only if you find it helpful in identifying the natural groupings of words within a clause or phrase.

A better understanding of sentence structure, and the ability to identify the main clause within a sentence can help in reading comprehension. Study the example which follows.

EXAMPLE:
Read through this short text. The main clause in each sentence has been highlighted in bold print. Now skim read just the main clauses in bold print, noticing how this helps you to understand the writer's main line of thought.

> **Darwin's theory of evolution put an end to a static view of the universe**, a static metaphysics. **This new view of the world has had enormous influence** which would be difficult to overestimate. From its humble origins in Darwin's journals, **it has become the dominant metaphor for understanding the universe. Everything is seen in evolutionary terms,** whether it be life, society, the Church, galaxies, everything! In the period of one century, from being a culture in which change was suspect, **we have moved to a culture which expects change**, where lack of change is suspect. **This is a significant challenge for the church,** which had in times past prided itself precisely on the fact that it did not change.
>
> [Adapted from Ormerod, 1990, p 30.]

Now apply your skill in identifying main clauses to the text below.

TASK 9: Highlight all the main clauses in the text below. Now skim read the highlighted clauses to get a summary of the writer's main line of argument.

Jesus and the purity system of the Jewish world

(The dominant social vision of Jesus' time was centred on holiness, equated with purity; Jesus' alternative social vision was centred on compassion.)

> Purity was political because it structured society into a purity system . . . Purity systems are found in many cultures. At a high level of abstraction, they are systems of classifications, lines and boundaries. A purity system 'is a cultural map which indicates a place for everything and everything in its place.' Things that are okay in one place are impure or dirty in another, where they are out of place. Slightly more narrowly, and put very simply, a purity system is a social system which is organised around contrasts or polarities of pure and impure, clean and unclean. The polarities of pure and impure establish a spectrum or 'purity map' which ranges from pure on one end through varying degrees of purity to impure at the other. These polarities apply to persons, places, things, times and social groups.
> ...
> In the context of a purity system that created a world with sharp social boundaries between pure and impure, righteous and sinner, whole and not whole, male and female, rich and poor, Jew and Gentile, we can see the sociopolitical significance of compassion. In the message and activity of Jesus, we see an alternative social vision, a community shaped by . . . compassion.
>
> [Adapted from Borg, 1995, pp 50, 53.]

TASK 10: To assist your reading comprehension, practise identifying the main clauses in texts you are required to read for your studies.
In particular, when you have read a paragraph and not understood it well, go back and identify the main clauses.

UNIT 10   COHESIVE DEVICES

Cohesive devices are used by writers to give coherence to a text. A text is coherent when the ideas between and within sentences, and with ideas elsewhere in the text are connected by cohesive devices in a way that makes the text easier to read and to understand.

The skill of recognising and interpreting cohesive devices is necessary for reading comprehension. Consider this sentence:-

> Before **that**, **they** had been unable **to do so**.

Because we do not know what '*that*' refers to, who '*they*' are, or what '*to do so*' means, we cannot understand this sentence by itself. But these words—cohesive devices—point us to some other place in the text where we can find the missing information.

There are a number of ways to achieve coherence in a text. In this resource book we list them as follows:-

1. The repetition of key words
2. Use of reference words (mainly pronouns)
3. Substitution
4. Ellipsis
5. Use of synonyms or alternative words
6. Discourse markers (ie 'signpost' words)
7. Logical ordering of ideas.

The text below entitled *Exegesis in the 20th Century* contains examples of all these cohesive devices. Discourse markers ('signpost' words) and the ordering of ideas in a text have been covered in Unit 4. In this Unit we examine the role of the other cohesive devices listed above as aids to reading comprehension.

1   Repetition of key words

The repetition of certain key words, usually nouns, helps to give clarity of meaning to a text. Read Lines 1-6 in the text below (*Exegesis*). You will see that the noun *exegesis* is repeated twice. Note also that in Line 14, by using the related noun, *exegetes* (ie persons who do exegesis), the writer maintains the focus on the central topic of the paragraph, namely, *exegesis*.

2   Reference words: mainly pronouns

<u>Pronouns</u>
A text is made easier to read by the use of reference words. These are usually pronouns (e.g. *this, that, those, they, hers, ours, it, one, another, all*) but may include certain adverbs and the definite article.

Pronoun reference words are used when it would be cumbersome to repeat the noun or noun phrase. In our text example below, in Line 1, instead of repeating '*the several branches of academic enquiry*', we use '*these*'.
In Line 3, instead of repeating the three branches again ('*the study of ancient languages . . . etc*', we use '*such scholarship*'.
In Line 15, '*this information*' refers back to the knowledge now made available through radiocarbon dating.

Unit 10 Cohesive Devices

<u>Definite article *the* as reference</u>
In Line 12 '*the*' in '*the scrolls*' is an example of the definite article used as a reference pointing back to '*the Qumran scrolls*' in Line 10. [Note: The definite article is explained further in the Grammar Revision section of Unit 14.]

<u>Adverbs</u>
Sometimes adverbs such as *here, there, then* are used to refer to some time or place already mentioned in the text. In Line 11 '*there*' refers back to '*the Holy Land*'.

3 Substitution

In Line 15 in our example below, the expression '*to do so*' is a substitute for '*to date critical documents with some precision*' in Line 14. By using the substitute phrase, the writer avoids cumbersome repetition. Other substitute expressions might include such examples as the following:

   Recent scholarship has concluded <u>the same</u>. (The same as what?)
   The Hebrews thought <u>so</u>. (What did they think?)
   The Romans <u>could not</u>. (Could not do what?)

Each of these sentences would require us to find the missing information elsewhere in a given text.

4 Ellipsis

Ellipsis refers to the omission of important information which is necessary for meaning, but which the reader is expected to understand from the text. As with *reference* and *substitution*, this cohesive device avoids unnecessary repetition. In Line 7 of our example below, '*one*' refers back to '*important advances*' in the previous line. The reader is expected to understand that the omitted word, indicated in the text by ^, is '*advance*'.

5 Use of synonyms or alternative words

Instead of repeating the same word or phrase, writers often use an alternative expression for the same thing. In Lines 6-7 the phrase '*the relevant areas*' is another way of referring to the '*several branches of academic enquiry*' (Line 1).

TASK 1: Now read the following text and then answer the questions on cohesive devices below.

Exegesis in the 20th century

1 **Exegesis** of the Bible depends upon several branches of academic enquiry. **These**
2 include the study of ancient languages, the findings of archaeology and a knowledge
3 of semitic cultural history. Without the support of **such scholarship**, **exegesis**
4 would be impossible. Consequently, meaningful access to the revelation of our
5 religious tradition would be largely closed. However, **exegesis** made great progress
6 in the twentieth century. During **that time**, important advances were made in all **the**
7 **relevant areas**. **One** ^ was the increase of available primary materials through
8 archaeological discoveries and **another** ^ ^ the breakthrough in deciphering the
9 script on **key ancient parchments**. Discoveries in the Holy Land in mid-century
10 were of particular importance in this quest for Biblical knowledge. The Qumran scrolls
11 found **there**, for example, have been an object of study ever since. But identifying
12 when **the scrolls** were written was an essential question for scholars to answer. A
13 **third advance** of **the century**, the development of radiocarbon dating, enabled
14 **exegetes** to date **these critical documents** with some precision. Before **that, they**
15 had been unable to **do so**. Now in possession of **this information**, biblical experts
16 have been able to tell us how the ancient texts illumine understanding of our own
17 scriptures.

English for Theology

Write in full the references or missing words for the following cohesive devices in the text, giving Line numbers.

1   Line 6: *'that time'*. What does *'that'* refer to? ....

2   Line 8: *'another ^^...'* (ellipsis). What are the two missing words?
       ....

3   Line 9: *'key ancient parchments'*. Find two alternative expressions for this in the text. ....

4   Line 13: *'the century'*. *'The'* refers back to what century? ....

5   Line 14: *'before that'*. What does *'that'* refer to? ....

6   Line 14: *'they'*. Who are *'they'*? ....

7   Find examples of three discourse markers in the text? What logical ordering of ideas does each one indicate. (Refer back to Unit 4 if necessary.)

       <u>Discourse marker</u>   <u>Logical order indicated</u>

       i) Line no. ....

       ii) Line no. ....

       iii) Line no. ....

TASK 2: Read the text which follows, noting the cohesive devices in bold type. Explain the references for each by completing the table below.

The question of the gospels as biography

1   The first critical approach to the story of Jesus was given systematic expression in
2   Germany by Hermann Reimarus, whose work was published posthumously in 1778.
3   **Reimarus'** thesis was that John the Baptist and Jesus were political insurrectionists
4   out to overthrow Rome; after the failure of **their** political ambitions **their** followers
5   invented the story of the resurrection and the figure Christ. **Reimarus'** book
6   provoked an immediate outraged response, and it could be said that modern New
7   Testament studies were to some extent born of the effort to refute **Reimarus'**
8   allegation that Jesus was a political revolutionary.
9   **This effort** produced a whole series of "lives of Jesus". Two facts soon emerged:-
10   (1) **These biographies** of Jesus tended to reflect the spirit of the age and the
11   theological viewpoint and temperament of the particular writer; and (2) the Gospels do
12   not always agree in their accounts.
13   Why, for example, does Matthew recount a saying of Jesus in circumstances different
14   from **those** in which Luke records the **same saying**? Even attempts at
15   harmonisation of the Gospels did not satisfactorily resolve the question of
16   discrepancies and inconsistencies. In fact, the attempt at connecting sections of the
17   four Gospels into a "harmony" tended to raise more questions that **it** answered; for
18   example, **it** revealed that the Gospel of John has a different chronological and
19   geographical framework from the Gospels of Matthew, Mark and Luke. **The latter**
20   **three** are called 'Synoptics' . . . because **they** have many elements in common in
21   **their** presentation of the story of Jesus. In John, Jesus sets out from Galilee to
22   Jerusalem three times, but in the Synoptics Jesus makes only one journey to
23   Jerusalem . . .
24   Is it then, simply a case of choosing between John or the Synoptics for an accurate
25   biographical account? **If so**, then how does one explain the nature of the 'inaccurate'
26   account?

27   Attempts to reconstruct Jesus' life and teaching from the sources available, namely,
28   the Gospels, and the difficulties to which **this effort** led, finally raised the question of
29   the nature of **these sources**. That John's concern was primarily theological was
30   recognised early. DF Strauss in **his** *Life of Jesus* (1835) underlined **this point**, and
31   went on to point out that because **this Gospel** was written from a primarily theological
32   perspective, it was not a suitable source for the historical understanding of Jesus.

[From Goosen, G & Tomlinson, M, (1994), *Studying the Gospels, An Introduction*, Dwyer, Sydney, pp 46-47.]

<u>Cohesive device</u>   <u>Reference in the text</u>

1 Lines 3, 5 & 7:   Note the repetition of the key name, *Reimarus*

2 Line 4, *'their'*:   Refers to whom? ………………………….

3 Line 9, *'this effort'*:   What effort? (Write in full) ……………….
                                       ……………………………………………

4 Line 10, *'these biographies'*:   This is both a pronoun reference and an
                                       alternative word for what? ……………….

5 Line 14, *'those'*:   Refers to what? ……………………………

6 Line 14, *'same saying'*:   Same as what? ……………………………

7 Lines 17, 18, *'it'*:   Write the reference in full: …………………
                                       …………………………………………….

8 Lines 19-20-21, *'the latter three'*,   Refers to? ……………………………
   'they', *'their'*
                                       …………………………………………….

9 Line 25, *'if so'*:   Write in full the expression for which *'so'* is a
                                       substitute. …………………………………….
                                       …………………………………………….

10 Line 28, *'this effort'*:   What effort?
                                       …………………………………………….

11 Line 29, *'these sources'*:   What sources?
                                       …………………………………………….

12 Line 30, *'his'*:   Who does this refer to?
                                       …………………………………………….

13 Line 30, *'this point'*:   What point? (Write in full)
                                       …………………………………………….

14 Line 31, *'this Gospel'*:   Which Gospel?
                                       …………………………………………….

TASK 3: In the next text you need to read for your studies, practise identifying and explaining the cohesive devices used by the writer. If appropriate, do this exercise together with other students.

UNIT 11 LEVELS OF MEANING AND AUTHORIAL VOICE

In Units 3 and 4, meaning in text was examined at the level of modes of discourse and organisation of ideas. This unit explains some further aspects of meaning.

All sentences in texts contain *conceptual*, *propositional* and *contextual* meanings. Some sentence functions may be expressed in the form of *rhetorical questions* which are reviewed in this unit. Sometimes it is possible also to identify *pragmatic* meaning, though this may be considered as simply another aspect of the functional or contextual meaning of a sentence

In addition to understanding the *literal meaning* of a text, that is, what the words actually say, a skilled reader will be able to understand some things not directly said, that is, to make *inferences* from the text.

Yet another comprehension skill is the ability to distinguish *authorial voice* from other voices or information conveyed in a text. All of these aspects of meaning are explained and illustrated in the examples which follow.

Conceptual meaning
The most basic level of meaning in a text is to be found in the concepts conveyed through individual words. For example, the words *rain forests, logging, destruction, cycle, begins* are concepts corresponding with things, actions or processes in the real world and can be readily understood.

Propositional meaning
When words are combined to form a sentence, we have propositional meaning. That is the meaning which can be understood when a sentence is read by itself.*   Here is an example:
The logging of rain forests can begin a cycle of destruction.
Propositional meaning, then,—*what* is said—is plain to anyone who understands the concepts involved. But *why* has this sentence been written?

Meaning in context
The contextual (sometimes referred to as functional) meaning of the sentence—the *why*—can only be understood in the context of the whole text. Here is the full text in which the above sentence occurs.

Theology and the environment

1 Ecological theologians take the view that the removal of rain forest from the earth's equatorial zones is, at base, a theological issue. **2 The logging of rain forests can begin a cycle of destruction.** *3 Soil erosion, river sedimentation, loss of habitat for wild life and loss of tree and plant species of benefit to humanity all follow the removal of forests. 4 This is a serious loss for humans who depend upon the environment for life. 5 But there is a more fundamental reason for stopping this destruction. 6 All creatures—plants, animals, the earth itself, as well as humans—are expressions of God's creativity and as such have intrinsic value. 7 Concerned people ask what is to be done in the face of this destruction. 8 To begin with, many more people, particularly in government and other regulatory bodies, need to take the problem seriously if damage is to be halted or even slowed. 9 But can we really expect progress on stopping logging any time soon? 10 If recent experiences in the Amazon Basin and Kalimantan are any indication, it seems, sadly, that greed and corruption will continue to reign.*

*In some circumstances where cohesive devices are used, the full meaning of a sentence can only be inferred from other parts of the text. An example is given in Unit 10 which illustrates the role of cohesive devices.

Within this text it is clear that the second sentence has the functional value of beginning the *explanation* of the claim made in the first sentence. In other words, the purpose of the second sentence is not simply to give the reader some botanical or biological information (the propositional meaning of the sentence) but to begin the explanation of why forest removal is a theological issue.

Each of the other sentences in the text above likewise has its own functional meaning or purpose, as set out below.

<u>Sentence number</u> <u>Sentence Function</u>
1 *Ecological theologians take the view ....* Statement of view (topic sentence)
2 *The logging of rainforests....* Explanation of stated viewpoint
3 *Soil erosion, river sedimentation...* Explanation of claim in sentence 2
4 *This is a serious loss...* Result or outcome of sentence 3
5 *But there is an even more fundamental...* Explanation
6 *All creatures—plants, animals...* Reason for viewpoint in sentence 1
7 *Concerned people ask what is to be done...* Comment on the situation
8 *To begin with, many more people...* Advice/suggestion/conclusion
9 *But can we really expect progress...?* Expression of opinion & frustration (Note: This is also a rhetorical question—see below.)
10 *If recent experiences in the Amazon ...* Opinion of likely outcome

Note that sentence functions are sometimes clearly indicated in a text by the use of 'signpost' words or discourse markers (see Unit 4). But often they are not.

Summary of common sentence functions in text
There are many possible sentence functions in English. The following partial list includes some of the more common ones.

description	statement of position	direction
assertion	instruction	prohibition
definition	example/illustration	exclamation
prediction	explanation	invitation
generalisation	emphasis	suggestion
speculation	comment	apology
hypothesis	reason	concession
contrast	purpose	result
………………..	………………..	…………………….
………………..	………………..	…………………….
………………..	………………..	…………………….
……………..	………………	…………………….

TASK 1: As you continue your studies, try to identify some further sentence functions and add them to the list above.

Rhetorical questions
Writers sometimes use sentences with the grammatical form of a question not in order to ask a question but for some other purpose. One common purpose is to introduce an explanation, enquiry or description which follows, as in these examples:-

> ***At what point in history did the deification of Jesus begin, in the time of Jesus or in the time of the early church?*** *For much of the twentieth century, scholars have argued that the deification or divinisation of Jesus was foreign to early Jewish Christianity. Etc . . .* [Evans, 1996, p.47.]
>
> *There is great inequality in the world today.* ***What are some of the indicators of this?*** *Life expectancy, level of education and average per person income are the more obvious measures but there are many others as well . . .*

The question form of a sentence may also be used to make a statement. For example, the question, *'Isn't it the case that so-called development has brought great damage to people and the environment?'* anticipates the answer 'yes' and therefore really means, *'It is the case that . . .'*

Likewise, *'We should acknowledge the great benefits of technological advances, shouldn't we?'* really means that *'We should acknowledge . . .'*

Sentence 9 in the text above is another example of a question which makes a statement. It is also an example of pragmatic meaning.

Pragmatic meaning*

A particular function which a sentence may have in a text is to evoke or invite some kind of interpersonal response on the part of the reader. This does not refer to the impact which information or persuasive argument may have on a reader. It refers to the situation where a writer conveys personal feelings or attitudes in a way intended to be appreciated by the reader. The writer assumes a personal interaction with the reader. The difference between pragmatic and other functional meaning is not always clearcut, but sometimes it is.

Sentence 9 in the text above - *But can we really expect progress on stopping logging any time soon?* — is an example of a sentence with pragmatic meaning.

It is also a rhetorical question. The writer's purpose is to make a statement not only about what she/he thinks, ie *we **cannot** expect any progress soon* — but also to convey something of his/her feeling of exasperation about the failure of authorities to take decisive action to stop destructive logging practices. And the writer wants the reader to appreciate those feelings. Consider the different effect if the writer had written instead:-

It is unlikely that much progress . . . will occur in the near future.

This is an academic and detached statement of opinion. It tells us what the writer *thinks* but nothing about the writer's *feelings or attitudes*.

While pragmatic meaning is more common in spoken language, it does occur in written text. Where it does occur, the reader needs to be alert to the interpersonal function of such a sentence or clause or phrase.

Literal and inferential meanings

The literal meaning of a text is what the words actually say. Sometimes the reader needs to be able to put information from the text together with her/his own general knowledge or reasoning powers to draw conclusions not directly stated in the text. This is called making inferences.

---

*This description draws on the approach outlined by Nuttal, C, 1982, *Teaching Reading Skills in a Foreign Language*, Heinemann, Oxford, p 81 ff.

Study this example:-

Mining and social justice

1 Large-scale mining in the island of New Guinea—east and west—has caused
2 enormous environmental damage and social dislocation and disadvantage.
3 Before the 1980s, some 20,000 villagers enjoyed a relatively affluent
4 subsistence life-style along the banks of the Ok Tedi-Fly River system in
5 Papua-New Guinea. Fish from the river, fruit and vegetables from the river-
6 bank gardens, and meat from the wild-life of surrounding forests were
7 plentiful. The dumping of mine waste and toxic tailings—cyanide, heavy
8 metal, sediment and sewage—in large volumes into the river system, subject
9 to flooding because of heavy rains and sediment build-up, changed all this in
10 a short time. Thousands of villagers were left impoverished and ultimately
11 displaced.

[Based on Jackson, R, 1993, *Cracked pot or copper bottomed investment*?, Dept Geog, Melanesian Studies Centre, James Cook University Queensland.]

This text contains certain information stated literally. For example, the text tells us (Lines 3-9) that before the 1980s, the villagers enjoyed a relatively affluent lifestyle with plenty of food, and that the dumping of mine waste into the river system changed this.

Questions such as *'How did the villagers live before the 1980s?'* and *'What happened to the river after mining began?'* can therefore be answered with information in the text.

However, a question such as *'Why were the villagers left impoverished and displaced?'* requires the reader to make some inferences. That is, if the river system was poisoned with mine waste, then this would poison the fish; if the poisoned river waters were used on gardens —or flooded the gardens during flood times—the fruit and vegetable would be poisoned or unable to grow. Animal life would be similarly affected. With no food, or insufficient food, the villagers would be impoverished and would have to leave their area in order to survive.

In this way, the reader links information in the text with his or her own knowledge and reasoning to draw conclusions not directly stated in the text.

Now practise making inferences from this text.

TASK 2: Read the text and answer the questions, both from information in the text and by making inferences based on your own knowledge/reasoning powers.

1 *In Nepal, where Suriyata lives with her child and works, thousands of*
2 *women and young girls are lured away from their families each year. They*
3 *are trafficked, or sold, largely into prostitution. Suriyata works to stop this*
4 *trade.*
5 *The girls, mostly from rural families, are promised by traffickers that they*
6 *will find employment if they leave their homes. They are, however, most*
7 *often sold to brothels, in either the capital of Nepal, Kathmandu, or into*
8 *India. They are forced to work as prostitutes at least until the amount of*
9 *money that the brothel owner paid the trafficker is repaid.*
10 *The reality of the life that these young women find in the city is*
11 *often vastly different from that of which they dreamed. Trafficking*
12 *devastates their lives. Many of them suffer both physical abuse and*
13 *psychological torment. Shame prevents many trafficked women from*
14 *returning to their villages. Many of the women also have contracted*
15 *HIV/AIDS, compounding their suffering.*
16 *Suriyata's work is to try and prevent trafficking. She visits communities*

17 *throughout Nepal and tells the people about the reality of trafficking. She*
18 *tells families stories of what could happen to their daughters as a result of*
19 *trafficking.* [Caritas Australia Newsletter, 2002, p 1, amended.]

Answer these questions. You will be able to answer some of them from information stated in the text. For others, you will need to make inferences. First identify which of the questions require you to make inferences from the text.

1   What do the traffickers promise the women and young girls?

....

2   Why are the girls who go with the traffickers mostly from rural areas?

....

3   What really happens to most of the women and young girls who go with the traffickers?

....

4   Why do many of the women not return to their villages?

....

5   Do you think that Suriyata's telling the families the truth about what happens to their daughters will stop the trafficking of women and young girls? Why/why not?

....

Discuss with other students the basis of the inferences you made to answer the questions. As you continue your study reading, practise being aware of information which can be inferred from the text.

Authorial voice
Interpreting or identifying the 'voice', or the point of view of the author (the writer), as distinguished from other points of view presented or information contained in a text, is another important comprehension skill.

Authorial voice in a text can be clearly identified by the use of first person and by emotive or feeling words. For example, "My position is that . . .", or "I hold the view that . . ." unambiguously state the writer's voice. Likewise, emotive words such as *tragically, unfortunately, happily*, or the *tragic events, the absurd situation, the lucky coincidence* give an indication of the writer's feelings or attitudes. Sometimes the choice of verb tense or mood (eg the definite *is* . . . rather than *may* . . . or *can* . . . ; the obligatory *must* or the advisory *should*) can indicate the writer's position.

The paragraphs used earlier in this unit contain several examples of authorial voice in the choice of vocabulary. Look again at the last sentence (10) of 'Theology and the Environment' at the beginning. The choice of such value-laden words as *greed* and *corruption*, together with the adverb *sadly*, tell us how the writer views this practice (logging). Consider the difference if sentence 10 had read as follows: *'If recent experiences . . . are any indication, it seems that the profit motive is dominant.'*

Likewise, the paragraph 'Mining and social justice' contains word choices which reveal the author's attitude. In Line 2, *enormous*, and in Lines 10-11, *impoverished* and *displaced* indicate the writer's feeling about the situation. Consider the difference if the words had been, say, *significant* (L2) and simply *affected* (L10-11). Verb tense and adverbial modification in Line 9-10 (*changed all this in a short time*) also reveal authorial position. That is, past tense claims established fact – no room for opinion—with compounded effects because the change was swift.

The choice of *lured* (L2) in the text in Task 2, instead of perhaps *persuaded* is a further example of authorial voice and purpose.

The reader, then, needs to be alert to vocabulary choices as indicators of the writer's voice and viewpoint. At other times, the reader needs to interpret whose 'voice' or viewpoint is presented from the context.

Consider this example:

1... The world is torn by wars, famines ... poverty, sufferings which find their origins not just in the fickleness of nature but in hardness of heart ... 2 One could say that there are two types of solution for this human condition, both sharing a common premise that our present situation is the result of a massive misuse of human freedom. 3 The first [solution] sees human freedom as the basic problem. 4 The solution then is to do away with freedom. 5 Such an abolition of freedom is achieved through a total, unquestioning ... obedience to a designated authority. 6 People must simply do what they are told to do, and if they fail they must be expelled from human society.
[Ormerod, 1992, p 3.]

The author's voice—his opinion—cannot be 'heard', that is, seen in this part of the text. The first two sentences are statements of well-known facts and opinions. Sentence 3 introduces the viewpoint of those who hold 'the first solution'. Sentences 4-6 then tell us what that viewpoint is. But there is nothing to tell the reader whether or not the author himself holds this view.

The above text continues:

*1 ... The second solution recognises that freedom is the cause of our problems but it also recognises that when freedom is drawn to evil, it is freedom itself which suffers. 2 The solution to this problem is not less freedom, but more freedom, the freeing of a freedom which has become trapped ... 3 While the first solution **despairs** in the human condition, the second **rejoices** in what is essential to human dignity, the full flowering of human freedom. 4 **Sadly**, we have seen too many attempts to implement the first solution.*

The first two sentences represent the 'voice' of those who hold the second solution but they do not reveal what the author thinks. In sentence 3, two words give the reader a clear indication of the author's evaluation, namely, *despairs* and *rejoices*. *Despairs* is a strong emotive word—it leaves absolutely no room for even a slightly hopeful view of the human condition, while *rejoices* is unambiguously positive. *Sadly* in the fourth sentence confirms what we have now understood, namely, that the author disagrees with the first solution. The author does not state that directly or literally, but if he is 'sad' about the many efforts to implement the first solution, then it can be safely concluded that he disagrees with it.

Here is another type of text where the authorial voice is clearly indicated by the use of the first person in the first paragraph. Other voices are represented by the use of third person. In

English for Theology

the fourth paragraph, the reader must interpret from the context that this represents the author's voice. All of the author's views are highlighted in bold print.

Trinitarian ecological theology

1 Some Christian thinkers (third person) have never transcended anthropocentrism, and their basis for judgement on all ethical issues is the dignity of the human person. **My (first person) argument is that the dignity of the human person is not the only criterion for ethical decision-making. The human person needs to be understood within a community of creatures, which have their own intrinsic value.**

2 On the other hand, some ecologists (third person) give no unique place to the human person. Some, like deep ecologists Arne Naess (third person) . . . argue for . . . Others, like J Baird Callicott (third person) argue that . . .

3 Ecofeminists (third person) stress the interconnections between creatures. They often reject hierarchical ordering, and some refuse to assert the rights of human beings over other creatures. There are those (third person) . . . who believe . . .

4 <u>**The trinitarian theology developed above**</u> **[ie in this book that I am writing] agrees with various forms of deep ecology and ecofeminism about the intrinsic value of all creatures.** <u>**It**</u> **is also in agreement with their critiques of exploitative and destructive human behaviour. As opposed to some, however,** <u>**it**</u> **suggests that a commitment to the intrinsic value of all creatures can and must go hand in hand with a respect for the unique dignity of human persons.** [Edwards, 1995, p 156.]

Note that in the last paragraph, even though the writer uses third person to talk about '*the trinitarian theology developed above*' followed by the third person pronoun *it*, because the reader knows that *above* means 'in this book I am writing', it is evident that the 'trinitarian theology' being described represents the writer's views.

TASK 3: Read this text and identify the author's voice. Look for indicators such as the use of first person, emotive words or other evaluative comments, emphatic words or verb tense which indicates definite rather than provisional view. Note also that writers sometimes use the viewpoints of others to convey their own position.

Christianity and the Pauline view of sin

1 The Christian religion has a lot to say about sin. Yet many people might feel that,
2 for all its concern about wrongdoing, Christianity fails to address real evil in the
3 world. It is not that people today have lost a sense of sin. It is more that the sense of
4 sin has undergone a change. People seem less inclined to catalogue, lament and
5 seek forgiveness for individual sins . . . They sense that what are customarily called
6 'sins' are really symptoms of a deeper malaise and that forgiveness must address this
7 basic level if it is to be lasting and effective in their lives.
8 On a wider scale people have a sense of a world trapped in irresolvable conflict . . .
9 [a world] locked in a vise of suspicion, greed and noncooperation. This for many
10 people today is sin . . .
11 What we find in Paul fits rather closely this modern sense of sin. Paul is not very
12 interested in sins. True, alongside virtues to be embraced, he can list for his
13 communities long lists of vices to be avoided (eg Gal 5:19-21, 22-23) . . . But such
14 things for Paul are really symptoms of a more basic ill . . .
15 Central to Paul's Christian vision . . . is the idea of human beings created in God's
16 image. Human existence is inconceivable except in relation to the Creator. For Paul,
17 then, sin is basically that which comes in from the human side to poison and frustrate
18 that relationship . . .Sin is ultimately a refusal to take responsibility—
19 or, rather, to share, be caught up in the responsibility of the Creator.
20 My sense is that this analysis of sin, inherited by Paul from Jewish reflection upon

Unit 11 Levels of Meaning and Authorial Voice

21 Genesis 1:26-27, has more rather than less validity at the present time. Since the late
22 1960s space travel has provided pictures and photographs of our world taken as a
23 whole – a powerful symbol of 'one world'. Advance in communications and transport
24 has made the sense of 'global village' a reality. We now have the means to grasp
25 imaginatively the extent of human responsibility for the fate of the world. This means
26 that the 'end of the world', once considered something God might bring about, is now
27 a frightening human possibility – whether it come about in one devastating blow
28 through nuclear exchange or through the slower but equally fatal onset of
29 environmental breakdown.

[Byrne, 1990, pp. 28, 29, 35.]

First underline those sections of the text which represent authorial voice. Then write the line reference numbers below.

....

....

TASK 4: Identify the author's voice in this text.

Is trinitarian faith still relevant?

1   Theologians . . . have had to address the question of what we really mean when we
2   pray to and speak of God as triune . . . They . . . have been obliged to consider again
3   how all aspects of our faith form an integrated worldview . . . Out of this quest have
4   come several common themes to be found in authors of the last decade or so.
5   The first of these common themes is that it is not out of speculation but out of
6   Christian spirituality that the doctrine of the Trinity emerges and becomes the central
7   pivot of the faith. The second common theme is the realisation that trinitarian ways of
8   thinking about God correspond to the insight that it is not self-determination as
9   isolated individuals but the capacity for relationship and community that is most
10 central in our own human personhood and identity . . .
11   A third common theme is the admission that we cannot, by the nature of the case,
12 have direct access to the intrinsic nature or being of God, as though God were an
13 object that could be observed and studied. What we can know is something of God's
14 dealings with us, as observed from our end of the relationship. That means that in the
15 final analysis discourse about the divine Trinity is really discourse about salvation
16 history . . . Therefore speculative theology about the trinity of God never
17 gets beyond the elaboration of analogies taken from our own lives . . .
18   A fourth common theme in the contemporary writers on trinitarian theology is the
19 understanding that we do not first come to know God as absolute being and then
20 extrapolate to the idea that God is love. It is rather the other way around. We first
21 come to know God as love—that is, as gracious self-communication—and then
22 extrapolate to the idea that God is ground of all being. ...
23   A masterly work dealing with such efforts to engage in trinitarian theology
24 responsibly and wisely is that of Dominican theologian William J Hill, . . . *The Three*
25 *Personed God*, 1982. Tracing the Hebrew sense of "Word of God" and "Breath (Spirit)
26 of God" through the variety of symbols for differentiation in God, Hill considers what
27 patristic, medieval and modern authors have made of this symbolism, coming to it
28 with their own prior expectations and their own characteristic sense of what is real . . .
29 Two aspects of his survey are astonishing: first, the number of theologians dealing
30 with trinitarian theology, of whom he discusses nineteen from the twentieth century,
31 many still living and writing; and secondly the convergence of these authors towards
32 taking the historical as the basis, and focusing on relationship, love and community as

33 the human experiences on which analogies for the divine must be built. The practical
34 implications of this have been spelled out at some length by several contemporary
35 authors.

[Hellwig, M, 1993, pp 155-159.]

Underline those parts of the text which represent the author's voice. Write the line reference numbers here.

....

TASK 5: Read this text and answer the questions below.

Theology in the nineteenth century

[Great changes have taken place in the Church's theology in recent times.]

1   The task now at hand is to examine what some of these differences are between
2   contemporary Catholic theology and the theology from which it immediately diverged.
3   This previous theology dominated the nineteenth century, though its roots go back
4   much further and unfortunately its branches reached well into the twentieth century.

Metaphysical
5   The key language of this theology was metaphysics, or the philosophy of being . . .
6   Being was conceived in static and hierarchical terms, truth was fixed and immutable
7   and generally held to be in possession.
8   Within this theological system, classical theological problems were solved by uses
9   of metaphysical categories of essence, existence, substance, potency, act, habit.
10 Thus the question of the real presence of Christ in the Eucharist was dealt with by
11 speaking of transubstantiation, a change in substance. The classical definition of the
12 Council of Chalcedon, that Christ is one person with two natures, was dealt with by
13 distinguishing between the existence and the essence of an object . . .
14 Coming to grips with this metaphysical system was a basic prerequisite for
15 studying theology! On the positive side, the use of metaphysics was an attempt to
16 find a mode of expression which was "transcultural", which transcended cultural
17 limitations.

Scholastic
18 Though this became a term of abuse, the scholastic methodology was simply to raise
19 and answer questions in a systematic manner. Typically, the question was posed,
20 objections were noted, an authority was cited and then the matter resolved. The
21 classical exponent on this approach is the *Summa Theologiae* of Thomas Aquinas.
22 Every article begins with a question, cites a number of authorities that would indicate
23 a particular answer, cites a single reference which refutes them, then proceeds to
24 give a reasoned response, together with answers to objections. This process
25 continues for hundreds of pages!
26 The line of questions was to find greater precision, eg when was the precise
27 moment when bread and wine became the Body and Blood of Christ. However, there
28 seemed to be a lack of discernment concerning the importance of various questions.
29 . . . The method fell into disrepute, the standard jibe being that the scholastics used to
30 ask how many angels could dance on the head of a pin. I have never seen any
31 evidence that Thomas Aquinas ever in fact asked this question!
32 Clearly, this style of theology predates the nineteenth century by hundreds of
33 years. Its persistence as a method is indicative both of its conceptual clarity and of
34 the failure of theology to come to grips with a changing intellectual climate.

[Ormerod, 1992, pp 25-27.]

Unit 11 Levels of Meaning and Authorial Voice

Answer these questions on the text. Identify words or phrases in the text, with line reference numbers, to support your opinion.

1. Identify the parts of the text where the author's 'voice' (ie opinion or comment) can be 'heard'.

   ....

2. Can you find any examples of sentences with pragmatic meaning? If so, identify the line number/s.

   ....

3. What is the author's attitude in general towards the theologies of the nineteenth century?

   ....

4. What does the author think of metaphysical theology?

   ....

5. What does the author think of scholastic theology?

   ....

6. What is the function of the sentence beginning *'Thus the question of the real presence...* (Lines 10-11)?

   ....

7. What is the function of the sentence beginning *'Every article begins...* (Lines 22-24)?

   ....

8. What is the function of the sentence beginning *'I have never seen any evidence...'* (Lines 30-31)?

   ....

9. What is the function of the sentence beginning *'Its persistence as a method is ...'* (Lines 33-34)?

   ....

TASK 6: Practise identifying authorial voice, literal and inferential meanings and the functions of sentences in the books you are presently studying.

SECTION 2

APPLYING READING SKILLS AND DEVELOPING SPEAKING, LISTENING AND WRITING SKILLS

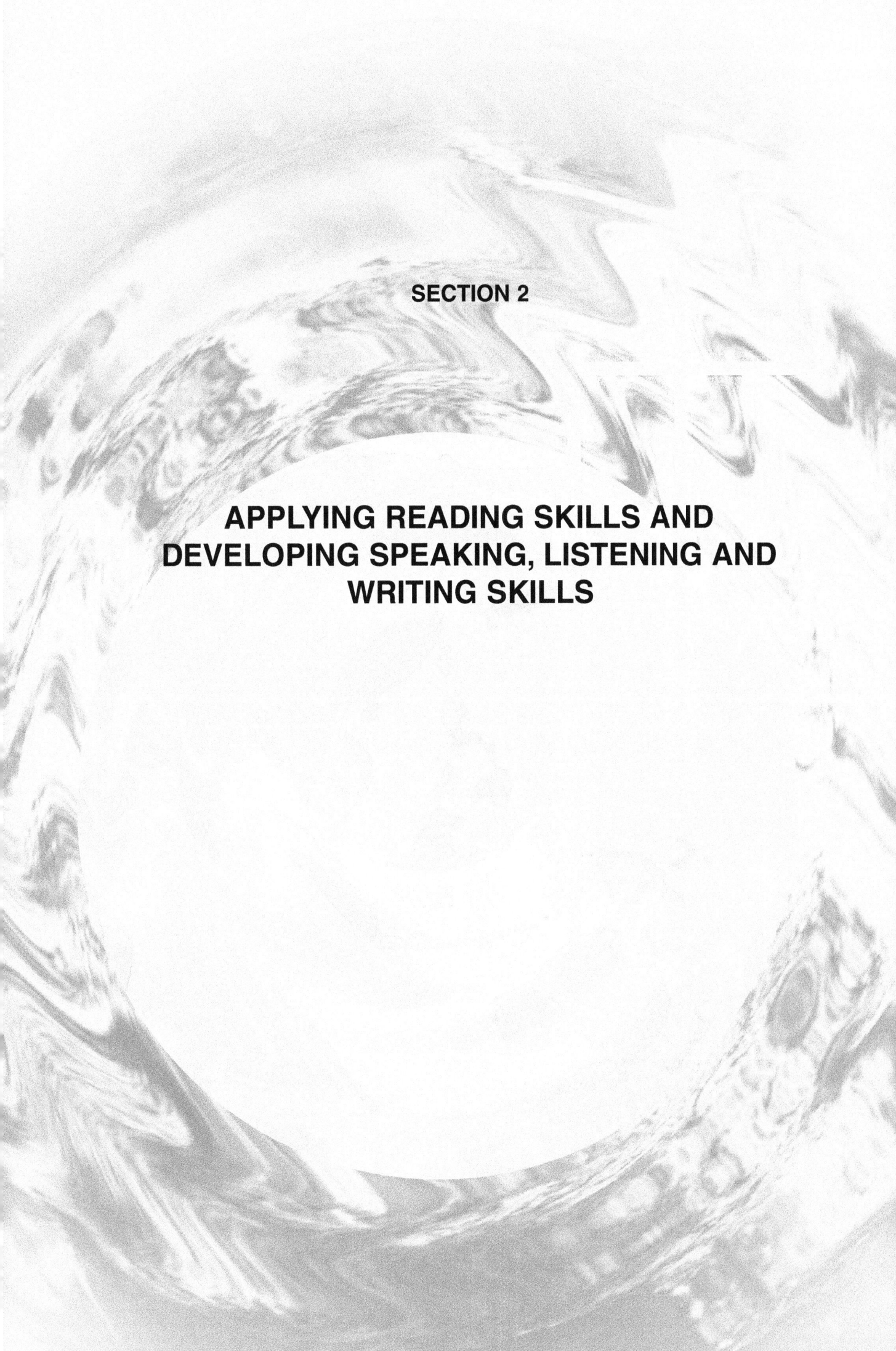

UNIT 12 FOCUS ON ASIA AND THE PACIFIC

PART 1

Preparatory discussion

"Asia" is a proper noun. What does it refer to in the world: a place, a concept, a culture, a people, or none of these? Discuss with two or three people around you.

If you had to choose five or six adjectives to describe the most significant qualities of Asia, what would they be? Write your choice of adjectives:-

……………………………   ……………………………   ……………………………

……………………………   ……………………………   ……………………………

Give reasons for your choices. Discuss in small groups and then with the whole class.

Listening

First read through the questions below. The questions ask you to listen for particular words, for specific information, or for the writer's opinion.

1   Which adjectives are used to describe Asia or Asians?..
    ....
2   What percentage of the world's land area does Asia occupy?..
3   What fraction of the world's population lives in Asia? ....
    <u>Say whether the next two statements are TRUE or FALSE according to the text</u>:-
4   There are very few traditional religions in Asia now.   TRUE/FALSE?
5   Christians are nowhere a majority in Asia.   TRUE/FALSE?
6   Does the writer express any opinions in the text?

Now listen to a short text about Asia and answer these questions.
Check your answers in Listening Text 1 in Appendix A.

Reading Comprehension

This text is the continuation of the text you have just heard. Read the whole passage and then answer the questions.

The face of Asia

1   Asia **is** multi-cultural. Rich and diverse traditional cultures **abound** in Asia. To some
2   extent many Asian societies have been influenced by the cultures of the west, made
3   possible in the past by colonisation, trade and commerce. These days, the
4   inroads of industrialisation, modernisation, tourism and mass media **foster** the
5   values of materialism, consumerism, secularism, individualism, and hedonism among
6   many Asian communities. This often **undermines** their traditional religious and
7   cultural values. Asia is where traditional and modern cultural values **meet** in creative
8   and at times destructive tension.
9   Asia **is** predominantly poor, though there **are** a few rich countries to be found in the
10 region: Japan, Taiwan, Singapore, South Korea and Hong Kong. From the end of the
11 colonial period, most of the Asian countries have been struggling to stand up on their
12 own feet in their respective socio-economic-political life, but the powerful rich nations of
13 the world still strongly **influence** them to the great disadvantage of the Asian countries
14 themselves. In effect, the new economic prosperity in many of our Asian societies
15 typically **benefits** the foreign capitalists and the few local elite, with very little benefit to
16 the majority of Asians. The plight of the poor masses **grows** worse because of the

English for Theology

17 pervasive practice of graft and corruption and by ineffective governance. This **results** in
18 the dismal delivery of basic social services. More tragic, the lack of planning and
19 monitoring of development programs in many Asian countries **leads** to ecological
20 devastation and disasters in many parts of the region.
21 On the bright side, however, Asia **is re-awakening**. There is a renewed consciousness
22 among Asian peoples of their respective identity and autonomy. In each nation, new
23 hope **is generating** a growing sense of appreciation and affirmation of one's ethnic,
24 political and national identity. Asian peoples **are becoming** more conscious of their
25 human dignity and human rights. There is a renewed affirmation among Asians of their
26 rich and life-giving cultural and religious values. A new confidence **is growing** in their
27 power and right to change the unjust structures of society. Asians **are** now
28 **collaborating** in various groupings and associations towards a better Asia.

[Adapted from Pedregosa et al, 1998, pp 1-3.]

1 Why were cultures of the west able to influence Asia?
....

2 Does the writer think that industrialisation and modernisation have been good for Asia? Why/why not?

....

3 Who receives most of the profit from Asia's new wealth?

....

4 What is one of the causes of environmental damage in the region mentioned in the text?

....

5 Why are Asian peoples now meeting social challenges with new confidence?

....

6 Do you think the writer of this text is a member of an Asian society or an outsider from another culture describing it? What evidence is there in the text for your answer?

....

Vocabulary Extension

1 Find the adjectives used in the text above to describe Asia. Together with the adjectives used to describe Asia in the listening text, how do these adjectives compare with your list made at the beginning of this Unit?
2 List any *other* adjectives you can find in the text, together with the noun which each one qualifies?
Example: *rich* cultures; *diverse* cultures

....

....

Revision of Grammar: Verbs – Present Simple Tense
We use the present simple tense to talk about
        i) general truths or states of affairs
        ii) situations which are more or less permanent
        iii) repeated actions or habits
Sometimes we use the present simple tense to talk about
        iv) future events which are part of a fixed plan or timetable.

The verbs in bold print in the first part of the text above and in the Listening text are in the present simple tense. Identify the function (in terms of the four categories above) of each highlighted verb.

Remember that for third person singular (affirmative), the verb ends in *–s* or *–es,* and sometimes in *–ies*. With the negative, you must use the correct form of *do/does not*.

REVISION EXERCISE 12.1

Complete these sentences with the present simple tense of the verb given in brackets. For each sentence, say whether the present tense verb is an example of i, ii, iii, or iv as explained above.

Example: Asia cover*s* (*cover*) thirty percent of the world's land area. (Example of i. state of affairs.)

1 Asia .... *(have)* the earth's highest mountain.
2 Many countries in Asia .... *(have)* mega-cities.
3 Beautiful beaches in the Pacific .... *(attract)* many tourists.
4 The sun .... *(rise)* in the east and ....*(set)* in the west.
5 She .... *(fly)* to Vanuatu tomorrow afternoon.
6 Their parents ....*(live)* in the village but their sister .... *(live)* in the city.
7 Adequate theology ....*(include)* the spiritual significance of land.
8 Actions .... *(speak)* louder than words.
9 He ....*(not speak)* Spanish; he ....*(speak)* Chinese.
10 Every day he .... *(catch)* a lot of fish.
11 A strong typhoon .... *(cause)* great destruction.
12 My friend .... *(watch)* television news each evening.
13 Maria .... *(go)* to school by canoe.
14 Most of the children ....*(not go)* by canoe. They .... *(walk)*.

Verbs – Present Continuous (sometimes called Progressive) Tense
We use the present continuous tense to talk about action in progress at the present time or a temporary situation. The present continuous form is:- verb *to be* + verb + ...ing.

Find some examples of present continuous verbs in Lines 21-28 of the text above.
Other examples:-   The social landscape of Asia **is changing** rapidly.
            They **are studying** in the library.
            I**'m walking** to school until my bicycle is repaired.

Sometimes we also use the present continuous tense to talk about future plans. For example:-
            Next month they**'re beginning** a new project in the village.
            He**'s driving** to the city next weekend
            What **are** you **doing** tomorrow evening?
(Note the position of the subject, *you*, when we ask a question.)

REVISION EXERCISE 12.2

Complete these sentences with the present continuous form of the verb.
1 Every year, multinational firms .... *(cause)* more changes in society.
2 Thousands of workers .... *(build)* the Three Gorges Dam in China.
3 Why ...... they .... *(stand)* there?
4 They .... *(wait)* for the bus to come.
5 In many countries, powerful spiritual movements .... *(rise)*.

Note: Some verbs are <u>not</u> usually used in the continuous form. These are verbs of thinking, eg *think, believe*, verbs of feeling eg *like, hate, love,* and verbs of perception eg *see, hear*, and so on. Consult a comprehensive grammar book for more detail.

Speaking

What do you think about the description of Asia above? Is it accurate? If you live in the Pacific region, does any of the description apply to your country? What is happening now in your country, and in neighbouring countries? (Talk about political, economic and religious happenings.) What would you like to see happen in the years ahead? Form discussion groups with members from two or three different countries if possible. A spokesperson for each country (or part of a country) may give a brief summary to the whole class.

PART 2

Preparatory Discussion

"The Pacific" is often used as a noun. What is it? Discuss with those around you questions similar to those in Part 1. For example, does "the Pacific" mean an ocean, a group of islands, a region, a culture? What is to be included and what is to be excluded from the idea of "the Pacific"?

Listening

Listen to a short text about some important ideas in traditional Pacific religion. Listen for the answers to these questions:-

1. Which two words/ideas belonging to the vocabulary of traditional Pacific religion have come to be prominent in the comparative study of religion? (Write them in the order that you hear them.) i……………………… ii……………………….
2. One of the two words referred to in question 1 has come to be widely used in ordinary English. What is that word?
   …………………………………………………………………………………………………
3. What is the meaning of each of these two words? (Complete the table below.)
4. Who was mainly responsible for the introduction of each of these ideas/words to the English speaking world? (Complete the table below.)

Word/idea	Meaning	Introduced to the English-speaking world by
i …………………	…………………………	……………………………………………
ii …………………	…………………………	……………………………………………

5. Who gave the second term 'a new psychological force' in the western world in the 20th century? ………………………………………………………………………………………

Check your answers by listening again or with the text in Listening Text 2 in Appendix A.

Reading Comprehension

Read the text below and answer the questions.

Dimensions of Polynesian religion

1 The most important distinction in Polynesian religion is that between the spiritual or invisible world
2 and the world which we can see and experience. The two are interwoven: the gods are the
3 various forces which lie behind visible events, such as thunder or menstruation, and by their nature
4 they are frequent visitors to the habitations of human beings. There is a distinction often drawn
5 between the heavenly world, the place where the gods are when they are not with us, and the
6 underworld whither the spirits of the dead pass.
7 Mostly, *rituals* are concerned with attempting some control of the gods. If they are to visit us,
8 then it is best that they do so where and when we want, so it is important to prepare dwellings for
9 them and form incantations to bring them hither, please them, and then (quite as important) send
10 them back to where they came from. Anything that has to do with the gods must be done with
11 great care. The taboos involved are simply a reflection of the fact that gods are dangerous. So
12 indeed is any person with great *mana* or inherent power. Thus in Hawaii the fact that chiefs
13 exuded tremendous power, and the fear of weakening that power by having lower-class spouses
14 mate with them, meant that there was sanction for brother-sister marriage. (This has been the

15   case in a number of other societies, notably in ancient Egypt.)
16   Naturally there were rituals for all propitious occasions, such as the planting of crops, the
17   beginning of a voyage, the start of a hunting or fishing expedition. Witchcraft—in the sense of
18   using ritual means to bring about bad results for others, rather than (like most rites) good results
19   for us—was widely practised also.

[Smart, 1989, p 164.]

Answer these questions on the text:-

1   In Line 2 there is a pronoun reference: "*the two ...*". What are the two things referred to here?
    i..   ii..

2   What are the *'habitations'* (Line 4) of human beings?..

3   What is the main purpose of ritual in traditional Polynesian religion?

    ....

4   In Line 8 there is a substitute expression. Write in full the verb and complement substituted by *'do so"*.
    ..it is best that they..

5   In Line 11 we read about taboos being connected with "*the fact that the gods are dangerous*". For whom is it a *'fact that the gods are dangerous'*?

    ....

6   Why were brother-sister marriages allowed in Hawaii in traditional times?

    ....

7   What is the main pattern of organisation of ideas in this text?
    i description   ii analysis
    iii explanation   iv argument   ....

8   Does the writer express any opinion or comment in this text? If so, give line reference number/s.

    ....

Speaking

Are there practices from traditional religion still common in day-to-day life in your society? What are they? What are some positive and/or negative effects of these practices in the community in general?

Writing

Write an 8-10 line description of your country for someone in another part of the world. Include the following information: location and size of your country, population, cultural and religious identities of the people, social conditions, and changes taking place at present. (Practise using the verb tenses reviewed in this Unit.)

PART 3

Preparatory Discussion

Several important international gatherings in recent years have focused on the Asia Pacific Region. Taking into account the views in the text in Part 1 of this Unit, and your own discussions in Parts 1 and 2, do you think there is a realistic basis for considering this as one region? Or should it be considered as many regions? What are the factors for and against a community of Asia-Pacific nations? Discuss.

Reading Comprehension

Read this text and answer the questions below.

The diversity of Asia

1   Do the countries of the Asia Pacific region have anything in common? Is it
2   realistic to consider this as a new geopolitical and economic community?
3   Impassable mountain ranges, vast areas of desert, flood-prone lowlands,
4   impenetrable tropical jungles and ocean deeps separating scores of island
5   groups present challenges to communication.
6   In addition, there are the cultural, religious and social differences. East from
7   India to China and Japan, and south through Asia to Australasia, millions of
8   people speak hundreds of languages. People pray to Allah, Christ, Buddha,
9   and Mammon. Socialists and capitalists vie for power. Silicon chip factories
10 thrive next to rice paddies ploughed by water buffalo. People live in Stone-
11 Age villages and crowded into futuristic cities. Many of these societies have
12 followed divergent traditions for centuries . . . However, despite the
13 incredible diversity of Asia Pacific, there are common themes, and changes
14 elsewhere are forcing countries in the region to rely more upon these
15 commonalities than their differences. In the future, the countries of Asia
16 Pacific won't be able to ignore each other. Nor will the rest of the world be
17 able to ignore a more united Asia Pacific.   [Note: Reference at the end of this unit.]

Answer these questions:-

1   On the basis of this text, which subject is the most likely main topic of the book from which this text comes?
    a comparative religion   b development and environment   c politics and economics.
    (Refer again to Unit 7 on Skimming if necessary.)

    ……………………………………   Give reasons for your answer.

2   What are the physical obstacles to easy communication in this region?

    ....

3   The writer lists many differences to be found in the Asia Pacific region. How many *classes* (categories) of difference are mentioned? What are they?

    ....

4   What does the author mean in Lines 8-9 by saying that 'people pray to . . . Mammon'?

    ....

5   In Lines 9-10 we read "Silicon chip factories thrive next to rice paddies ploughed by water buffalo". This is first of all a description of a fact. What is the functional meaning (the purpose) of this sentence within the paragraph? Explain.

    ....

6   The writer asks two rhetorical questions at the beginning of this text (Lines 1-2). What is the writer's purpose in using these questions (ie what is the function of the sentences)? (Refer back to Unit 11 on the functions of rhetorical questions.) What does the writer think about the answers to these questions? What is the evidence in the text?

    ....

    ....

    ....

Vocabulary Extension – Lexical Transformation

Make a table in your notebook as below. Several verbs (in the infinitive form) used in the passage are listed in the left-hand column. Complete as many of the other columns as possible. (Note: Not all verbs can be transformed into nouns or adjectives.)

Infinitive	Simple Past Tense	Noun	Adjective/Past Participle
eg *consider*	*considered*	*consideration*	*considerate/considered*
separate	....	....	....
present	....	....	....
speak	....	....	....
pray	....	....	....
force	....	....	....
rely	....	....	....
ignore	....	....	....

PART 4

Preparatory Discussion

Apart from churches, mosques and temples, are there other sacred places in your country? Where are they? Why are they considered special, that is, how did they come to be associated with spiritual qualities? Did something special happen there? When do people go there and what do they hope to receive? Discuss these questions in small groups.

Reading Comprehension

Read this passage and then answer the questions below, according to the text.

Land, place and theology

1 The theological significance of place is a constantly recurring motif across the
2 centuries of human and religious history. Sometimes this notion finds
3 expression in the idea of a land promised by God to a particular people, as in
4 the case of the Israelites. At other times, it is the belief of a people that, in the
5 wisdom of the Great Spirit, it is they who belong to a certain land, and this
6 belonging carries with it the sacred duty of protecting and caring for the land.
7 This is the experience of the Australian Aborigines, and indeed of some other
8 tribal peoples. Sometimes this numinous quality of the land is attributed to
9 particular localities, where sacred places, such as groves, caves, hills,
10 springs and rivers draw the faithful for prayer and healing. For many people,
11 the sacred place of religious pilgrimage may be associated with the lives of
12 great religious leaders or prophets. Jerusalem and Mecca are two such
13 places for millions of people around the world. This same motif of the
14 theological significance of land is carried over into the convenient practice of
15 people themselves building sacred places, such as temples, churches and
16 mosques. Wherever and however people give expression to this idea, it
17 surely reflects a common human belief that our place or our land and all
18 earth's creatures and plants, with their life-giving and beautiful qualities, are
19 gifts of God and a mysterious reflection of the divine. Our lands are thus a
20 gift in trust and they call for our reverence and gratitude.

Answer these questions on the text:-

1 Which people believe that they belong to the land? ………………………………..

2 Why do some people go to special caves, rivers or hills?

   ……………………………………………………………………………………………

3 Is this statement true or false, according to the text?
   It is mainly the tribal or animist religions which consider places to have spiritual significance.   TRUE/FALSE…………….

4 In Line 12 of the text there is a pronoun reference, *"two such places"*. What does *"such"* mean here? Write out the full meaning of the phrase.

   ……………………………………………………………………………………………

5   Which of the following statements best expresses the writer's *main point* in this text? Note that all of the statements are true according to the text.

a   The Israelites believed in a land promised by God. ❏

b   Jerusalem and Mecca are very important religious places in the world. ❏

c   Tribal peoples are very aware of the need to care for the land. ❏

d   The idea that some places are especially holy is widespread in human history. ❏

e   Peoples of many different faiths usually worship in buildings these days. ❏

Writing
Write a half to one page describing a sacred place in your country. Say where and what it is (eg a river, hill, cave), with a short description, why it came to be considered a holy place, when people go there, what they do while there and what they hope to gain from their visit. Check your work carefully before finishing. Make sure subjects and verbs are in agreement.

[Reference for text in Part 3 of this Unit. Based on Dobbs-Higginson, 1993, pp 3-4.]

UNIT 12 VOCABULARY

Add to the list any more new words that you want to remember in connection with the topics in this Unit.

Nouns	Verbs	Adjectives	Other
influence	thrive	major	predominantly
extent	host	minor	
modernisation	abound	multi-cultural	
prosperity	undermine	ancient	
plight	foster	primal	
graft	generate	traditional	
corruption	collaborate	elite	
devastation	vie	prone	
motif	embark	numinous	
rituals	exude	inherent	
incantations	interweave	propitious	
notion	sacralise		
sanction			
…………………	…………………	………………………	…………………
…………………	…………………	………………………	…………………

UNIT 13 THEOLOGY AND SPIRITUALITY

PART 1

Preparatory Discussion

What is *your* definition of theology? How is it different from philosophy? What are some specific theologies which developed in the twentieth century (eg liberation theology), and in the centuries before that? What *might* be some theologies of the twenty-first century? Work together and list as many as you can.

Theologies

Before the 20th century	20th century	21st century ?
....	....	....
....	....	....
....	....	....
....	....	....

Reading Comprehension

Read the text. Work in small groups to answer the questions. Share your ideas with the class.

Vocabulary preparation: *neutral, piety, authoritarianism, dogmatism, fideism, existential*

A classical definition of theology

1 Probably the most well-known definition of theology is St. Anselm's definition. In the
2 Middle Ages, he said that theology is *faith seeking understanding*. According to one
3 author, there are advantages in this brief definition. Firstly, it makes clear that, unlike
4 religious studies, theology is not a neutral activity. A faith stance **is taken** by the
5 theologian. Secondly, the provisional nature of theology **is indicated** in this definition.
6 Theology **is** never **finished**. Rather, it is a continuing search for understanding because
7 new questions **are being generated** as history unfolds. Thirdly, intelligence and reason
8 **are involved** in this search. This makes theology quite different from piety,
9 authoritarianism, dogmatism or fideism. "Theology is the meeting place of faith and
10 reason."
11 At the same time our author points out some of the gaps in this definition of theology. For
12 example, what exactly is faith? By what criteria **is** faith **determined?** Is it a matter of
13 intellectual assent only, or do we assert that a fully existential commitment **is involved**?
14 Whose faith **is being considered**—that of the fundamentalist, of the theologian, of
15 church leaders? 'Truth claims' **are made** by some people? What is truth, and can such
16 claims be made? The tensions created by these issues **are not** easily **resolved.** Yet
17 exploration of difficult questions must go on.

[Based on Ormerod, 1990, pp 3-5.]

1 What is the difference between theology and religious studies?

   ....

2 What is the writer's explanation of the 'provisional nature' (Line 5) of theology?

   ....

3 Why is theology never finished (Line 6)?

   ....

4 How is theology different from piety, authoritarianism, dogmatism and fideism?

   ....

5   What are some of the problems with this definition of theology?

    ....

6   What is the writer's main purpose in this text:- *to argue, explain, or evaluate*?

    ....

7   What is the writer's attitude towards the difficult questions of theology?

    ....

Vocabulary extension

In Line 11, a figurative word, *gap*, is used about the definition of theology? What does *gap* mean in this text? What is the literal meaning of the word *gap*? What other words could be used to convey a similar meaning?

<u>*gap* (literal meaning)</u>
words of similar meaning   ……….   ………...   …………

<u>*gap* (figurative meaning)</u>
words of similar meaning: ………..   ………...   …………

Revision of Grammar : Verbs – Passive voice – Present and Continuous

The passive form is used to indicate that the grammatical subject is not doing the acting but receiving the action. The present passive is formed by the verb *be + the past participle*. For the continuous form, we use *be + being + past participle*.

Example:

   Theology **is studied** by many people these days.   (Present passive)
   Questions on that issue **are being raised** by the faithful. (Present continuous passive)

The text above contains many examples of present passive verbs. Find examples of the present passive continuous form? (Give Line references.)

Note that the active and passive forms of a sentence, though they seem to convey the same information, do not mean exactly the same thing.

Example: *The Portuguese introduced Christianity to the island of Flores.*
             Christianity was introduced to the island of Flores by the Portuguese.

 What is the difference in meaning between these two sentences?

Consult a comprehensive grammar book for more detail on passive verbs.

English for Theology

REVISION EXERCISE 13.1
Lexical transformation:
Complete the table for each verb as in the example given.

Infinitive verb	Simple Past Tense	Noun	Adjective/Past Participle
eg *indicate*	indicated	indication	indicative/indicated
use	....	....	....
give	....	....	....
generate	....	....	....
involve	....	....	....
determine	....	....	....
assent	....	....	....
commit	....	....	....
consider	....	....	....
create	....	....	....
resolve	....	....	....
examine	....	....	....
explore	....	....	....

REVISION EXERCISE 13.2
Change these sentences into the active form.
eg Truth claims *are made* by some people.   *Some people make truth claims.*

1   New questions are generated by unfolding history.
....

2   By what criteria is faith determined?
....

3   The use of intelligence and reason is involved in theology.
....

4   A faith stance is required by theology.
....

5   Theological development is retarded by the failure to examine difficult questions.
....

6   Many people are disturbed by the uncertainties of modern life.
....

Change these sentences into the passive form.

1   An ecclesial community often supports the theologian.
....

2   Everything we do expresses our spirituality.
....

3   Culture and history influence theology and spirituality.
....

4   Careful discussion often <u>resolves</u> misunderstanding.

   ....

5   The theologian systematically <u>studies</u> revelation.

   ....

6   Different people <u>understand</u> revelation in different ways.

   ....

Speaking

Here is another definition of theology:-
   *A theology mediates between a cultural matrix and the significance
   and role of religion in that matrix.*   [Lonergan, 1971, p xi.]

How does this definition differ from St Anselm's. (*Theology is faith seeking understanding.*) If culture is relevant, what other realities or ideas (besides faith) are included in theology by Lonergan's definition? What are some questions raised by Lonergan's definition?

One of these two definitions might be described as a definition of *function* (ie what role theology plays in society, what it <u>does</u>), and the other as one of *essence* (what it <u>is</u>). Which description—of function or essence—applies to Anselm's definition and which to Lonergan's?

Writing

Choose ONE of the twentieth century theologies you listed at the beginning of this Unit. In about 8-10 lines, describe the focus of that theology and mention particular persons, places or situations associated with it. Which of the two definitions of theology—essential or functional—(St Anselm's or Lonergan's) better describes the theology you have selected and why?

PART 2

Preparatory Discussion

Discuss in small groups: How is theology related to spirituality? Is it a part of spirituality, is spirituality a part of theology, or is neither of these the case? In pairs, write down all the words which come into your mind in relation to spirituality. (Two minutes only.) (Keep this list for later.) Are there different spiritualities? Share your ideas with the whole class.

Listening

Listen to a short text on spirituality. You will hear the passage three times. Do not attempt to write everything you hear but take brief notes on the main ideas. Work with two or three people to reconstruct in your own words the meaning of what you heard. Share your version with other groups in the class.

[Afterwards, check your accuracy by referring to Listening Text 3 in Appendix A.]

Reading Comprehension

Read these two texts on spirituality and answer the questions below.

Spirituality

A

1   Spirituality focuses on that inner dimension of the person which is called
2   "the spirit" by certain traditions. This spiritual core is the deepest centre of
3   the person. It is here that the person is open to the transcendent
4   dimension. It is here that ultimate reality is experienced by the person.
5   The study of spirituality explores how this core is discovered, the dynamics
6   of its development, and its journey to the ultimate goal.

[Based on preface, McGinn & Meyendorff, editors, 1985, p xiii.]

B

1   Long ago, Isaiah described the fundamental human impulse which is the
2   basis of spirituality everywhere: *My spirit within me earnestly seeks you.**
3   The terms in which different peoples understand the meaning and the
4   'object' of that search may vary. Yet it is clear that this inner experience
5   . . . is common to all people . . . This experience encompasses more than
6   mere self-expression. There is always an element of response, more or
7   less consciously, towards that *hidden power which hovers over the course*
8   *of things.*** It is this movement of the human spirit towards the other,
9   though the "Other" is deep within, towards what is to become, in this
10   striving for self-expression and self-transcendence, that we find the proper
11   arena of spirituality. Most religious traditions unhesitatingly name the
12   source and the term of this life impulse as God.

[Kelly, 1992, p 99.]

*   Isaiah 26:9   ** Vatican II, Declaration on Non-Christian Religions, para. 2.]

1   These two texts, A and B, could be described as an *explanation* and a *definition*. Which description better applies to each text? Why?

Text A could be described as ……………………. because………………………………

………………………………………………………………………………………………

Text B could be described as …………………… because………………………………

………………………………………………………………………………………………

2   In Text A, the place adverb *here* is used twice (Lines 3 and 4). Where is *here*, according to the text (ie what does *here* refer to)?

    ……………………………………………………………………………………….

3   In text B, the writer refers to *'this movement'* (Line 8). The writer gives two explanations of what is meant by *'this movement'*. What are they?

    ……………………………………………………………………………………….

    ……………………………………………………………………………………….

4   Are these statements TRUE or FALSE (T/F) according to Text B?

    i) Isaiah's description of spirituality applies only to the Hebrew Scriptures, ie the Old Testament.   T/F?   ………..

    ii) People everywhere understand the spiritual search in the same terms. T/F?   ……..

English for Theology

PART 3

Preparatory Discussion

Has the understanding and practice of spirituality changed in your country over the past thirty or so years? Make two columns, headed *earlier spirituality* and *spirituality now*. Brainstorm as many characteristics of each as you can. Consider language, rituals, pious practices, actions, hymns and any other aspects you can think of. Is all change good? Discuss with others in the class.

Listening

1 First, skim read the text below to gain a general idea of what it is about.
Then from your general knowledge of the topic, try to predict what words might fit the blank spaces. Work with a partner if you wish.

What is Christian spirituality?

1   Christian spirituality is essentially a following of the Will of God as revealed in Scripture which
2   culminates in the words, the deeds and the Person of Jesus Christ in the Gospels. The history of
3   Christian spirituality demonstrates the .... **1** of ways in which the Gospel teaching has
4   been ....**2**, adapted and ....**3** to the needs of nations, ...**4**
5   and ....**5**. Spirituality involves the twin elements of **6**
6   and ....**7** where traditionally practice .... **8** on the fruits
7   of ....**9**. Contemplation is a ....**10** **11**
8   and ....**12** on God's revelation with the hope that God's will would become
9   ....**13** for one's life and world. It is the...**14**
10 of God's will for one's life and world that ....**15** **16**
11 in Christian spirituality. In essence, there should only be one Christian spirituality since there is
12 only one ....**17** who is Jesus Christ. The appellations *old* and *new*
13 spirituality only point to the .... **18** and .... **19** in the
14 understanding of God's Will ....**20** through Jesus Christ and its applicability to a
15 ....**21** changing ....**22** which may be characterised by **23**
16 ....**24**.

[Ojoy, pp 20-21.]

2   Now listen to the complete text as it is read, completing the blank spaces with the words you hear. Check your accuracy with the full text in Listening Text 4 in Appendix A.

Reading Comprehension

Read through the above completed text again. Answer these questions.

1. What is the author's definition of 'contemplation'?..

2. What explanation does this author give for differences in Christian spirituality?

   ....

   ....

3. The author states that 'there should be only one Christian spirituality' (Line 11) and later refers to 'old' and 'new' spiritualities (Line 12). What do you think is the author's attitude towards 'new' spiritualities—is the author in favour of 'new spiritualities' or not in favour? What is the evidence in the text for your opinion?

   ....

PART 4

Preparatory Discussion

With a partner, prepare a list of five of your favourite writers—or mentors or gurus—on spirituality. What country do they come from? What time in history do they represent? Are they men or women? How do any of these things (time, place, gender) influence what they write? Discuss in small groups and then share with the class.

Reading Comprehension

Read the passage and answer the questions.
Vocabulary preparation: *holistic, seldom, convention, conviction*

Spirituality

1 Spirituality can be described as the whole of our deepest religious beliefs, convictions, and patterns
2 of thought, emotion and behaviour in respect to what is ultimate, to God. Spirituality is holistic,
3 encompassing our relationships to all of creation—to others, to society and nature, to work and
4 recreation—in a fundamentally religious orientation. Spirituality is larger than a theology or set of
5 values precisely because it is all-encompassing and pervasive. Unlike theology as an explicit
6 intellectual position, spirituality reaches into our unconscious or half-conscious depths. And while
7 it shapes behaviour and attitudes, spirituality is more than a conscious moral code. In relation to
8 God, it is who we really are, the deepest self, not entirely accessible to our comprehensive self-
9 reflection. In a Christian context, God's love goes before us in a way we can never fully name.
10 Spirituality can be a predominantly unconscious pattern of relating seldom reflected on, activated
11 only in certain situations . . . As such it is a dimension of life for the most part unexamined,
12 resting on convention, upbringing or social expectations. But spirituality can also be made
13 conscious, explicitly reflected on, developed, changed, and understood in a context of growth . . .
14 Christian spirituality entails the conviction that God is indeed personal and that we are in immediate
15 personal relationship to another, an Other who "speaks" and can be spoken to, who really affects
16 our lives.

[Carr, 1986 p 49-50]

Are the first 3 statements true or false according to the text?

1 Spirituality is mainly about our relationship to God? TRUE or FALSE?   …………..
2 Spirituality is another term for moral behaviour. TRUE or FALSE?   …………..
3 Many people may not be aware of their spirituality. TRUE or FALSE?   …………
4 How does this writer explain the difference between theology and spirituality?
   ………………………………………………………………………………………..
   ………………………………………………………………………………………..

According to this writer, why is spirituality 'for the most part unexamined' (Line 11)?
………………………………………………………………………………………..
………………………………………………………………………………………..

Vocabulary Extension – Lexical Transformation

Complete this table as far as possible.

Infinitive verb	Simple Past	Noun	Adjective/Past Participle
describe	………………	………………	………………………………
encompass	………………	………………	………………………………
pervade	………………	………………	………………………………
shape	………………	………………	………………………………

Writing

Make brief notes of what you consider to be the three or four most important ideas about spirituality from the texts in this unit. Refer back to your list of words in relation to spirituality in Part 2, Preparatory Discussion, in this unit. Using your own words (not quotations from the texts), write your definition of spirituality in no more than five lines.

UNIT 13   VOCABULARY

Add to the list any more new words that you want to learn and remember.

Nouns	**Verbs**	**Adjectives**	**Other**
definition	hover	neutral	unhesitatingly
stance	culminate	provisional	precisely
piety	demonstrate	transcendent	seldom
criterion	characterise	applicable	
dimension	entail	ultimate	
dynamics	shape	holistic	
arena		pervasive	
appellation			
………………	………………	………………	………………..
………………	………………	………………	………………

UNIT 14   THEOLOGY AND LANGUAGE

PART 1

Preparatory Discussion

What do you know about the origins of language, about the different language groups in the world today, about the influence of culture on language? What is the language *group* of your first language (L1)? (Is it Japanese, Dravidian, Austro-Asiatic, Tai, Sino-Tibetan, Indo-Iranian, Germanic or something else? Consult the appendices of a major dictionary.) Does your language have dialects? Can the speakers of different dialects understand each other? Share your knowledge in a brief class discussion.

Listening

Listen to a text on the origins of language. Take notes and then answer these questions.
1. What do we know about the origins of language? ………………………………………
2. When in the history of the world did language probably begin?………………………...
3. What are some of the theories of how and why language began?
   ………………………………………………………………………………………………

Check your answers in Listening Text 5 in Appendix A.

Reading Comprehension

Read the passage and answer the questions.

………………?……………..

1   Language, with its complex relationship to thought and culture, is always somewhat **paradoxical.**
2   It is the tool which enables humans to give expression to thought, yet it cannot **encompass** all
3   forms of human consciousness. As we say, some experiences are 'beyond words'. Language can
4   reflect rational consciousness. However, scholars like James, Polanyi and Lonergan have shown
5   that human consciousness is much greater, more **'polymorphic'**, than its merely rational
6   **dimension**. When we search for truth, cultural influences on our thinking and language must
7   also be taken into account. Theological language is especially challenging because it **explores**
8   realities which transcend the human mind. As Porter has said, "the nature of religious language is
9   to be problematic".* He has pointed out that two developments in the twentieth century have
10 further complicated the problems of religious language. One has been the very great increase in
11 primary materials—for example, Greek papyri, Semitic language sources—available for scholars of
12 both the Old and New Testaments. Another has been the large number of philosophical questions
13 raised about religious language by philosophers and linguistic analysts. One of the most
14 **fundamental** of these questions is whether God 'exists', whether it is even meaningful to speak of
15 God.   *[Porter, editor, 1996, p 20.]

1   Word matching:

For each of the words in the text in bold print, find a word from this list which could be used in its place. Try to do this without using your dictionary.

examines …………   *contain* ……………   *basic* ……………

aspect …………..   *contradictory* ………..   *multiform*…………

Answer these questions:

2   The writer states that language is 'paradoxical' (line 1). What explanation does the writer give for 'paradoxical'? ………………………………………………………………………
………………………………………………………………………………………………

3   Why is theological language a special problem? (Lines 7-8.)

………………………………………………………………………………………………

93

4   What particular problems has the twentieth century added to religious language?

    ....

    ....

5   Which of the following titles would be the most suitable heading for this text? Give your reasons.
    a. Complexities of language and culture   ❑
    b. The rational dimension of language   ❑
    c. The challenges of theological language.   ❑

    Reasons? ....

Revision of Grammar: Articles

In the English language, the scope of reference intended for nouns is indicated or determined by words called 'determiners'. For example, in referring to the noun *book,* we would want to indicate which book: *this book, your book, most books, the book, a book,* and so on. Articles in English are a sub-set of these determiner words and they are of two kinds: **indefinite (*a, an*)** and **definite (*the*)**. When articles are used, they always come before the noun. If the nouns are qualified by an adjective, then the article precedes the adjective: eg *the English language, an ancient language, a countable noun, an item, a particular item, the discovery.*

The definite article: *the*

The definite article is used when both the writer and the reader (or speaker and listener) know what is being referred to. There are four situations where this shared knowledge occurs.

[Ref Leech & Svartvik, 1975, pp 52-53.]

1 REFERENCE BACKWARDS
This occurs when there has already been mention of the noun in an earlier part of the text (or conversation).
For example: *She arrived by **bus** yesterday evening. **The bus** was two hours late…*(ie the bus already referred to).
OR   *He borrowed **a book** from the library. **The book** was in great demand.*

In these examples, the definite reference comes in the sentence immediately following the original reference. Often, there may be one or more sentences between the first and following references to a noun.

NOTE: If the subsequent use of the noun is generic (ie referring to the whole class of things) rather than specific, then zero article—no article—is used.
Examples: ***A new insight** (this is specific use) into 'original sin' has followed recent sociobiological discoveries. **New insight**, (this is generic use) however, takes a long time to translate into pastoral practice.*

   ***A lasting peace** (specific use) among the tribal groups can only be brought about through justice, but **lasting peace** (generic use) often seems to be an impossible dream.*

2 REFERENCE FORWARDS

The definite article is used when the identity of a noun is made clear by what follows.
For example: ***The language problems*** *which have arisen in the twentieth century....*
Here we are talking about not just any language problems, but specifically those 'which have arisen in the twentieth century'.

3 UNIQUE REFERENCE

When everybody knows that what we are talking about is the only one or group of its kind in our world, or in the particular context, we have the unique use of the definite article.
For example: ***The Qumran scrolls*** *have contributed greatly to biblical scholarship..*
      Also: *the Bible... **the** human race.... **the** ozone layer... **the** sun*...etc.
In a given context, we would know that *the President, the Prime Minister* or *the library, the common room* referred to a specific person/place understood by all.

4 INSTITUTIONAL REFERENCE

This use of the definite article occurs when we refer to something commonly shared or experienced by society.
For example: *He wanted to use **the** telephone to contact headquarters.*
          ***The** elections will be held later this year.*
          *It was reported in **the** newspaper.*
          *We saw it on **the** television.* (Note: We can also say *We saw it on television.*)

The definite article can be used with all kinds of nouns, that is, singular, plural, countable or uncountable nouns. Eg *the book, the students* (countable*); the water, the rain* (uncountable)

GENERIC USE

A particular use of the definite article occurs with countable nouns when we refer to what is general or characteristic of a whole category.
Example: ***The** scripture scholar must be familiar with the ancient biblical languages.*
       ***The** pastoral worker often meets painful personal situations.*
       *In some countries these days, **the** priest is a vanishing species.*

Here we are talking about scripture scholars, pastoral workers or priests in general.

Example

In this text, note the various uses of the definite articles as indicated below:

In **the** Scriptures (1)... we read over and over again **the** words (2): "Listen!", "If you but listen to **the** voice (3) of **the** Lord (4)...," if you remain alert and attentive you will hear something after all. **The** imperative (5) to "hearken," to remain receptive to a revelatory "word" is pervasive in **the** Hebrew and Christian (6) (as well as **the** Islamic 7) texts.

[Haught, 1988, p 5.]

1   Unique reference- we all know we are referring to the Judaeo-Christian scriptures.
2   Forward reference- the following word tells us which word.
3   Forward reference- of the Lord.
4   Unique reference- we all know this is a reference to God.
5   Forward reference- to hearken.
6   Unique reference
7   Unique reference

The indefinite article: *a/an*

The indefinite article is used 1) when we refer to something for the first time (in the next mention we use *the* [Backward reference]) or 2) when it is not clear from the context which particular thing/item we mean.

1) Example - First mention: ***A useful book*** *for introducing Christology is "Consider Jesus".* ***The book*** *takes a chronological approach to developments ….*

OR ***A man*** *lame from birth sat daily by the temple gate. One day, after speaking with somebody,* ***the man*** *got up and walked away, praising God.*

2) Example - Identity not clear from context: *I'll try to find* ***a book*** *on that subject.*

OR *If you want to know the meaning of* ***a word****, look up* ***a dictionary****.*

Indefinite article with definitions

The indefinite article often occurs in definitional statements (see Unit 4).

Examples: *Liberation theology is <u>a type of theology</u> which emphasises the motif of liberation…*
<u>A sacrament</u> is <u>a visible sign</u> of God's presence. It is <u>a sign through which</u> the church manifests….
Pelagianism is <u>a heresy</u> with roots in the fifth century……

The indefinite article is used only with singular countable nouns. We use ***a*** if the following word begins with a consonant, or if the pronunciation of the following vowel is more like a consonant. For example: *a book, a teacher,*
but also *a European theologian, a university.*
We use ***an*** if the word following the article begins with a vowel, if the pronunciation sounds like a vowel, or if the word begins with silent *h*.
For example: *an open question, an MA degree in theology (but a Master's degree), an hour.*

Countable and Uncountable Nouns

Students will already be aware of the general rules for article use in relation to countable and uncountable nouns, and of the fact that some nouns may be both countable and uncountable in different contexts.
For example, *wine, coffee and cheese* can be both countable and uncountable.

In the area of theology, some nouns may be both countable and uncountable, depending on the context. For example, we can talk about the study of *theology*—or *philosophy*—(uncountable) and we can also refer to a particular *theology* or *theologies*—metaphysical, biblical, liberation (countable). *Church* is another noun which may be both countable or uncountable. For example, we can talk about the *church* in general, or we may refer to particular *churches*—this or that denomination or building.

For more detail on the uses of the definite and indefinite articles, consult a comprehensive grammar book.

In the exercises which follow, use the information about articles above to decide whether you need ***the*** or ***a/an*** in the space. Where you need the indefinite article, use spelling—or pronunciation—to decide whether you need ***a*** or ***an.*** Check your answers in the back of the book.

REVISION EXERCISE 14.1
Fill in the blank spaces in this text with the appropriate definite or indefinite article.

1....... word ecology is derived from 2...... Greek word, *oikos*, which means 'house' or 'place in which to live'. According to Eugene Odum in *Fundamentals of Ecology*, it is literally 3 .... study of organisms 'at home'. Included in this 'at home' is 4........ study of living beings, 5 .... place in which they live, and 6 .... interaction among and between 7 .... living and non-living components of 8 .... place being studied. So ecology attempts to understand 9 .... complex web of linkages, relationships and interdependencies in 10 .... particular environment or ecosystem. 11 .... ecosysem being studied might be 12.......... meadow, 13 .... freshwater lake, 14........... mangrove swamp, 15 .... island, 16 .... continent, 17 .... ocean or finally 18........... Earth itself.

[McDonagh, 1986, p 17.]

REVISION EXERCISE 14.2

In the space write whether the definite article reference is **backwards, forwards, unique** or **institutional.**

Humans are bringing about changes in **the atmosphere** [1................] which can affect **the global climate** [2…………..]. A temperature change of a few degrees one way or another is all that is needed to bring about a new ice age or to melt **the polar ice caps** [3 …………..]. **The climatic changes** [4 ……………]which might be expected to follow from temperature change will adversely affect some of **the world's most fertile agricultural lands** [5……………]

[*Ibid*, pp 26-27]

REVISION EXERCISE 14.3

A   Complete the blank spaces with the appropriate articles.

There can be two approaches to social analysis. Let's call one "academic" and the other "pastoral". 1 .... academic approach studies 2 .... particular social situation in 3............ detached, fairly abstract manner, dissecting its elements for 4………….. purpose of understanding. 5………….. pastoral approach, on 6……….. other hand, looks at 7…………. reality from 8…………. involved, historically committed stance...

[Holland & Henriot, 1986,. 7.]

B   Find examples in this text of the definite article *(the)* used as Backward reference? Write the relevant number/s (1-8) here:
....

PART 2

Preparatory Discussion

What do the *garuda,* the *dragon* and the *kangaroo* have in common? Can you add to this list? What is the literal meaning of these words? What symbolic meaning do they have? Why do we use symbols? Do you have a favourite personal symbol? Share with others in the class.

Reading Comprehension

Read this text and answer the questions below.

The idolatry of religious language

1 On the issue of the truth of religious language, there are continuing powerful, conservative religious
2 movements which insist on the literal reference of language to God. Religious conservatism is a
3 widespread tendency within contemporary culture, not restricted to groups which call themselves
4 "evangelicals" or "fundamentalists." This tendency is linked with fear of relativising Scripture
5 through historical criticism and a refusal to accept a plurality of interpretive perspectives. The Bible,
6 says this movement, *is* the Word of God; the Bible is inerrant or divinely inspired; the words and
7 images of the Bible are the authoritative and appropriate words and images for God. The Bible is
8 a sacred text, different from all other texts, and not relative and pluralistic as are all other human
9 products. The Bible becomes an idol: the fallible, human words of Scripture are understood as
10 referring correctly and literally to God. Even where these sentiments are not expressed clearly or
11 in such extreme fashion, religious literalism remains a powerful current in our society. And it does
12 not stem only from a fear of relativism and plurality. It also derives from the understanding of what
13 counts as "true" in our culture. What is "true" in our positivistic, scientifically oriented society is
14 what corresponds with "reality," with the "facts." Translated into artistic terms, this means realistic
15 art; the "true" painting or sculpture is a copy of what it represents. Translated into religious terms,
16 "true" religious language is also a copy of what it represents; in other words a literal or realistic
17 representation of God's nature . . .
18 But there is, I believe, an even deeper reason why religious literalism runs rampant in our time. It is
19 not only that many people have lost the practice of religious contemplation and prayer, which alone
20 is sufficient to keep literalism at bay, or that positivistic scientism has injected a narrow view of
21 truth into our culture. While both are true, it is also the case that we do not think in symbols in the
22 way our forebears did. That is to say, we do not see the things of this world as standing for
23 something else; they are simply what they are. A symbolic sensibility, on the contrary, sees
24 multilayered realities, with the literal level suggestive of meanings beyond itself.

[McFague, 1982, pp 4-5]

1 What is '*this* tendency'(Line 4)? Write out the full meaning………………………………..
2 The text contains both facts and opinions, from the viewpoint of the author and/or of the conservatives. Identify whether the statements below are facts or opinions, and according to whom. NB. This is not a question about your opinion but about what the text is saying.

Statement from author's text		Fact or opinion	According to author OR religious conservatives
Religious conservatism is a widespread tendency in contemporary culture (L2-3)	Example:	*fact*	*according to author*
1) The words and images of the Bible are the authoritative and appropriate words and images for God (L6-7)		………………	………………
2) Religious literalism … stems from … a fear of relativism and plurality (L11-12)		………………	………………

3 The author gives a number of reasons (in addition to fear of relativism and plurality) why 'religious literalism runs rampant in our time'. What are these reasons?

………………………………………………………………………………………………

According to the author, what is the most fundamental of these reasons?

………………………………………………………………………………………………

PART 3

Preparatory Discussion

In groups of three or four, list as many images of God (that is, words we use for God) as you can in a couple of minutes. Do you know the origin of each image? Do you have some favourite images? Does it matter what images we use for God? Discuss.

Reading Comprehension

Read this text and answer the questions below.

'To speak rightly of God'

1 What is the right way to speak about God? This is a question of **unsurpassed** importance, for
2 speech to and about the mystery that surrounds human lives and the universe itself is a key
3 activity of a community of faith. In that speech the symbol of God **functions** as the primary
4 symbol of the whole religious system, the ultimate point of reference for understanding experience,
5 life and the world. Hence, the way in which a faith community shapes language about God
6 implicitly represents what it takes to be the highest good, the **profoundest** truth, the most appealing
7 beauty. Such speaking, in turn, powerfully **molds** the **corporate** identity of the community and
8 directs its *praxis*. A religion, for example, that would speak about a warlike god and extol the way
9 he smashes his enemies to bits would promote aggressive group behaviour ...
10 In our day interest in right speech about God is **exceptionally** alive in a new way ... The
11 women's movement in civil society and church has shed a bright light on the **pervasive** exclusion
12 of women from the realm of public symbol formation and decision making, and women's
13 consequent, strongly enforced subordination to the imagination and needs of a world designed
14 chiefly for men. In the church, this exclusion has been effective virtually everywhere: in ecclesial
15 creeds, doctrines, prayers, theological systems, liturgical worship, patterns of spirituality, visions of
16 mission, church order, leadership and discipline. It has been stunningly effective in speech about
17 God. While officially it is rightly and consistently said that God is spirit and so beyond identification
18 with either male or female sex, yet the daily language of preaching, worship, catechesis and
19 instruction conveys a different message: God is male, or at least more like a man than a woman,
20 or at least more fittingly addressed as male than as female. The symbol of God functions. Upon
21 examination it becomes clear that this exclusive speech about God serves in **manifold** ways to
22 support an imaginative and structural world that excludes or subordinates women. Wittingly or not,
23 it **undermines** women's human dignity as equally created in the image of God.

[Johnson, 1994, pp.3-5.]

Answer these questions on the text:-
Word matching:- Without using a dictionary but from the sense of the text, match each of the words in bold print in the text with one from this list:-

a) in all places................. b) deepest....................... c) many...................

d) takes away .... e) of top priority............... f) works..................

g) influences .... h) very much .... i) group ....

2 The writer states that symbols/words used for God influence people's behaviour. What example does she give?...

....

3 According to the text, why is there new interest these days in right speech about God?

....

4 In Line 23 we read ... "**it** undermines..." What is the noun phrase represented by this pronoun (**it**)? ....

PART 4

Preparatory Discussion

Work with a partner to sort these words and phrases into two columns headed as below:- *Word of God, rising sun, sceptre of Israel, key of David, cornerstone, sun of justice, root of Jesse, son of God, light of the world.*

Do any of these words and phrases belong in both columns? Discuss with the whole class.

Denotative/Univocal/literal	Connotative/Non-univocal/non-literal
....	....
....	....
....	....
....	....

Listening

Listen to the dictation of a short text about metaphorical theology. Write down what you hear. Check your work as the text is read for the second time.
What well-known religious metaphor is mentioned in the text?........................
Check with Listening Text 6 in Appendix A.

Reading Comprehension

Read the text and answer the questions.

Analogical affirmations

1   The first experience I want to talk about is the experience that all theological statements ... are
2   analogical statements. This goes without saying for any Catholic theology. It is explicitly stated, on
3   one page or another, of every theology and, since Erich Przywara, has become even more self-
4   evident for theologians. Nevertheless, my conviction is that this principle is continually overlooked
5   in individual theological assertions. I want to share my alarm about this kind of oversight.
6   Let me begin in a rather simple way. A very basic, simple understanding of the concept of
7   analogy runs along the following lines: an analogical way of thinking is characterised by the fact
8   that, with the help of such an approach, an assertion about a specific reality is legitimate and
9   unavoidable. However, at the same time, the assertion must always be negated in a certain sense.
10 Were we merely to apply this concept alone to the reality at issue without negating it, without
11 acknowledging this strange and uncanny back and forth between affirmation and negation, we
12 would be mistaking the real object and end up in error. But this mysterious and uncanny negation
13 necessary for the truth of an analogical statement is more often than not left unclarified and
14 forgotten. It is not possible here to develop an actual metaphysics of knowing analogical
15 statements. By so doing, we could counter the unsophisticated and naïve belief that an analogical
16 term is simply an amalgam between an ordinary univocal utterance on the one hand and an
17 equivocal utterance on the other. A true understanding of analogy, however, would acknowledge
18 the fact that analogy comprises a fundamental and basic structure of human cognition.
19 Here I touch on the essence of analogy—something too frequently overlooked and, in particular
20 instances, altogether ignored—namely, the negation of an affirmative statement of conceptual
21 content precisely in its affirmation. The Fourth Lateran Council clearly stated that from the
22 perspective of this world, that is from any starting-point we might conceive of based on human
23 knowing, nothing substantial of a positive nature about God can be stated without, at the same
24 time, perceiving the radical inadequacy of such affirmative statements. Yet time and again in our
25 theological praxis we forget this. We talk about God, about God's existence, characteristics, about
26 three persons in God; we speak of God's freedom, of God's binding will, and so forth. Of course,
27 we need to proceed in this manner; we cannot simply keep silent about God. Indeed, it is only
28 after we have first spoken that it is possible—really possible—to be silent. But in such discourse
29 we usually forget that any statement made about God is legitimate only to the extent that it is
30 always simultaneously negated. It is a question here of enduring the uncanny suspension
31 between affirmation and negation as the true and only fixed term of our knowledge. In so doing,
32 our theological assertions descend into the silent incomprehensibility of God's very self. Our

33 theoretical statements then share the same existential destiny as we do, namely, that of a loving,
34   trusting self-surrender to the unfathomable reign of God, to God's merciful judgement and sacred
35 incomprehensibility.
36 I think—I hope—that no theologian will seriously dispute what I have just said. But at the same
37   time it is so often the case with us theologians that this single, formal proposition is simply
38 mentioned somewhere in our theology alongside other things. This theological truism is hardly a
39 vital force that really radically and inexorably pervades our entire theology in all of its statements.
40 So often from our lecture podiums and our pulpits and from the Church's sacred dicasteries our
41 pronouncements do not give the clear impression that they are replete with the complete humility of
42 a creature. Only with such humility can one truly speak about God. Only then does one recognise
43   that all discourse about God can only be the final moment before that blessed silence that fills the
44 heavens with the pure vision of God face to face.

[Rahner, 2000, pp 4-6.]

Answer these questions from evidence in the text. Give line reference numbers in your answers.

1   The author states that he wants to talk about the experience that all theological statements are analogical statements (L 1-2).
    a What <u>reason</u> does he give for wanting to talk about this?..............................

    ....

    b How does the author <u>feel</u> about this? ....

2   The author repeats his reason for wanting to write about this, or the need to do so, at least three more times in this text. Identify in full the statements where the author repeats his reason. Give line reference numbers.
    i ....

    ii ....

    iii ....

3   Which of these statements represents the author's position on analogy?
    a The concept of analogy is 'an assertion about a specific reality' ...
       [that] must always be negated. (L8-9)   ❑

    b An analogical term is simply an amalgam between an ordinary
       univocal utterance . . . and an equivocal utterance . . . (L15-17)   ❑

    c Nothing substantial of a positive nature about God can be
       stated . . . (L23).   ❑

4   What is *"this theological truism"* (Line 38)?

    ....

Writing

Write a short explanation (about half to one page) in your own words of the problem of theological language and how theologians deal with this problem.

UNIT 14 VOCABULARY

Add to this list any more new words that you want to learn and remember.

Nouns	Verbs	Adjectives	Other
papyri	transcend	paradoxical	naively
scientism	relativise	complex	
conservatism	attest	polymorphic	
relativism	constitute	problematic	
perspective	deny	fundamental	
idol	intend	inerrant	
sentiment	characterise	fallible	
bay	negate	positivistic	
conviction	dispute	rampant	
		uncanny	

UNIT 15   RELIGION AND CULTURE

PART 1

Preparatory Discussion

What were the earliest known religions or belief systems in your country? When did other religions begin to develop and how were they introduced? What are some major events in the history of religion in your country? What religions are practised in your country these days? Is there a predominant faith? How are minority religions treated?

Form groups of three or four students, from different countries or regions if possible, and share your knowledge.

Listening

Listen to a text about the people and religions of Indonesia. Listen for the answers to these questions and write them in your notebook. [Note: Sailendra was the name of a ruling dynasty in early Indonesia.]

1 Which religions are mentioned in this text? ………… ………….. …………..
   ………….. …………….   …………………. …………….   ……………..
2 What three religious elements have blended to form Javanese mysticism and religious practice? ……………..   ………………….. …………………
3 In which century did the Islamic faith spread throughout Indonesia? ………………….
4 Who first introduced Christianity to Indonesia? ……………………………………...

Now check your answers in Listening Text 7, Appendix A.

Reading Comprehension

Read this passage about the religions of India and answer the questions below.

Religion on the Indian sub-continent

1   India's religious history is distinguished by a number of sacred texts and eminent persons. In
2   the millennium before the Christian era there **were** the ancient Hindu texts known as the *Rig*
3   *Veda* and the *Upanishads*. In those centuries, the teachings of Mahavira the Jain **made** a
4   deep impact on many people and continue to do so today. Around 500 BCE, Gautama the
5   Buddha **emerged** as a leading religious figure. Over time, his teachings **developed** into a
6   religion of world-wide significance. Buddhism **was** once the main religion of India, but
7   eventually Hinduism **became** the predominant belief system. Since its origins in the seventh
8   century, the Islamic faith has become a major religion in the sub-continent. Numerous
9   minority religions also flourish in India, including Christianity. According to tradition, this
10 faith **was introduced** to southern India by St Thomas the Apostle quite early in the
11 Christian era. Certainly, groups of Thomas Christians have existed there since the third
12 century CE.   [Based on Smart, 1989, pp 42-45 .]

1 Which eminent persons are referred to in this passage?………………………….………
2 When did the Moslem faith begin to influence people on the sub-continent?…………...

Are the following statements TRUE or FALSE (T/F) according to information in the text?

3 The teachings of Jainism were significant only before the Christian era. T/F? ………
4 Buddhism is the main religion of India. T/F? ………………………
5 Which of these two descriptions best fits this text:
                           a) an expression of opinions   ❑
                    OR   b) a narration of facts   ❑

English for Theology

Vocabulary extension – lexical transformation

Complete as many of the columns below as you can.

Infinitive	Simple Past Tense	Noun	Adjective/Past Participle
distinguish	…………………	………………	…………………
impact	…………………	………………	…………………
emerge	…………………	………………	…………………
develop	…………………	………………	…………………
dominate	…………………	………………	…………………
originate	…………………	………………	…………………
introduce	…………………	………………	…………………
exist	…………………	………………	…………………

Revision of Grammar: Verbs – Simple Past Tense

We use the simple past tense to narrate or tell what happened in the past or to talk about past situations. Note the examples in the above passage.

To form the past tense for regular verbs, add *–ed*. Note that sometimes the spelling changes as well. For example, for one-syllable verbs, where the last three letters are consonant-vowel-consonant, double the last consonant for past tense. Eg *chop, chopped; stop, stopped; pat, patted*.

Irregular verbs have different forms for simple past: eg *come, came; go, went; see, saw; bring, brought*. Consult a chart of irregular verbs or make up your own for revision.

REVISION EXERCISE 15.1

Complete the blank spaces with the simple past tense of the verb in brackets.

The year of Mahatma Gandhi's birth **1**………. *(is)* 1869. He **2** ……… *(grow up)* in Kathiawar in western India and **3** ……… *(have)* close contacts both with Hindus and non-Hindus. His mother's religion **4** ………. *(is)* a kind of evangelical devotionalism, within the *bhakti* tradition, somewhat influenced by Islam. The area he **5** ……….*(come)* from was one of the main Jain regions and the Jain ideal of non-violence **6** ………… *(influence)* him. At the age of nineteen he **7** ………… *(go)* to London to study law and there **8** ………… *(come)* into contact with the Theosophical movement, which **9** ………. *(combine)* Eastern motifs with a concern for comparative religion.

He also **10** ………*(have)* contact with followers of Tolstoy. After his return to India, Gandhi **11** ………… *(practise)* law unsuccessfully in Bombay (Mumbai) before being offered a job in Durban, Natal, South Africa. He **12**……….. *(go)* there in 1893. He **13** ……….*(work)* for twenty-one years in South Africa until 1915. It was there he **14** ……… *(work out)* the methods of nonviolent political resistance which he later **15**…….. *(use)* against the British in India. It was in South Africa that he **16** ………. *(take on)* the garb and mien of a saintly holy man. But he was not a recluse. What he **17** ……… *(do)* in effect was to give the old Jain and Indian idea of *ahimsa* (non-violence) a political context and meaning. He also **18** ……… *(give)* the notion of renunciation a new social context. The main point of his practices . . . was to prepare himself spiritually for the struggle against oppression and injustice. The most important single thing that he **19** ……………*(teach)* was that our motives in such struggles must be pure. … He was influenced by the Christianity of the Gospels: "Love your enemies" **20** …………… *(become)* for him a prime precept.

[Smart, 1989, pp 400-401, adapted.]

REVISION EXERCISE 15.2

Phrasal verbs

There are three examples of phrasal verbs in exercise 15.1 above, each ending with a different adverbial particle, ie *up, out, on*. Make three columns in your notebook like this.

grow up	*work out*	*take on*	?	?	?
…………	…………	…………			
…………	…………	…………			
…………	…………	…………			
…………	…………	…………			

Add as many more phrasal verbs as you can under each heading in three minutes. How many more columns can you make with phrasal verbs ending with different adverbs?
Consult a comprehensive English grammar for more detail on phrasal verbs.

Verbs – Past Simple Continuous

The form of the Past Simple Continuous (or Progressive) is: *was/were* + verb + *ing*.
The past simple continuous is often used together with the simple past when telling about what happened during a period of time past.

Eg While Gandhi ***was living*** in South Africa, he ***met*** the Trappist monks.

REVISION EXERCISE 15.3

Join the ideas in Columns A and B by using *when* or *while* and the past simple/past simple continuous tense. Note that the *when/while* clause may come either in the first or the second position.

Example: 1 *I lived at the college while I was studying theology.*
     OR *While I was studying theology, I lived at the college.*

	A	B
1	I (study) theology	I (live) at the college
2	Archbishop Oscar Romero (say) Mass	The soldiers (shoot) him
3	The earthquake (strike)	Most of the people (sleep)
4	Relief supplies (come)	The villagers already (starve)
5	She (complete) her postgraduate studies	She (teach) at the university
6	They (guard) their sheep	They (discover) the ancient scrolls

1 ....

2 ....

3 ....

4 ....

5 ....

6 ....

REVISION EXERCISE 15.4

Complete the blank spaces with the simple past tense of the verb in brackets.

The effect of history on theology

The nineteenth century **1**...........*(see)* an explosion of critical historical studies, which **2**..........*(throw)* into confusion many dogmatic certainties. Such studies **3**............*(are)* critical in the sense that they no longer **4**............*(take)* sources at their face value. Everything, every authority, **5**...............*(is)* subject to the closest scrutiny. A hermeneutics of suspicion had been discovered! In ecclesial circles, this critical historical investigation **6** .... *(result)* in dogmas being studied in their historical context, the condemnation of past figures being called into question—nothing **7** .... *(escape)* historical examination. A key Catholic figure in this movement **8** ....*(is)* the German historian Doellinger, who eventually **9** ....*(leave)* Catholicism after Vatican I's declaration of Papal infallibility. Doellinger **10** ....*(feel)* he **11** .... *(can not)* accept it on historical grounds.

This interest in critical history **12**.............*(give rise)* to the "quest for the historical Jesus", the attempt to use the methods of critical history to uncover the "real" story of Jesus of Nazareth.

[Ormerod, 1990, pp 31-32.]

REVISION EXERCISE 15.5

Make a list of all the irregular verbs in the text above. Complete the chart below for each one.

Infinitive	Simple past	Past participle
....	....	....
....	....	....
....	....	....
....	....	....
....	....	....
....	....	....

PART 2

Preparatory Discussion

What words come into your mind when you hear the word *culture*? Make a list of some of these words and talk about why you associate them with *culture*. Do this in small groups or with the whole class. Attempt to define what culture is and then compare your definition with at least two others.

Listening

Listen to a text on the relationship between human life and culture. Answer these questions, using this outline to assist you.

1   *Why do human beings need culture?* ....

2   *What is the scope of meaning of the word "culture"?* ....

   It means ....

   It includes ....

   Finally, it is ....

3   *Hence, it follows that*..

Now work in groups of three or four students and try to reconstruct a version of the text in your own words. Compare your version with others in the class. Finally, compare your version with the original in Listening Text 8, Appendix A.

Reading Comprehension

Read this text and then answer the questions below.

Culture and theology

1   Firstly, we must ask what do we mean by culture—do we have a normative or empirical notion of
2   culture? A normative definition of culture takes one culture, [usually one's own] as the norm by
3   which all other cultures are to be judged. One either lives up to the standards set by this culture, in
4   which case one is considered civilised, or one fails to live up to it, in which case one is considered
5   a barbarian. Within the confines of a normative notion of culture, theology will be seen as a
6   permanent achievement, a lasting accomplishment. The sole task of later generations will be to
7   stand in awe at the achievement of the past. Any variation from its canons will be seen as sure
8   signs of decadence and imminent collapse. However, one may have an empirical notion of
9   culture. Here, a culture is seen as a set of meanings and values which inform and structure a way
10 of life. Here, one compares and contrasts cultures, evaluates their weaknesses and strengths,
11 studies how they give meaning and purpose to peoples' lives. No one culture can be seen as a
12 definitive and permanent achievement, since all are open to development and change, progress as
13 well as decline. Given an empirical notion of culture, theology can be seen to be an ongoing
14 process. Here, theology is located as an activity within a culture. As culture changes, so will
15 theology. A theology suitable for a mediaeval culture will not necessarily be suitable for a
16 contemporary culture, since the basic thought forms, the meanings which inform a culture, can be
17 quite different.   [Ormerod, 1990, p 9.]

Answer these questions on the text:-

1. Which of the following descriptions best apply to this text (you may tick more than one box)?

    Narrative ❏
    Problem-solution ❏
    Contrastive ❏
    Definitional ❏
    Analytical ❏

2. Which of the two views of culture, namely, normative or empirical, do you think this writer prefers? What is the evidence in the text for your opinion? ....

    ....

3. What is the writer's attitude towards a theology which is seen as 'a permanent achievement, a lasting accomplishment' (Lines 5-6)?

    ....

Speaking

Here is a definition of culture from a well-known anthropologist. After reading it, talk about its similarities and differences with your own ideas about culture and with those expressed in the Listening Text in Part 1 of this unit.

> . . . the culture concept to which I adhere has neither multiple referents nor, so far as I can see, any unusual ambiguity: it denotes an historically transmitted pattern of meanings, embodied in symbols, a system of inherited conceptions expressed in symbolic forms by means of which [people] communicate, perpetuate and develop their knowledge about and attitudes towards life.
>
> [Geertz, 1973, p 89.]

Writing

Choose one of the topic sentences below and write a paragraph of 8-10 lines, developing the idea. Refer again to Unit 8 to help you with the structure of your paragraph.

* *There are many examples of the way in which history has influenced religion and theology.*

* *Culture continues to be an important influence on theological thinking in today's world.*

PART 3

Preparatory Discussion

Given the ideas so far in this unit, what influence might culture have on the truths of revelation and the passing on of the gospel, as expressed in theology: a little influence, a lot of influence, or hardly any at all? Think of some examples where culture has had an impact on theological interpretations, either at different stages of history, or in different cultures co-existing today in the world? Discuss in small groups and then share with the whole class.

Reading Comprehension

Read the text and answer the questions.

Culture and the gospel

1 ... the process of evangelisation in the history of the world was conceptually comparable to
2 the way the Logos became incarnate, that is to say, to the way the Word of God became
3 human in Jewish culture at the time of the Roman Empire. Looked at this way the concept
4 of inculturation becomes clearer ...
5 Inculturation can, therefore, be defined as the dynamic process that develops when the gospel is
6 preached in a culture which is older than the gospel itself and different from the cultural
7 background from which the gospel emerged. This process is reciprocal. Both elements, the culture
8 and the gospel message, because of mutual interaction, begin a process of change in order to
9 achieve, at the very least, a symbiotic, harmonious merger. The paradigm of the incarnation, as
10 expressed in the letter to the Philippians,
11 *who, though he was in the form of God, did not regard equality with God something to be*
12 *grasped. Rather he emptied himself, taking the form of a slave, coming in human likeness,*
13 *and found human in appearance (Ph 2:6-7),*
14 can serve as a model for the preaching of the Christian message in other cultures. The gospel
15 empties itself of its historical-traditional character and takes on a new shape in a lifestyle so alien to
16 it, but without losing its identity as the gospel of Jesus Christ.
17 It is to be noted that both poles, the gospel and the cultures in which it is preached, will undergo
18 a process of change, without losing the identity of each. That sounds like a paradox, but it does
19 not have to be. After all, both the gospel as well as cultures stand constantly in the changing flow
20 of history but do not have to give up their identity as a consequence. Culture change is a striking
21 phenomenon of the present times and because of cultural contacts and all the possibilities of
22 communication between cultures has become so extensive and, indeed, is accelerating so rapidly
23 that the present generation has become very aware of it. In the same way, the literary history of
24 the way the Christian message came to be written and edited as well as the way the message has
25 been interpreted through time even to the present day are proofs to many who are conscious of
26 this that the Christian message has also undergone a process of change.

[Piepke, 1999, pp 43-53.]

Answer these questions on the text.

1. Which of these is the writer's main purpose in this text?
   i) to explain that the Word of God became human in a particular culture and time (ie Jewish, Roman empire) ❑
   ii) to assert that cultural change these days, because of extensive communication, is very rapid ❑
   iii) to argue that the interpretation of the gospel has changed and will continue to change with the flow of history ❑

2. What is *'this process'* referred to in Line 7? ....

3. What is the function of the sentence beginning *'both elements....'* (Lines 7-9)?

   ....

4. There are two subjects (incl. phrases/clauses) of the verb *'are (proofs.)'* in L25. Write each one below in full. Then identify the key parts or words in each by underlining

   i) ....

   ii) ....

PART 4

Preparatory Discussion

Culture, nationality and religion are the sources of our full human development. But too often they seem to be sources of conflict—or are they? Think of some conflicts in the world today. Do you think the problems are cultural, national or religious, or something else? Discuss in small groups and then share with the class.

Reading Comprehension

Read the text and answer the questions.

Christianity and Asia

A..

1 The experience and renewal of Christianity in Asia is bringing to the fore some very far reaching
2 questions. Asian theology shares with the rest of the Third World the critique of the Western Euro-
3 North American theology. Beyond these and the general feminist critique there are specific issues
4 arising from the multi-religious context, the extreme poverty, the massive populations and the
5 experiences of Marxist regimes specially in China.

B ....

6 The crucial issues are in relation to the nature of the Absolute, divine revelation, the sources of
7 theology, the person of Jesus, the role of the Christ, the nature of the human predicament – the
8 'fall', original sin, redemption in Jesus, grace, the mission of the Church, Christian liturgy,
9 proclamation witness and dialogue, justice within nations and world justice.

C..

10 The traumatic experience of Christianity in Asia makes present day theologians question
11 radically some positions which are taken for granted in most of the rest of world Christianity. The
12 consciousness of the Church having blundered during several centuries in Asia in its failure to see
13 God's presence in other faiths brings about an understandable and radical questioning by Asian
14 theologians. They are increasingly suspicious of the very presuppositions on which the Western
15 construct of Christian theology has been built up over centuries.

D ....

16 Concerning *revelation* many Asian theologians—particularly in India and Sri Lanka—hold that
17 God need not be limited to the Bible in her/his revelation to humanity. The sacred texts of other
18 religions can be a source of divine revelation. At the same time both these and the Bible need to be
19 studied critically to exclude elements which cannot be from God—such as an excessive
20 ethnocentrism or 'religionism' (a concept developed by the present writer in *Planetary Theology*).
21 God has spoken to all the peoples of the world in diverse ways and continues to do so today too.
22 This raises a major hermeneutical issue concerning the nature of revelation, the sources of
23 theology and their interpretation.

E........

24 The non-theistic thinking of Theravada Buddhism, and the pantheistic perceptions in Hinduism,
25 influence Asian Christian theologians to search for deeper meaning concerning the nature of the
26 Absolute. The affirmations concerning *God*, the *creation* of the universe, the beginning of human
27 life and life beyond death are being rethought in the dialogue with other religions (and secular
28 ideologies). Theologians see that what can be said concerning the divine nature is so relative to
29 our human experience and philosophical schools. Alternative interpretations are possible
30 concerning human knowledge of the Transcendent and about the relationship of God to human life.

[Balasuriya, 1988, pp 42-43.]

Answer these questions.

1 This text explores some of the special questions facing Christian theologians in the Asian context. Select the most appropriate heading from the list below for each of the five paragraphs of the text. Write the heading in the spaces labelled **A** to **E** above.

i) The role of sacrament and image
ii) Legacy of religious imperialism
iii) Ultimate mysteries and limits of language
iv) Social and religious context
v) Feminist critique in Asian context
vi) Philosophical and doctrinal concerns
vii) Church structures and governance
viii) Is God really partisan?

2   What do you think is meant by the expression "the traumatic experience" of Christianity in Asia (Line 10)?

3   What is the function of the sentence beginning "They are increasingly suspicious...." (Lines 14-15) in relation to the other sentences in that paragraph?

4   On the basis of this author's attitude and thinking as revealed in this text, which of the following three would be the most likely ending to this sentence in his view?

The forms and practices of Christianity planted in Asia through the historical efforts of missionaries from abroad have been for Asian people

a) an unfortunate experience
b) a mixed blessing
c) a great gift

Support your opinion with evidence from the text.

Speaking

Read this definition of religion from a well-known anthropologist.

... A religion is a system of symbols which acts to establish powerful, pervasive, and long-lasting moods and motivations in [people] by formulating conceptions of a general order of existence and clothing these conceptions with such an aura of factuality that the moods and motivations seem uniquely realistic.

[Geertz, 1973, p 90]

Talk about the meaning of this definition. For example, what does it mean to 'formulate conceptions of a general order of existence'? What general formula did the early Hebrew people have? What does the Hindu 'formula' look like? What does the Buddhist formula look like? What about the Christian or Islamic formula?
What does it mean to 'clothe' a conception with 'an aura of factuality'?
In what way does Balasuriya's text above provide a reflection on the idea of religion as 'formulating conceptions of a general order of existence . . .".

Writing

Write about 1-2 pages on the topic:- *A critical issue for Asian Christians.*
Identify and explain what the issue is (relate the issue to your own region) and why it is an issue; explain the approach which theologians or church people are taking to address the issue; what are the obstacles and the likely outcome in the immediate future.

UNIT 15   VOCABULARY

Add to this list any more new words that you want to learn.

Nouns	Verbs	Adjectives	Other
minority	civilise	eminent	eventually
explosion	consider	predominant	
scrutiny	confine	normative	
confines	define	empirical	
decadence	accelerate	sole	
inculturation	blunder	definitive	
merger		incarnate	
paradigm		reciprocal	
		symbiotic	

UNIT 16   REVELATION AND THEOLOGISING

PART 1

Preparatory Discussion

In an earlier Unit (12) we looked at a definition of theology as *"faith seeking understanding"*. This raises the question of what exactly is the content of the faith we seek to understand or to study. The simple answer is that revelation is the content of faith, and theology is the systematic study of revelation. But this, in turn, raises the question: What is revelation? What words and ideas come to your mind when you think of 'revelation'? Discuss this with a few people around you and share with the whole class.

Listening

Listen to a short text on Revelation. Take brief notes of the main ideas as you listen. Then work together with a small group to reproduce one text in complete sentences (not necessarily the exact words you have heard).

Use these questions to guide your listening:-
1   What is revelation, and why are we able to accept it?
   ....
2   In what manner or how (listen for adverbs) is God disclosed to us?
   ....
3   Where (in what 'places') does revelation occur?......................................
   ....
4   What are the two aspects of revelation?..
   ....

When each group has completed its reproduced text, share with the whole class. Compare your text with Listening Text 9 in Appendix A.

Reading Comprehension

Read the text and answer the questions.

Revelation

1   ... I would propose that we consider revelation in the following terms. Revelation is a
2   hermeneutic process, that is, a process for the uncovering and transmission of
3   meanings and values which arise in relation to the life, death and resurrection of
4   Jesus of Nazareth. Primarily, these meanings and values are the meaning and value
5   of the person of Jesus himself and the meanings and values he passes on to his
6   disciples. The further process of recovering and transmitting those meanings and
7   values is then carried on under the inspiration of the Holy Spirit. Thus, revelation is
8   God's self-communication in Word and Spirit.
9   This understanding of revelation should not be seen as restricting revelation to the
10 Christian experience. Other cultures, other **peoples** may experience the revelation of
11 God. They may uncover meanings and values totally consistent with those found in
12 Christian revelation. However, **it** does take a normative stance, that Jesus is THE
13 revelation of God so that other revelatory experiences find their true meaning and
14 fulfilment in him.

[Ormerod,1990, p 46.]

1   This writer defines revelation as 'a hermeneutic process'. How does he explain this process?

   ....

2   In the first paragraph of this text (Lines 1-8), the writer explains revelation by identifying three aspects or stages which centre around *the meanings and values of Jesus*. What are these three aspects or stages?

    1st..
    2nd...
    3rd...

    What is the necessary condition for the third stage to occur?.....................

3   Is this statement TRUE or FALSE according to the text?
    Revelation is restricted to the Christian experience.   T or F ....

4   Why does the writer use the plural *'peoples'* instead of *'people'* in Line 10?
    ....
    What is the difference in meaning between the two words—the singular and the plural?
    ....

5   In Line 12, to what noun or noun phrase does the pronoun **'it'** refer?
    ....

Revision of Grammar: Prepositions

As the prefix *pre-* indicates, prepositions are words which are placed before a noun/noun phrase. They indicate a particular type of relationship or connection (of what went before) with the noun/noun phrase following the preposition. The most common relationships are about place, time, direction and movement.

Examples: *That book is **in** the library.*   *The train leaves **at** six o'clock.*
            *They walked **towards** to river.*   *They do not eat **until** sunset.*

Here is a list of commonly used simple prepositions:-
about, above, across, after, against, along, among, around, at, before, behind, below, beneath, beside, between, beyond, by, down, during, for, from, in, into, near, of, off, on, over, round, since, through, till, to, towards, under, underneath, until, up, upon, with, within, without.

Add to this list as you work through this Unit.

    ....
    ....

Complex prepositions, with more than one word, include the following:-

in comparison with	*except for*	*owing to*
according to	*because of*	*by means of*
in relation to	*due to*	*on top of*

Try to extend this list of complex prepositions *as a result of* your reading.

    ....
    ....

Prepositions may also indicate relationships other than time, place and so on. For example, the prepositions *of* and *with* may indicate a relation of having something:-

    *She is a scholar **of** distinction.*
    *He is a person **with** many friends.*

Of may also indicate a relation of belonging:-
>*Relativity was the idea **of** Einstein.*
>*Jesus was the son **of** Mary and Joseph.*

Of is also used to introduce apposition-like phrases or clauses. For example:-
>*Scholars have worked on the issues **of cultural variations in religion**.*
>*World leaders must work on the problem **of what to do about poverty**.*
>*Theologians are examining the question **of Christianity in relation to world religions**.*

For a detailed account of the range of prepositions and their uses, consult a comprehensive grammar book.

Use of prepositions in theology

Within the discipline of theology, as in many other areas of everyday use, unless the subject matter is dealing with concrete physical realities (eg Jesus and the disciples rowed *across* the lake; they found the scrolls *near* Qumran), the use of prepositions of place, direction, distance and movement will generally be abstract or metaphorical. For example:-

>*Suffering plays an important role **in** the thought of Schillebeeckx.*
>*Without an understanding of metaphor, we are **in** danger of distorting the truth.*
>*God is a mystery **beyond** our understanding.*

REVISION EXERCISE 16.1

Complete these sentences with a suitable preposition. There may be more than one correct answer.

1 At Passover time, Jesus walked along the road .... Jerusalem.
2 They nailed him .... a cross before the Sabbath.
3 As they walked to Emmaus a few days later, the disciples were talking .... everything that had happened.
4 Then Jesus himself came up and walked .... them.
5 Those disciples encountered Jesus face to face. Today we can encounter him .... his words and deeds recorded in Scripture, and .... the traditions of Christian experience.
6 Theologians have been studying the Scriptures .... two thousand years.

REVISION EXERCISE 16.2

Complete the blank spaces with the most suitable prepositions.

The intimate connection.................1 our religious heritage and our lives makes theological reflection a vital resource .... 2 Christians who seek to experience more fully the power ....3 their religious heritage as they seek to cooperate daily .... 4 God's actions ....5 history. It also makes theological reflection an important resource .... 6 pastoral ministers [and others] who walk .... 7 people .... 8 their journeys ....9 faith.

   While this book is written .... 10 and .... 11 the Christian tradition because that is the author's own, what it says .... 12 theological reflection can be extended .... 13 appropriate modifications ....14 other religious heritages as well.

[O'Connell Killen & de Beer, 1995, p ix.]

PART 2

Preparatory Discussion

What do you know about revelation outside of Christian experience? Are there examples of non-Christian revelation in the religious and cultural experience of your country? Share your knowledge and ideas about this and discuss briefly.

Reading Comprehension

Read this text and answer the questions.

Jesus and revelation

1 In the Christian experience of revelation in Jesus Christ, God not only told us that
2 [God] was inextricably bound with us through love but also showed us what it means
3 to live in this love by the word becoming flesh. As divine, or, as St Paul says, as 'the
4 image of the invisible God' (Col 1:15), Jesus is the revealer of God's love par
5 excellence; as human, he is the hearer of God's word par excellence. Thus, if we
6 want to know what God is like and how God has involved [Godself] with us, then we
7 look to Jesus. Likewise, if we want to know what humanity is like and how we are
8 involved with God, then we look to Jesus. ....
9 On the one hand, the revelation of Jesus is constrained by a particular history. It
10 remains situated in time at about 30 AD [ie 30 CE] and in a place between
11 Galilee and Jerusalem in the Middle East. On the other hand, the revelation of Jesus
12 escapes any particular history and continues as true for us today as it was then. Only
13 our relationship, not the content, has changed. Instead of encountering a Jesus who
14 walks and talks with us, who not so incidentally was rejected by many who saw and
15 heard him, we encounter his words and deeds recorded in Scripture and the
16 experiences of Christian believers who have verified his revelation over two thousand
17 years. As in the first century, so now [two thousand years later], we authenticate in
18 our own lives the revelation of Jesus.

[Mueller, 1984, pp 8-9.]

1 The first paragraph of this text (Lines 1-8) consists of an explanation of how God is involved with us in and through Jesus Christ. The writer uses traditional Christian metaphorical language to do this. Identify as many of these metaphorical words and phrases as you can. (Refer back to Unit 3 if necessary.)
Eg Line 1: God *told* us (This is metaphorical because the literal meaning 'tell/told' involves having a physical human voice.)

    ………………………………..   ………………………………
    ………………………………..   ………………………………

2 What does the writer mean by saying that the revelation of Jesus is *constrained* by a particular history?…………………………………………………………………….

3 The second paragraph of this text (Lines 9-18) uses a different mode of discourse. Which of these modes best describes the language of the second paragraph:-
    i) metaphorical   ❑
    ii) metaphysical   ❑
    iii) existential.   ❑

   Give evidence from the text to support your opinion.

4 Why does the writer say in Line 14, that *'not so incidentally'*, Jesus was rejected?
   ……………………………………………………………………………………………

PART 3

Preparatory Discussion

Many cultures have stories about a holy person who went away or apart from society for a time to pray or to seek wisdom. Can you think of examples of such people in your own culture or in another culture? When such a person returns to society, they have sometimes gained much wisdom (which they want to share). Does this count as *revelation*? Discuss in small groups and then share with the whole class.

Listening

Listen to a brief description of a number of different 'models' of revelation.
Take notes as you listen. After you have listened, work with a small group to write one text which includes the main ideas you have heard. Your text should include:-
The number of models of revelation mentioned.
A definition or brief description of each one.

Check your text with Listening Text 10 in Appendix A.
Does this change the views you expressed in the Preparatory Discussion or not?

Reading Comprehension

Read the following text and answer the questions.

Recent theologies of revelation

1   In the history of theology 'revelation' has often been understood as an inner
2   "illumination" or as a sort of divine teaching and instruction. At other times it has been
3   understood according to a "propositional" model. That is, "revelation" has been
4   taken to be the communication of information capable of being expressed in
5   sentences or propositions. Today, however, the central model for understanding the
6   idea of revelation has shifted to a more "personal" one, at least in most important
7   theological reflection. Revelation is understood by theology today, and especially
8   Catholic theology, fundamentally as God's *self*-revelation. It is first of all the gift of
9   God's own self, and only derivatively is it the propositional unfolding of the event of
10 this divine self-gift. Revelation is not primarily the uncovering of information that is
11 otherwise inaccessible to reason and ordinary experience. Such a "gnostic" idea,
12 tempting though it has been since very early in the history of Christianity, trivialises the
13 idea of revelation, making it appeal more to our sense of curiosity than to our need for
14 transformation and hope. Instead revelation means essentially God's gift of self.
15 And the awareness of such a self-giving God is "revealed" to faith not as a proposition
16 or doctrine but as a *promise* of ultimate fulfilment. The sense of God's revelation in
17 history happened first to people whose lives swelled with a sense of expectation.
18 Today as well, any meaningful sense of revelation would occur only to those of us
19 who can share this same sense of promise and the hope that accompanies it.

[Haught, 1988, pp 13-14.]

1   How many models of revelation does this writer consider? What are they?

    ....

    ....

2   Which of these models does this writer prefer? ....
    Does the text tell us explicitly or is this information implicit in the text?

    ....

English for Theology

What is the evidence in the text supporting your answer?

....

3   In Line 11, the writer refers to 'such a "gnostic" idea'. What is the 'gnostic' idea referred to? (Note: You can find the answer in the text without reference to a dictionary. Take note of the cohesive device *such*.)

....

4   This text mentions or implies a number of possible roles or purposes for revelation in our lives, eg
   i) Revelation gives us information.
   ii) Revelation is a response to our sense of curiosity.
   iii) Revelation can help change our lives.
   iv) Revelation can give us hope for the future.

Which of these purposes does the writer believe are important? How do you know?

....

....

5   According to this writer, what condition is necessary for a person to have a meaningful sense of revelation?

....

Speaking

Find out what you can about *gnosticism* and have a class discussion on the topic. Use these questions to guide your search. What is the dictionary meaning of *gnostic*? What is the meaning of *gnosticism* within Christian history? Does *gnosticism* occur today?

PART 4

Preparatory Discussion

What is the difference between theology and theologising? Which one comes first? Who can study theology? Who can theologise? What are some of the earliest results of Christian theologising? What are some of the most recent results of Christian theologising? Discuss these questions in small groups and then with the whole class.

Reading Comprehension

Read this text and answer the questions.

Theological reflection

1   When we talk about theological reflection we mean this:

2   *Theological reflection is the discipline of exploring individual and corporate*
3   *experience in conversation with the wisdom of a religious heritage. ...*

4   Theological reflection puts our experience into a genuine conversation with our
5   religious heritage. This conversation opens the gates between our experience and
6   our Christian heritage. It helps us [to] access the Christian tradition as a reliable
7   source of guidance as we search to discover the meaning of what God is doing now
8   in our individual and corporate lives. It assists us to clarify and deepen our
9   relationship to the Christian tradition, especially when we struggle with its sinful and
10 oppressive aspects. This conversation also enriches and strengthens our
11 experiences of the tradition's sustaining wisdom and power. Further, it trains us to
12 discern the presence of God's spirit in the social events and movements of our time.
13 ... today, perhaps more than at any other time, people of faith must learn to tap
14 the wisdom of their heritage, if the Christian tradition's powerful resources for life are
15 to succour and sustain the welfare of human beings and the planet. Unless adult
16 Christians engage in critical and conscious theological reflection, the Christian
17 community's faithfulness to the gospel and its authentic witness to that gospel in the
18 world diminishes. It even becomes counterproductive of gospel values. Why?
19 Because our capacity to comprehend and to live faithfully as Christians exists in
20 direct proportion to our capacity to notice, describe, and discover the revelatory
21 quality of our human experiences. Our capacity to live rich, authentic, human lives
22 depends on our capacity to befriend and enter deeply and openly into our Christian
23 heritage. Tapping the inherently dynamic and energy-filled connection between our
24 lives and the Christian heritage is crucial to the survival of our world, our planet and
25 our church.

[O'Connell Killen & de Beer, 1995, pp viii-ix.]

1   Which one of these statements most adequately reflects the writer's position on how best to live a faithful Christian life today?

    i)   Prayerfully reflect on revelation as it is found in the ❑
         Christian tradition and act accordingly.
    ii) Critically reflect on our religious heritage and on our ❑
         human experiences today.
    iii) Prayerfully reflect on the revelation given through our ❑
         everyday human experiences.
    iv) Rely upon the presence of God's spirit in our lives now. ❑

Be prepared to explain not only your choice, but your reasons for <u>not choosing</u> the other three.

2   Are these statements TRUE or FALSE according to the text?   T/F
    i) The Christian tradition can be a reliable
       source of guidance for our lives today.   ....
    ii) The Christian tradition can train us to
        discern God's presence in our lives.   ....
    iii) The Christian tradition can support human
         life but not the environment.   ....
    iv) The Christian tradition contains sinful and
        oppressive elements.   ....

3   What is the predominant mode of discourse of this text?

    i) empirical   ❏

    ii) existential ❏

    iii) symbolic   ❏

    Give evidence from the text in support of your answer.

Speaking

What do you understand by the term "sign of the times"? Do you know where to find the gospel origins of this phrase? In the modern age, why has it taken on further meaning? What does it have to do with the idea of revelation? Discuss these questions in small groups or in the whole class.

Writing

In about one to two pages, write in your own words an explanation of revelation. Include the following information:- A short definition; the range of models of revelation; the model of revelation which has most meaning for you.

UNIT 16 VOCABULARY

Add to this list any more new words that you want to remember.

Nouns	Verbs	Adjectives	Other
illumination	transmit	hermeneutic	inextricably
curiosity	restrict	authentic	likewise
transformation	constrain		derivatively
heritage	authenticate		
capacity	trivialise		
	discern		

UNIT 17   CHRISTOLOGY

PART 1
Preparatory Discussion
What is your understanding of *christology*? We often encounter this term qualified by various adjectives, for example, *biblical christology*. How many different *christologies* can you list? When in history did each one develop? Where in the world did they originate? Spend a few minutes working in pairs to fill in a table in your notebook like the one below. Share your ideas with other students. [You may wish to add to this table as you work through this Unit.]

Type of Christology	Stage in history	Part of the world
....	....	....
....	....	....
....	....	....
....	....	....
....	....	....
....	....	....

Do you think there could be new *christologies* in the 21st century? What adjectives might describe them? Where might they come from?

Listening

Listen to a text which reflects on the significance for Asian Christians of three questions asked in the gospels about Jesus.
Listen for the answers to these questions.

1   What did John the Baptist say? ....

2   What did the Magi say? ....

3   What did the Greek worshippers at Jerusalem say? ....

4   What does John the Baptist's question tell us about how some Asian Christians feel about Jesus (according to the writer)?

    ....

5   What do the other two questions tell us about the hopes and desires of Asian Christians in relation to Jesus?

    ....

Compare your answers with those of other students around you.
Check your answers with Listening Text 11 in Appendix A.

Reading Comprehension
Here is an account of one of the earliest portrayals of Jesus. Read the text and then answer the questions below.

Jesus in Mark's Gospel

1 The Jesus (1) <u>who</u> is portrayed in [the] opening chapters of Mark's gospel is a strong, vibrant, yet
2 vulnerable character, keenly aware of the mission entrusted to him by the One (2) <u>who</u> calls him Son
3 and Beloved. The possibilities and promise contained in the notion of the reign of God find expression
4 in Jesus' teaching, in his healing miracles, in his power to forgive sin, and in his invitation to all to be
5 part of the discipleship circle. He seeks out and attracts not those (3) <u>whose</u> status would normally
6 permit them access to the channels of power but rather those (4) <u>who</u> might have considered
7 themselves excluded from those blessed by God. Where health, gender, family or good fortune might
8 once have determined (5) <u>who</u> was worthy of the God of Israel, now in the person of Jesus all such
9 requirements are swept away. The God (6) <u>whom</u> Jesus reveals will not be bound by such
10 prescriptions.

[Kiley, 1995, pp 31-32.]

1 Why does the writer use the definite article, ***the***, to refer to Jesus in Line 1?
   ....

2 The writer uses four adjectives to describe Jesus as he is represented in the first part of Mark's gospel. What are they? Explain in your own words what each adjective means.
   ....

3 What explanation is given to the phrase "reign of God" (Line 3) in the text?
   ....

4 In Lines 8-9 we read: "all such requirements are swept away". What exactly are these "requirements"? Why were they swept away? ....
   ....

5 Several words in this text have been underlined, namely, *who, whose, whom*. What is the grammatical name of these words? ....
   Name some other words in the same group. ....

6 Which of the following best describes the organisation of ideas of this text (see Unit 4):-
   a*) argument*   b) *description*   or   c) *evaluation?*   ....

Revision of Grammar: Relative clauses

You were probably able to identify the words in Question 5 above as relative pronouns, which are used to introduce a relative clause.

A relative clause describes a noun or pronoun in the independent (main) clause of a sentence. Relative clauses (sometimes called adjectival clauses) are usually introduced by the relative pronouns *who, which* or *that*. We use *who* for people and *which* for things or places. We can also sometimes use *that* instead of *who* and *which*.* Here are some examples where the relative pronoun is the subject of the relative clause.

Examples: The person (noun) ***who* wrote the book** is giving a seminar in the holidays.
           (We could also say, The person *that wrote the book*....)
           Those (pronoun) ***who* want success** should study hard.
           The discoveries (noun) ***which* took place at Qumran** have been very helpful to scholars.
           (We could also say, The discoveries *that took place*....)

*Note: Australian and British English allow the use of *which* or *that* as explained. However, in the United States, according to Microsoft standards, *which* is used only in non-restrictive (non-defining) relative clauses—see below. *That* is used in all other cases.

When the relative pronoun is the object in the relative clause, we use *whom* (for persons) and *which* for things. When the relative pronoun indicates possession, we use *whose*.

Examples:　　The person **_whom you asked_** is not here. (You asked whom..)
　　　　　　　The books **_which Jo borrowed_** were mine. (Jo borrowed which..)
　　　　　　　The students **_whose essays are finished_** may play sport. (The essays of whom..)

When the relative clause gives necessary information about the noun/pronoun, as it does in all the examples above, it is called a Restrictive relative clause (sometimes called Defining). These clauses are **not** separated from the main clause by commas.

Sometimes the information given may not be essential to the meaning of the sentence. This is called a Non-Restrictive or Non-Defining Relative clause. In such sentences, the relative clause is preceded and followed (unless it is at the end of a sentence) by a comma.

Examples:　The Qumran scrolls, **_which were discovered over fifty years ago_**, continue to be very important for biblical scholars.
　　　　　　Java, **_which is by no means the largest island_**, is the most densely populated island of Indonesia.
　　　　　　Edward Schillebeeckx, **_whose name is familiar to many people_**, wrote some classic studies in Christology.

The relative pronoun may also be the object of a preposition in a Restrictive or Non-restrictive relative clause.

Examples:　The factory **_in which they process coffee beans_** is very large. (Restrictive)
　　　　　　The scriptures, **_on which we depend for our spiritual well-being_**, need careful study and patient meditation. (Non-restrictive)
　　　　　　Bioethics is a subject **_about which few books_** have yet been written. (Restrictive)

Note: Sometimes a relative clause may be introduced by a relative adverb, eg *where, when, why*, when these mean the same as *in which, on which* or *for which*.

Examples:　The library **_where_** (= in which) **_we study_** has few books.
　　　　　　I will never forget the day **_when_** (= on which) **_I arrived here._**
　　　　　　The reason **_why_** (= for which) **_I enrolled in this course_** was to improve my English.

For more details on relative clauses, consult a comprehensive grammar book.

REVISION EXERCISE 17.1

The text in Part 1 (Jesus in Mark's Gospel) has six relative clauses. Write out below each of these clauses in full and indicate by a tick whether the clause is Restrictive (R) or Non-restrictive (NR) and whether the relative pronoun is subject (Subj.), object (Obj.) or possessive (Poss).

Relative clause in full	R or NR	Subj.	Obj.	Poss.
1 Eg *who is portrayed in the opening chapters of Mark's gospel* ✓		✓		
2………………………………………………				
3………………………………………………				
4………………………………………………				
5………………………………………………				
6………………………………………………				

REVISION EXERCISE 17.2

For each pair of sentences below, write one sentence including a relative clause. Indicate whether the clause is Restrictive (R) or Non-restrictive (NR) by circling the appropriate letter/s. Use *who, whose, whom* for persons and *that* or *which* for things.

Examples:
* The women remained near the cross. They had accompanied Jesus from Galilee.

  The women who had accompanied Jesus from Galilee remained near the cross. R

[Note: This could also be understood as Non-Restrictive. In this case it would be preceded and followed by a comma.]

* The eminent theologian will give a public lecture next week. Her book was published recently.

  The eminent theologian, whose book was published recently, will give a public lecture next week. NR

1 Mark's gospel tells the story of a woman. She had been suffering for twelve years.
....R/NR

2 The woman was cured. She touched Jesus.
....R/NR

3 Has anyone seen the book? I left it on the table.
....R/NR

4 The scriptures tell us that Judas committed suicide. His kiss had betrayed Jesus.
....R/NR

5 Gustavo Gutiérrez is one of the founders of liberation theology. He lived in South America.
....R/NR

6 Ecological theology is gaining more attention. It has developed because of the poor state of the environment.
....R/NR

REVISION EXERCISE 17.3

Identify each relative clause in the text below by underlining and placing a number in the margin beside it. Indicate below for each one whether the relative pronoun is subject or object, and whether the clause is Restrictive or Non-Restrictive.

Developments in Christology

1 As a wave is created at sea . . . and breaks as it comes close to land, so too it seems that successive
2 understandings of Christ have formed, swelled, and broken upon Catholic consciousness since the mid-twentieth
3 century. The first wave in the 1950s consisted in remembering the genuine humanity of Jesus Christ, a memory
4 stirred up by the 1,500th anniversary of the ancient council of Chalcedon which had declared the christological
5 dogma. A decade later biblical scholarship began to flourish, triggering critical discovery of the history of Jesus.
6 Both of these waves overlapped as they arrived in a church that was incorporating concern for justice into its
7 sense of mission. Before they had time to recede, a third wave formed as the voice of the poor began to be
8 heard doing theology from the "underside of history" and so claiming Jesus Christ as liberator. Almost
9 simultaneously the movement of feminist theology stirred yet another wave to life, swelling as the majority of the
10 church's members who had long been left out of the conversation about Christ began to articulate their insights.
11 Even more recently a realisation of the vastness of the world and its peoples has arisen, and looms as a
12 question about the universal influence of Jesus the Christ. Under threat of ecological disaster, global vision now
13 grows even wider to incorporate the view that not only human beings but all creatures of the earth and the
14 universe itself are destined for final blessing in Christ. [Johnson, 1990, pp x-xi.]

1) .... 2) etc ....

PART 2

Preparatory Discussion

What do you know about Gustavo Gutiérrez, Jon Sobrino, Leonardo Boff and Juan Luis Segundo? What do they have in common? Can you add any other names to this list? Discuss with those around you and share with the whole class.

Listening

First read through this partial text. Try to predict what might complete the blank spaces. Now listen to the text and complete the blank spaces according to what you hear.

```
1   The realisation that concern for justice is an intrinsic part of christology receives a sharper and
2   more critical focus when it is articulated by people who are actually suffering from injustice. The major
3   Catholic theologians who developed transcendental christology in the 1960s, recovering the
4   genuine humanity of Jesus, and narrative christology in the 1970s, recovering the .....................
5   ..........................., have a great deal in common: they are all white, well-fed, well-educated,
6   prosperous, privileged, European males. They all theologise, however ..............................., out of
7   an experience of political, economic and ............................................ Starting in the 1970s and
8   moving into the 1980s, a third wave of renewal in Catholic christology has developed as the
9   ...............................................in the world have begun to find their voice. On virtually every
10  continent, reflection on faith from the "........................................" has resulted in forms of theology
11  collectively known as ................................. It is a new way of doing theology, one which
12  draws on the experience of systematically ....................................................... peoples.[ ....]
13  ...................... theology originated in ........................................ after the .......................
14  although its roots reach back into the ........................................................ begun decades
15  earlier.                                                                                    [Johnson, 1990, p 83.]
```

Check your completed text with Listening Text 12 in Appendix A.

Reading Comprehension

Read the text and answer the questions below.

Christology from an Asian woman's perspective

```
1    In the light of Asian women's reality in general, a liberational, hope-filled, love-inspired, and
2    praxis-oriented Christology is what holds meaning for me. In the person and praxis of Jesus are
3    found the grounds of our liberation from all oppression and discrimination: whether political or
4    economic, religious or cultural, or based on gender, race or ethnicity. Therefore the image of Jesus as
5    liberator is consistent with my christology. On the other hand, in view of what I have written, it would
6    be inconsistent to hold on to the title and image of "lord" in reference to Jesus, because of the
7    overtones of the word as used today. In Asia, the word "lord" is connected with the feudal system
8    which in my own country is one of the root causes of the poverty, injustices, inequalities, and violent
9    conflicts that exist there today, many of the victims being women. It is also a colonial term for the
10   British masters which is still used in countries like Pakistan for those who have taken their place.
11    "Lord" connotes a relationship of domination, which is opposite to what Jesus taught
12   and exemplified. "The rulers of the gentiles exercise lordship over them . . . but not so with you" (Lk
13   22:24). His apostles called him "teacher" and "lord", yet Jesus preferred to be remembered as one who
14   serves (cf Jn 14:13-16). Asian women have been "lorded over" for centuries and all the major
15   religions including Christianity have contributed to this sinful situation. The title "lord" would not be in
16   keeping with a liberating Jesus.                                                      [Fabella, 1993, p 218.]
```

Answer these questions on the text:-

1   What is the writer's main purpose in this text:
    a) analysis   b) description   c) argument   OR   d) evaluation. ……..………..

2   Which type of christology (out of those identified so far in the unit) does this writer prefer? Give the line reference/s for your opinion. ……………………………………
    Why does this writer prefer this christology? Refer to evidence in the text.
    ……………………………………………………………………………………………

3   This writer says it would be inconsistent to use the title or image of "lord" in reference to Jesus (Line 6). What arguments does she use to support this view?
    ……………………………………………………………………………………………
    ……………………………………………………………………………………………

4   In Line 9, to what noun does the pronoun *it* refer? ……………………………………..

5   Identify all the relative clauses in this text, by underlining and numbering them. How many can you find? ……………...…………………………………………

6   What is "this sinful situation" referred to in Line 15?
    ……………………………………………………………………………………………

Writing

Choose an Asian theologian—woman or man, living or dead—whose life and work you admire. Write about one page on the life, work and theological contribution made by this person. Include information about the person's place of origin, and the conditions which may have influenced the development of the person's theology. Mention any notable events in the person's life, and evaluate if possible how this person's theology has improved the lives of people in the surrounding society.

Speaking

Prepare a short talk for the class on the theologian you have chosen to write about. (You may use notes to help you but avoid reading your talk.)

English for Theology

PART 3

Preparatory Discussion

Recall your earliest memories of hearing and learning about Jesus Christ. Which approach or type of christology do you think those learnings represented? Do you find one or other of these christological approaches more helpful to you than others? Why? What about people in your parish, your city, your country—do you think they would have a preferred approach? Discuss briefly.

Listening

Listen to part of a story told by a Chinese church leader, KH Ting, about some church experiences in China during the Cultural Revolution. The story is part of an address given to European Christians.

Listen for the answers to these questions about how the Christians used to meet together.

1 Where did the Christians meet? ……………………………………………………..

2 How often did they meet? ………………………………………………………….

3 How many people usually gathered in the groups? ………………………………….

4 What did they do during their meetings? ……...…………………………………….
…………………………………………………………………………………………

5 How did they conduct their meetings, ie how did they relate to one another? ……….
…………………………………………………………………………………………

6 Without Bibles, how did they get access to the Bible, ie the Scriptures? ……………...
…………………………………………………………………………………………

7 Why did they not have Bibles? ……………………………………………………....

8 How does the speaker describe what he believes is the essential nature of the church?
…………………………………………………………………………………………

Check your answers in Listening Text 13 in Appendix A.

Reading Comprehension

Read the text and answer the questions.

Jesus, Christology and Asia

1 Images of Jesus imported to Asia are so wrapped up in various christological configurations that one
2 often overlooks the fact that Jesus came from Asia, or to be precise, west Asia. He was raised up and
3 engaged in brief public activity in and around the villages and cities of Palestine. Early on, there was a
4 strong eastward thrust of the Jesus movement through Persia and Afghanistan, but much of this was
5 disintegrating by the time of the emergence of Islam, leaving only a struggling minority in South India
6 and a church precariously established in China and ultimately disappearing in a welter of civil war. It
7 took nearly fifteen hundred years before the rest of Asia could feel the full impact of Jesus' personality
8 and the significance of his teaching. It was only through the Western missionary irruption beginning in
9 the fifteenth century that the rest of Asia came to know Jesus.
10 When Jesus made his belated second visit to the eastern part of Asia, he did not come as a Galilean

11 sage showing solidarity with its seers and wisdom teachers. Rather, he came as an alien in his own
12 home territory, and more tellingly, as a clannish god of the *parangis* (a term used by Indians during the
13 salad days of the empire to describe the foreigners) sanctioning the subjugation of the peoples of Asia
14 and their cultures. He was projected and paraded as the totem symbol of the privileged and the
15 powerful.
16 Since then there have been a number of attempts by Asian Christians to counteract this imperial,
17 supremacist and absolutist understanding of Jesus. These discourses try to re-Asianise and refashion
18 Jesus on Asian terms to meeting the contextual needs of Asian peoples . . .
19 [For example, these essays] weave a wide variety of cultural symbols, philosophical insights and
20 social concerns of Asia into their christological articulations. These understandings of Jesus indicate
21 that as fresh horizons open up, the perceptions of Jesus that emerge may not resemble either in form
22 or content portrayals of him depicted in the Christian scriptures. They also raise the question of why
23 Jewish thought patterns have to be the norm for the christological enterprise of people who are not
24 familiar with their nuances. It is not that Asians are reluctant to learn from or utilise the hermeneutical
25 resources of the Jewish people. The point of the Asian articulations of Jesus is that if the Christian
26 church in the fifth century was successful in delicately maintaining the enigma of Jesus in the
27 language, mood and the spirit of that hellenistic period, why should not Asians draw on their own
28 hermeneutical reservoir to fashion Jesus for their own time and place?

[Sugirtharajah, 1993, p viii-ix.]

Answer these questions on the text.

1 Which of these statements best expresses the writer's main point in this text?
   Note: They are all true statements according to the text.
   i) Asians are very ready to learn from the original
      Jewish community of Jesus.   ❏
   ii) Jesus was often presented to Asians in Western images
       and this tended to conceal the reality that Jesus was in
       fact Asian (west Asian) himself.   ❏
   iii) Jewish and hellenistic thought patterns have been
        successfully used to interpret Jesus.   ❏
   iv) The philosophical insights, symbols and concerns of
       of Asia need to be applied to the interpretation of Jesus.   ❏

2 The writer refers to Jesus' 'second visit' to Asia (Line 10). When did this happen?
   ....

3 When and where was the first visit? ....
   ....

4 The writer notes that Western missionary activity from the 15th century brought knowledge of Jesus to a large part of Asia (Lines 8-9). What is the writer's opinion of much of that activity? Support your opinion with evidence from the text. ....
   ....

5 What does the writer mean by a 'hermeneutical reservoir' (Line 28). ....
   ....

PART 4

Preparatory Discussion

Recent years have seen considerable discussion and some controversy about the idea of developing Asian theologies. What do you know about these developments? Who is involved? What is being achieved? What are some of the important concerns. What are your hopes for these developments? Discuss in small groups and then share with the whole class.

Reading Comprehension

Read the text and answer the questions below.

'Coconut Christology'

1. The coconut theology is another theology that can be identified in the Pacific. Everyone in the Pacific
2. knows and literally lives on coconut. It is a tree of many uses, and a tree of life for Pacific islanders. If
3. Jesus had grown up and lived in the Pacific, He could have added another identification of himself—I
4. am the Coconut of Life.
5. The tree has many uses, as drink, food, housing, shelter, fuel, mats, etc. Once it bears fruit it
6. continues to bear fruit every year. The fruit is round and it has a tendency to roll down to the lowest
7. possible level. When the coconut rolls down it rolls down with its many lifegiving possibilities. It rolls
8. down with food, drink, husks, shells, money and industry. Sometimes it falls into the ocean and it floats
9. to another island to take food etc. to the people there. It floats as long as there is life in the coconut. It
10. has a protective shell and a soft kernel. It has eyes, a mouth and features like those of a human head.
11. When one drinks from it one draws nourishment by 'kissing' it. In the coconut there are so many
12. Biblical concepts. The fullness of time *(kairos)* is there. No one can push back the time when it will
13. ripen, nor make it ripen any earlier: only at the fullness of time will it fall.
14. Many people when they are late talk about Fijian time or Tonga time, but the best suggestion is to
15. call it the Coconut time, for it does not matter whether one is early or late. The important thing is that
16. the task is done and the mission fulfilled.
17. The full Christology can be seen in the coconut. The Incarnation and the Virgin Birth is in the
18. coconut. The full potential of new life is in the coconut and when it is ready (fullness) the new life
19. breaks through in sprouts and, rooted in the soil, it grows towards heaven. There are glimpses of death
20. and resurrection: "a seed must die in order to live." At the end, the authorities forced Christ to the
21. earth's womb, intending to keep Him there with the Roman seal (power), and to say the end had come.
22. But instead of the end they had expected, the shell cracked and resurrection took place. A new full-
23. grown coconut came to its own.
24. The concept of *one Spirit* could be illustrated by what we use in building houses. The whole
25. structure is tied up with the sennet. We may use artistic designs, but the fact is that they are held
26. together by only one string. The churches are held by only one string: the Holy Spirit.
27. When we think of the Eucharist, the coconut is more relevant than the bread and wine. In the
28. Hebrew context, the pilgrims had to use the unleavened bread and wine, because they were simple to
29. make and within their means to use. But, for the people of the Pacific, bread and wine are foreign and
30. very expensive to import. The wheat and the grapes are two separate elements. The coconut has
31. both the drink and the food from the same fruit, like the blood and flesh from the one and the same
32. body of Christ.
33. I am convinced that if Christ had grown up and lived in the Pacific, He would have used the coconut
34. to represent the body which was bruised and crushed, and the juice for the blood as elements of the
35. Holy Eucharist.

[Havea, 1987, pp 14-15.]

Answer these questions on the text, after re-reading the text in Part 3 of this unit.

1. Compare and contrast this text of Havea with the text (Sugirtharajah) in Part 3 of this unit. Identify similarities and differences in the main ideas expressed. To assist you, consider the use of positive and negative evaluations, and the use of general principle and/or concrete details. Make your responses under these headings:-

Similarities	Differences
…………………………………	…………………………………
…………………………………	…………………………………
…………………………………	…………………………………
…………………………………	…………………………………

2. What is the writer's (Havea's) attitude towards failure to be on time?

   …………………………………………………………………………………

3. What is 'the sennet' (sometimes *sennit*, Line 25). Guess its meaning from the context if you do not know. What do you suppose it is made of?

   …………………………………………………………………………………

4. The writer thinks that for Pacific people the coconut is more relevant for the Eucharist than bread and wine. What reasons are given for this opinion?

   …………………………………………………………………………………

   …………………………………………………………………………………

Speaking

In small groups, talk about what local items or features (plant, animal, landscape feature) or cultural practices have been used in your country or region to enculturate better (i.e. make more meaningful) the Christian message.

What local symbols or practices *could* be used which are not yet used?

Writing

Write about a half to one page on the topic "A local item/practice as symbol of the Christian message." (The item must not be the coconut.)

Describe what the local item or feature is, and explain what qualities or aspects can be symbolic of the Christian message in some way.

UNIT 17 VOCABULARY

Add to this list any more new words that you want to remember.

Nouns	**Verbs**	**Adjectives**	**Other**
vastness	portray	vibrant	simultaneously
praxis	articulate	vulnerable	
overtones	loom	implicit	
domination	overlook	worthy	
anarchy	irrupt		
configuration	subjugate		
nuance	depict		

UNIT 18 THE PROBLEM OF SUFFERING

PART 1

Preparatory Discussion

"As a religious problem, the problem of suffering is, paradoxically, not how to avoid suffering but how to suffer . . . how to make pain . . . bearable, supportable . . . sufferable."*
Do you agree or disagree with this statement? Is this opinion sufficient from a Christian point of view? Discuss.

* [Geertz, C quoted in Richard, 1992, p 2-3.]

Listening

As you listen to a text on suffering, write down brief notes about the main ideas you hear. Then work with a small group to reproduce the meaning of the text in your own words.

Check your text against Listening Text 14 in Appendix A.

Reading Comprehension

Read the text and answer the questions.

The nature of suffering according to Edward Schillebeeckx

1   Suffering is a complex reality as it is perceived in the history of humanity. Suffering is not always a
2   negative reality although it may be perceived as such. In fact, "A world in which there was no place
3   for suffering and sorrow, even for deep grief, would seem to be inhuman, a world of robots, even an
4   <u>unreal</u> world."* Certain suffering when borne with courage and dignity can contribute to the maturity of
5   an individual. There is also the suffering for a good cause, a suffering motivated by sacrificial love.
6   'Suffering is the likely consequence in this world of any whole-hearted sacrifice for a great cause:…'
7   There is also suffering brought about because of the perceived absence and hiddenness of God.
8   While there can be certain benefits to suffering, there is far too great an "excess" of suffering in the
9   world to ever justify its existence. Always confronting humanity, there is the <u>unmerited</u> suffering, the
10 suffering of the innocent, for which there cannot be any rational or logical explanation. "There is
11 suffering which is not even suffering 'for a good cause', but suffering in which men/women, without
12 finding meaning for themselves, are simply made the crude victims of an evil cause which serves
13 others."* That kind of suffering provokes scandal, a scandal which cannot have "a specific structural
14 place in the divine plan."* That kind of scandalous suffering cannot be categorised simply as a problem
15 that cannot simply be solved, because before such suffering human logic stands <u>mute.</u>
16 For Schillebeeckx, the only meaningful response that can be made to such suffering is to resist it.
17 Evil has no right to exist and such a refusal is "consistent and coherent if it is linked with a powerful
18 involvement in resistance against all forms of evil." * Yet there can be no total victory over suffering, no
19 complete resistance, for there is always death. "**Death above all shows that we are <u>deluded</u> if we**
20 **think that we can <u>realise</u> on earth a true, perfect, and universal salvation for all and for every**
21 **individual."***

*Schillebeeckx, 1980, pp 724-726.   [Richard, 1992, pp 30-31.]

Answer these questions:-
1   Several kinds of suffering are identified in this text. For example, there is
     i) 'certain suffering'(Line 4) (what might this be?) which leads to maturity;
     ii) 'suffering for a good cause' (Line 5).
     List the other kinds of suffering mentioned and give the Line reference numbers.
       iii) …………………………………..
       iv) …………………………………..
       v) …………………………………..

2   In Line 16 reference is made to 'such suffering'. What does 'such' refer to here?..

3   Without using a dictionary, match the words underlined in the text with one from the list below:
    a. silent   b. mistaken   c. attain   d. illusory   e. undeserved
    ....

4   In this text we 'hear' the voice of the theologian Edward Schillebeeckx, mostly indirectly but sometimes in direct quotes from his book.
    Read through the following statements and decide whether each one would accurately reflect the thinking of Schillebeeckx or not, according to the text above. Be prepared to give evidence from the text to support your opinion.

Statement	Reflects Schillebeeckx's thought: Yes/No?
i Throughout history, humans have perceived suffering as a many-sided reality.	....
ii Suffering, sorrow and grief seem to make the the world an inhuman place.	....
iii Commitment to a cause is certain to bring suffering.	....
iv All suffering has a place in the divine plan.	....
v All suffering must be resisted.	....

Revision of Grammar: Nominal or noun clauses

A nominal or noun clause is a dependent clause which stands in place of a noun or noun phrase. A noun clause may therefore function in any of the ways in which a noun or noun phrase can function.

The last sentence in the Reading text above (Lines 19-21) contains examples of two noun clauses, one within the other.

A noun clause must have: Subordinating word/Subject + Verb + Complement.
Two common types of noun clause are:-
1   Declarative noun clauses, ie those which make a statement.
2   Interrogative noun clauses, ie those which ask a question.

[Note: There are other types of noun clauses. Consult a comprehensive grammar for more detail.]

1   <u>Declarative noun clauses</u>
The subordinator *that* is used in noun clauses which make a statement.
Examples:-
   The lecturer noted ***that many religions flourish in Asia.***
   Death shows ***that we are all equal in the end.***

Unit 18 The Problem of Suffering

Sometimes the subordinator *that* may be omitted without changing the meaning of the sentence.

    Eg Death shows ***we are all equal in the end.***

Verbs which often introduce declarative noun clauses include verbs like these:-

report	*state*	*explain*	*advise*	*tell*	*demonstrate*
realise	*think*	*remember*	*promise*	*notice*	*conclude*
maintain	*argue*	*allege*	*claim*	*assume*	*declare*

You may wish to add to this list of verbs by including those you identify in your reading.

………….   ………….   ………….   ………….   …………..   ………….

………….   ………….   ………….   ………….   …………..   ………….

In the above examples, the noun clause is the object of a main verb, ie *noted* and *shows*. Declarative noun clauses may also follow an adjective or a noun, as in the following examples.

He was <u>sad</u> ***that the people were so poor.***   (Adjective)
They were <u>amazed</u> ***that he healed people of their sicknesses.*** (Adjective)

He went ahead in the <u>hope</u> ***that things would improve.***   (Noun)
It was the people's <u>belief</u> ***that the government would assist them.*** (Noun)
He enrolled on the <u>assumption</u> ***that he was accepted.***   (Noun)

A noun clause may also be the subject of the main verb in a sentence, as in the following examples:-

That he healed the sick amazed the people in all the villages.
That tropical forests are being destroyed worries scientists and others around the world.

2   <u>Interrogative noun clauses</u>

There are two main types of interrogative noun clause:
    i) Those which ask a *wh-*question.
    ii) Those which ask a *yes-no* question

Like declarative noun clauses, interrogative noun clauses may occur as either object or subject of the main verb in a sentence.

    i) Subordinators used to introduce a *wh-*question noun clause include the following:-
       who, whoever, where, wherever, when, what, whatever, how

Examples
    (Object)   He could not remember ***<u>where</u> he had left the book.***
                        She want to know ***<u>who</u> had finished the exercises.***
                        The teacher asked ***<u>how</u> he had travelled.***

    (Subject)   ***How he had travelled*** was not important. He had arrived safely.
                        Whoever studies hard will succeed.

ii)   Subordinators used to introduce a *yes-no* question are *whether* (*or not*) and *if*.

English for Theology

Examples

(Object)　　　The travellers inquired ***whether the boat sailed every day.***
　　　　　　　The student wanted to know ***whether or not he was qualified to enrol.***
　　　　　　　She asked ***if she could borrow that book.***

(Subject)　　　***Whether you leave early*** is your decision.

For more detail about noun clauses, consult a comprehensive grammar book.

REVISION EXERCISE 18.1

Identify the noun clauses in the following sentences by enclosing them with brackets. Indicate for each one whether the noun clause is
　　　i) declarative or interrogative, and
　　　ii) the subject or the object of the main verb.

The first two are completed as examples.

1　Theologians have concluded (that suffering cannot be explained.)
　　　i) Declarative noun clause
　　　ii) Object of main verb.

2　(Whether humans will find a cure for cancer soon) depends on many factors.
　　　i) Interrogative
　　　ii) Subject

3　Archaeologists explained that the parchments were over two thousand years old.
　　　i) ……………………………………….
　　　ii) ……………………………………….

4　Many theologians have discovered that suffering is the beginning point of their theologising.
　　　i) ……………………………………….
　　　ii) ……………………………………….

5　Death shatters any illusion that we can find complete happiness for all on earth.
　　　i) ……………………………………….
　　　ii) ……………………………………….

6　That many people in the world are poor is a simple fact.
　　　i) ……………………………………….
　　　ii) ……………………………………….

7　The traveller asked how far away the train station was.
　　　i) ……………………………………….
　　　ii) ……………………………………….

8　Whether you pass the examination or not depends on your effort.
　　　i) ……………………………………….
　　　ii) ……………………………………….

PART 2

Preparatory Discussion

"Nowadays the cross, the most important symbol in Christianity, has become a problem for many women. The tortured body of Christ on the cross, and his death—interpreted as an atoning death—no longer give them any strength . . . The cross as it is often preached has often had fatal consequences for women . . ."

[Moltmann-Wendel, 1994 in Tesfai,Y, p 87.]

Why might the cross, 'as often preached' have had 'fatal consequences' for women? What might be these 'fatal consequences'? Discuss in small groups and then with the whole class.

Listening

Listen for the answers to these questions in the text you will hear.

1. Who developed his theology on the experience of suffering?..............................
2. What two kinds of suffering are mentioned in the text? 1st..............................
   2nd..............................
3. What is the effect of each kind of suffering? 1st ....
   2nd ....
4. What attitude towards suffering (of the second kind) is demanded by belief in Jesus? (Use the words you hear in the text.) ....

Check your answers in Listening Text 15 in Appendix A.

Reading Comprehension

Read the text and answer the questions.

[Dorothy Soelle, a German theologian residing in the US, has written one of the most provocative books on theology and suffering in recent years. (Richard, 1992, p 73.) The following text represents some of her thinking on the subject.]

Suffering – a feminist perspective

1 While there is a suffering from which we can learn, there is a suffering that cannot be given a meaning
2 and that is the suffering of the innocent. It is such suffering that leads to atheism. "Wherever people
3 are confronted by senseless suffering, faith in a God who embodies both omnipotence and love has to
4 waver or be destroyed." Such innocent suffering goes against faith and trust in a loving God, so
5 "atheism arises out of human suffering." But this negation of God is not a negation of the God of Jesus
6 but a theism "that has nothing to do with Christ."
7 Innocent suffering poses the theodicy question most starkly and preempts any possibility of
8 perceiving God as directly or indirectly involved with such innocent suffering. Dorothy Soelle is very
9 severe toward the traditional position of theodicy.

10 We have to guard against facile theological interpretations of suffering. From a Christian point of view, suffering does
11 not exist in order to break our pride, demonstrate our impotence, or take advantage of our dependency. The purpose
12 of suffering is not to lead us back to a God who attains to [God's] greatness only by reducing us to insignificance.*

13 It can never be affirmed that God can cause suffering in any way. On this point Dorothy Soelle is
14 quite critical of Jurgen Moltmann's position. She perceives Moltmann as affirming that God the Father
15 is the author of Jesus' suffering, the omnipotent Father who delivers the Son to suffering. For Soelle,
16 Moltmann's position remains problematic. It cannot resolve the tension between the loving God of the
17 incarnation, the one in solidarity with us, and the wrathful God of the cross. For Soelle Jesus simply
18 cannot have suffered because of God. For Soelle the cross is not the symbol of the relation of the
19 Father to the Son, but of Jesus to the world. The cross is above all a symbol of reality: love that
20 confronts oppressive structures usually ends on a cross. Love does not cause suffering or produce it,
21 although it must necessarily seek confrontation.
22 Dorothy Soelle's criticism of the apathetic God-Father led her to a greater emphasis on the person
23 of Jesus Christ . . .

24 For Soelle our only way to God is through Jesus: God can only be experienced in the powerlessness of
25 Jesus Christ. In the gospels, Jesus as the human face of God is truly the powerless one, the man for
26 others. He is the one who refused to come down from the cross. "The only capital with which he
27 came into the world was his love, and it was as powerless and as powerful as love is."

*Soelle, D, 1984, *The Strength of the Weak*, The Westminster Press, Philadelphia, p 29.

[Richard, 1992, pp 81-83.]

Answer these questions on the text.

1 Check your understanding of *theism* (Line 6) and *theodicy* (Line 9).

2 What is meant by the apparent contradiction that *'this negation of God is not a negation of the God of Jesus'*? (Lines 5-6) That is, what is the difference, in the text, between God and the God of Jesus?

3 Compare Soelle's ideas about suffering as described in this text with those of Schillebeeckx outlined in the Reading Comprehension text in Part 1 of this Unit. Use questions and a chart like this to make comparisons:-

	Schillebeeckx	Soelle
i Can suffering ever be justified?	*Yes, suffering which leads to maturity; suffering for a good cause*	....
ii What sort of suffering can never be justified?	....	....
iii What is God's role in unjustified suffering?	....	....
iv What might be the effects of unjustified or unmerited suffering on human beings?	....	....
v Other?	....	....

Writing

Using information from the exercise above and from both Reading texts in this Unit so far, in your own words write about a page describing the views on suffering of EITHER Schillebeeckx or Soelle. Begin with an introductory statement and include paragraphs on suffering which can be accepted (for what reasons?), suffering which can never be accepted and what should be the Christian response to such suffering.

PART 3
Preparatory Discussion

Two categories of suffering were mentioned in the Listening exercise in Part 2. Working in small groups, spend a few moments listing some examples of each kind of suffering. Eg

1st kind of suffering	2nd kind of suffering
....	....
....	....
....	....
....	....

Which list is longer? Share your lists with the whole class.

Reading Comprehension

Read the text.

The religions in Asia and the problem of suffering

1 Asians are religious people. Religious feeling is deeply imbedded in their hearts so that the whole of
2 their life, their attitudes and their thinking, are enduringly inspired and directed by it. In other words, the
3 activities of Asian people can only with difficulty be separated from their religious experiences.
4 All human problems, including suffering, are viewed from a religious perspective. Through religion
5 people try to understand the significance of life with all its ups and downs. They try to find answers to
6 their destiny. All these attempts can be seen as nothing other than human strivings to achieve
7 salvation.
   ...
8 In addition to Buddhism, which Pieris calls *pan*-Asian due to its cultural integration, numerical
9 strength and geographical extension (. . .), other religions are also adhered to by Asian people and
10 continue to exert influence on their lives.
   [These include Hinduism, Islam, Shintoism, Shamanism, Confucianism and Taoism.] ...
11 The problem of suffering plays a significant role in each of these religions. This fact, however, need not
12 surprise us, since the problem of suffering is very closely related to the question of human destiny.
13 Reflections on suffering made by these religions are efforts to answer this question, so that people
14 may come to a better understanding of the significance and meaning of their lives.
15 To pose questions about suffering in connection with human destiny, within the framework of
16 religions, may also be important because religions are ambivalent about suffering. On the one side,
17 religions can preserve ways of release from suffering. On the other side, however, religions can lock
18 people into suffering permanently. Using Pieris' words, religions, like poverty, have at the same time
19 their liberating and enslaving faces, psychologically as well as sociologically. In its psychologically
20 enslaving face, religion becomes superstition, ritualism, dogmatism, transcendentalism, while in its
21 sociologically enslaving face, it tends to legitimise an oppressive status-quo. On the other hand, while
22 the psychologically liberating face of religion can be seen in interior liberation from sin (mammon,
23 antigod, *tanha*, exploitative instincts), its sociologically liberating face is seen in religions' potential for
24 radical social change.
25 In Hinduism . . . the destiny and aim of life is none other than to escape this process of becoming
26 (reincarnation) . . .
27 In Buddhism . . . to gain release from suffering, one must also be freed from desire, whose root lies in
28 human existence itself. The one who succeeds in this will reach the status of *nirvana*.
29 In Confucianism . . . evil is seen as unnatural. So suffering, which is seen as an expression of evil, is
30 also understood as unnatural.   [And so on.]
   ...
31 From the foregoing, it is quite clear that the problem of salvation is a crucial one. We can also see
32 that in attempts to give answer to the problem of suffering, salvation has become the focus of attention
33 for most religions in Asia. In connection with this issue, A Pieris points out that the soteriological

English for Theology

34 power of the non-Christian religions in Asia is so strong that we have to treat them seriously . . .

35 The concept of salvation does not, however, come only from the religious angle. The socio-
36 economic and socio-political situation in Asia has been forcing people to rethink the meaning and
37 significance of salvation. The development plans launched by the governments of the Asian countries
38 can also sometimes be understood within the framework of reconceiving salvation. There are,
39 accordingly, at least two understandings of salvation seen here: religious and political.
40 The question which can be raised here has to do with the character of salvation. Does the salvation
41 offered by the various religions and development plans really constitute a breakthrough in solving the
42 problem of human suffering? This question is still being discussed by theologians and thinkers in Asia.

[Yewangoe, 1987, pp 15-18, 20.]

1   What is meant by the statement, *'religions are ambivalent about suffering'*? (Line 16) What explanation is given in the text?

   ....

2   Clarify through class discussion any further questions you have about this text.

3   What do you think Schillebeeckx (Part 1) or Soelle (Part 2) would say about viewing salvation not only from a religious angle (Line 35) but also from a socio-economic and socio-political angle? Mention evidence from the texts to support your opinion.

Speaking

Salvation in this world and/or the next? Continue the discussion begun in response to question 3 above. What are some church documents which have something to say about this question? What do they say?

PART 4

Preparatory Discussion

With reference to religions in general, the Reading text in Part 3 above notes Pieris' view that *'religions ... can have at the same time their liberating and enslaving faces.' ... 'Religions can preserve ways of release from suffering ... [and] religions can lock people into suffering permanently.'* Is this true of Christianity or not? Does Christianity have anything distinctive to offer humanity on the problem of suffering? Discuss.

Reading Comprehension

Read the text and answer the questions.

Paul's response to tragic suffering

1   Among the biblical responses to suffering and hope, Paul's response is particularly impressive.
2   In making a clear distinction between two dimensions of suffering—suffering at the hands of human
3   injustice and suffering at the hands of the power of death—Paul combines a prophetic and an
4   apocalyptic response to suffering and hope.
5   1. Suffering because of human injustice and idolatry evokes Paul's *prophetic response*.
6   The church is here called to redemptive suffering, that is, to resist human idolatry and injustice and to
7   suffer redemptively in the world *against* the world *for* the world.
8   2. Suffering because of the power of death evokes Paul's *apocalyptic response*—grounded
9   in the sure knowledge that God's victory over death in the cross and resurrection of Christ has
10 inaugurated the definitive glory and victory of God. This triumph will seal the final defeat of the
11 mysterious and evil power of death in God's world.
12 Paul's way of interweaving prophetic and apocalyptic response to suffering and hope marks his
13 distinctive contribution to our topic. This becomes clear when we compare Paul with the responses of
14 the book of Revelation and 1 Peter (see chap 3).
15 To be sure, the book of Revelation also proclaims a dynamic interrelation between the prophetic
16 and apocalyptic responses (the actualisation of hope after suffering), but the *apocalyptic* so dominates
17 this book that the *prophetic* response is muted and is limited to a passive stance of Christians in the
18 world. As a consequence, the book of Revelation is unable to achieve a proper integration between the
19 realms of suffering and hope. Suffering is here not permeated by hope in such a way that hope is able
20 to motivate "hopeful" strategies in and for the world. Although the book of Revelation emphasises that
21 suffering can be endured and hope can be maintained, this emphasis occurs at the price of combining a
22 purely passive suffering with an elitist hope for the remnant of the faithful—a hope which is permeated
23 by a vengeful disposition towards the world of the Roman oppressors. "Hope" for the world is here
24 turned upside down: all that the world can "hope" for is its total destruction at the hour of God's last
25 judgement.
26 First Peter demonstrates as well a dynamic relationship between the prophetic and apocalyptic
27 responses to suffering and hope. Social and political circumstances which cause extensive and severe
28 suffering are nevertheless able to stimulate hope. As we have seen (chapter 3 above), the suffering of
29 the church in the world has here a redemptive character because it signifies the enfleshment of its
30 hope in God's coming triumph over evil and suffering. First Peter, therefore, stimulates hope by linking
31 it with the necessity of suffering for the sake of the gospel of God's coming kingdom.
32 Thus 1 Peter, along with Paul, promotes and fosters—in a much more positive sense than the book
33 of Revelation—the dignity of human life in this world. Indeed, both 1 Peter and Paul establish a mutual
34 relation and interdependence between suffering and hope in their prophetic and apocalyptic
35 responses. In accordance with this, 1 Peter and Paul view suffering in the world not just as a witness
36 *against* the world, as in the book of Revelation, but also as a witness *for the sake of* the world. ...
      ...
37 ... The proper balance between suffering and hope is ... inherent in any authentic Christian
38 interpretation of God's redemptive action in the suffering death and hope-engendering resurrection of
39 Jesus Christ. And in my view the depth of Paul's perspective on suffering and hope is the result of such
40 an "authentic" interpretation.

[Beker, 1994 pp 103-105.]

Answer the questions on the text.

1. In Line 16 there is an example of ellipsis. What word has been omitted, but which is to be understood? ……………..

2. Lines 15-25 outline the Book of Revelation's approach to suffering, as understood by Beker. How does this approach compare or contrast with the ideas of Schillebeeckx and Soelle?

   ....

   ....

3. Do you think Paul, as represented in the above text, would agree or disagree with Schillebeeckx and Soelle?

   ....

   ....

Speaking

What are some specific examples of suffering—of any kind—among people in your town, your region, your country? What is being done to respond to this suffering? What else could be done?

Writing

Describe in about one to two pages one socio-economic or socio-political project in your region or country which is directed at the alleviation of suffering. Begin with a brief description of the suffering and how widely it affects people. Outline the causes of the suffering. Describe the project aimed at responding to the suffering, including who is responsible for planning and carrying out the work involved, and how successful the project is.

UNIT 18 VOCABULARY

Add to this list any more new words that you want to learn.

Nouns	**Verbs**	**Adjectives**	**Other**
robot	motivate	mute	starkly
scandal	permeate	coherent	
omnipotence	provoke	facile	
negation	delude	apathetic	
theodicy	waver	ambivalent	
	pose	soteriological	
	preempt	elitist	
	adhere		
	inaugurate		
……………	……………	……………	……………..
……………	……………..	……………	……………..
……………..	……………..	……………	……………..
……………	……………..	……………	……………..

UNIT 19   GRACE

PART 1

Preparatory Discussion

Grace is one of those words which belong to the specialist theological vocabulary. (Refer to Unit 1.) It is therefore likely to have many connotations. Spend a couple of minutes noting down any other words or ideas which come to mind when you think of *grace*. Now share some of these words with the whole class, explaining why they are connected in your mind with the word *grace*.

Listening

Listen to a short text which describes grace and how we might experience it.
Listen for the answers to these questions:-
Which two adjectives are used to describe grace?   Grace is …………………..
                                                     Grace is …………………..

In this text the writer mentions three ways that people might experience grace.
    What are they?   ………………………   …………………….   …………………….

Check your answers in Appendix A, Listening Text 16.

Reading Comprehension

Read this text and answer the questions.

Charis: A polyvalent symbol

1   Our English word 'grace' translates the Latin *gratia*, which translates the Greek *charis* of the Christian
2   Scriptures. A continuity in meaning is present, but not without complexity. Each word had and has
3   still its own contexts and range of meanings. Hence we **must** view the continuity as one of
4   overlapping areas rather than as a straight line or a convergence point. As for the English word
5   grace, there is little interplay between its secular and theological uses. In a theological context we do
6   not have in mind the poise of a . . . ballet dancer. On rare occasions, where a connection is made, it
7   hardly advances theological understanding or influences theological language. One **might** even claim
8   that the interplay of secular and religious uses of the word "grace" are improper, for the Christian
9   Scriptures hardly ever draw a connection between *charis* and an aesthetic quality, though secular
10 Greek usage **might** allow such a connection. We **must**, however, [leave aside] the problem of
11 whether it is appropriate to extend a theological term by allowing it to assume meanings drawn from
12 secular contexts not envisaged in the biblical context. Suffice it to say that *charis, gratia*, and "grace"
13 have travelled different historical roads, though efforts have been made in the theological enterprise
14 to control the use of the English "grace" (and its foreign language equivalents) by the term *charis* as it
15 is employed in the Christian Scriptures.

[Duffy, 1993, p 29.]

Answer these questions according to information in the text.
1   What is the origin of the theological term "grace"?
2   Which of the following diagrams best represents what the writer is saying about the similarity and/or differences in meaning of *grace, gratia* and *charis*?

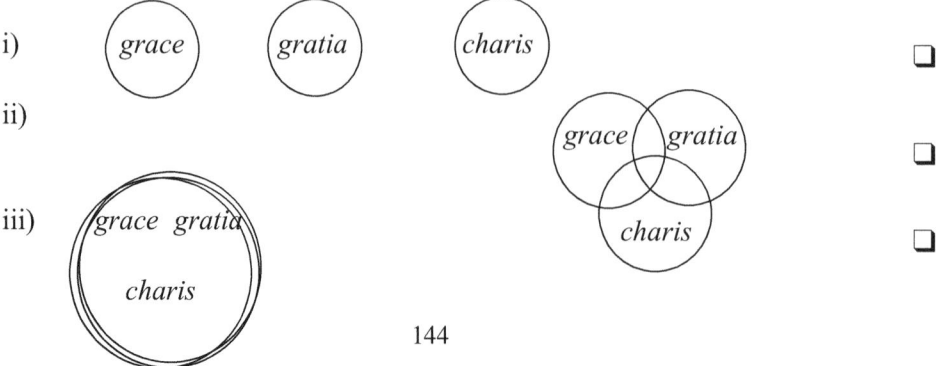

3   The writer states that there is "little interplay" between the theological meaning of *"grace"* and the secular or everyday use of the word. What example does the writer give to explain his view on this? ……………...........................…………………..

4   The writer even says that it may be "improper" to mix or interchange the theological and secular uses of "grace". What reason does the writer give for this opinion?

    ………………………………………………………………………………............…………

5   What does the writer mean by saying that *grace, gratia and charis* "have travelled different historical roads"? Does the clause have an empirical or metaphorical meaning?

    ………………………………………………………………………………............…………

6   Why is the heading for this text *charis* and not *grace* or *gratia*?

    ………………………………………………………………………………............…………

Writing

In no more than two or three short, simple sentences, give some idea of what you mean by *grace* for a person from a non-Christian faith who has never heard of the word.

Revision of Grammar: Modal auxiliary verbs

Modal auxiliary verbs are used to talk about possibility, permission, probability, willingness, ability, offers, requests, obligation, certainty, necessity, advice, future time.
The modal auxiliaries are:- *can, could, may, might, will, would, shall, should, ought to, must, used to, need* and *dare*. (Note: *Need* and *dare* may also function as main verbs.)
Consult a comprehensive grammar book for a detailed explanation of the uses of modal verbs.

Must and *might* each appear twice in the Reading Comprehension text in Part 1 above. Identify which modal function is intended there (ie possibility, ability, permission etc). What is the main verb to which each modal auxiliary is linked?

The following sentences contain examples of some common uses of modal verbs. The function is indicated in brackets.

1   You may borrow the books for a month at a time. (permission)
2   You may develop new insight if you read widely. (possibility)
3   You should study hard if you want to succeed. (advice)
4   She can read the original text in Greek. (ability)
5   The class is finished. You can go now. (permission)
6   I would help you (willingness) *with the translation if I could (help).* (ability)
7   Further study of ancient scrolls should shed more light on Christian origins. (probability)
8   You must return the books to the library after four weeks. (obligation)
9   You ought to study culture if you want to understand how theology has developed. (advice)
10 Theology will develop further as humanity evolves. (future time)
11 If you dare to have a truly open mind, your theological understanding may grow (possibility) *deeper and truer.*
12 The evidence is overwhelming; it must be true. (certainty)

English for Theology

REVISION EXERCISE 19.1

Identify in the following examples the function of each of the modal verbs underlined.

		Function
1	You <u>may want</u> to improve your reading skills for study purposes.	....
2	You <u>must study</u> Greek if you want to advance in scripture studies.	....
3	You <u>may enrol</u> for further studies after completing this course.	....
4	An adequate theology <u>must embrace</u> the whole cosmos.	....
5	We <u>could solve</u> the problem of poverty if we had sufficient resolve.	....
6	Nations <u>ought to collaborate</u> against injustice in the world.	....
7	An increase in just economic relations <u>should promote</u> peace.	....
8	The world <u>should find</u> other energy sources besides fossil fuels.	....
9	This government <u>might not be</u> an improvement on the last one.	....
10	You <u>needn't have</u> perfect pronunciation in order to be understood.	....
11	You <u>mustn't cross</u> the street on a red light.	....

REVISION EXERCISE 19.2

Complete the following sentences with the most suitable modal verb. Use the negative form where necessary. More than one choice of modal verb is possible in most sentences.

1. He hasn't come to class today. He .... be sick.
2. She .... read the book in German, because she is fluent in that language.
3. If you are finding that subject difficult, perhaps you .... spend more time in study.
4. You .... come to class tomorrow—it's a holiday.
5. The teacher has told us that we .... work together with another student if we want to.

Present perfect tense verbs

We use the present perfect tense in these situations:-
- i) to talk about an action or situation which started in the past and which continues into the present;
- ii) to talk about things which have happened during a period of time, or experiences in life up to now; or
- iii) to talk about the effects or results of a past action which continue into the present.

The present perfect tense is formed with *have/has + past participle*

Examples:

- i) *Christians <u>have lived</u> in India for nearly eighteen hundred years.* (They are still living there now.)
- ii) *She <u>has passed</u> all her examinations this year.* (During a period of time up to now.)
  He <u>has visited</u> the caves at Qumran in Israel. (An experience in life up to now.)
- iii) *Theologians <u>have realised</u> that theology must develop to take account of new discoveries in the universe.* (They realised this in the past and the effects of that realisation continue into the present.)

Note: In questions, the order of words is:- *have/has + subject + past participle*

Example: *Have you visited* the caves at Qumran yet?
Has she passed her examinations?
Have they experienced life in other countries?

REVISION EXERCISE 19.3

Complete the following sentences using the present perfect tense of the verb in brackets.

1 It is traditional Christian belief that God .... *(reveal)* God's self in Jesus and in the Holy Spirit.
2 Theologians .... *(develop)* this belief into doctrines about the Trinity and about grace.
3 These students .... *(live)* in the college for three years already.
4 The professor .... *(teach)* systematic theology for twenty years.
5 The findings of archaeologists ....*(contribute)* greatly to scriptural studies.
6 Every believer .... *(hear)* about grace from an early age.
7 In that country the Buddhists and Christians .... (*build up*) a fine tradition of collaboration.
8 They .... *(find)* that solving problems through dialogue is a better way.
9 When we say that God .... *(speak),* we are speaking metaphorically.
10 Many theologians ....*(write)* on the subject of human suffering.

REVISION EXERCISE 19.4

Complete these sentences with the present perfect tense of the verb in brackets. Then turn the statement into a question.

1 Tom .... *(finished)* writing his essay.

   Question: ....?

2 You .... *(read)* that book before.

   Question ....?

3 They .... *(fly)* in aeroplanes before today.

   Question: ....?

PART 2

Preparatory Discussion

In the Listening Text in Part 1, we heard that 'grace functions in a distinctive way in the God-human relationship'. Where, how and when do you experience God relating to you, or in other words, God being *gracious* to you? Reflect for a few moments and share with those around you.

Reading Comprehension

Read this text and answer the questions.

The Spirit of life

1 The simple question: when did you last feel the workings of the Holy Spirit? embarrasses us. The
2 Spirit's "holiness" fills us with religious awe. We are conscious that the Spirit is something apart from
3 secular life, and **sense** our own remoteness from God. Religious experiences, as we all know, are not
4 everyone's line of country.
5 It is a different matter if we are asked: when were you last conscious of *"the spirit of life?"* Then we
6 can answer out of our own everyday experiences and **can talk** about our consolations and
7 encouragements. Then "spirit" is the love of life which delights us, and the energies of the spirit are the
8 living energies which this love of life awakens in us.
9 The Spirit of God is called *the Holy Spirit* because it makes our life here something living, not
10 because it is alien and estranged from life. The Spirit sets this life in the presence of the living God and
11 the great river of eternal love. In order to bring out the unity between the experience of God and the
12 experience of life, I shall be talking in this book about *"the Spirit of life"*, and I should like to invite
13 readers to open themselves for their own experience, and to look at them for what they are.
   ...
14 The operations of God's life-giving and life-affirming Spirit are universal and can be recognised in
15 everything which ministers to life and resists its destruction . . . [Moltmann, 1992, pp x-xi.]

1 Why does this writer say we are embarrassed if asked whether we feel the workings of the Holy Spirit? ....

2 What answer do you think Moltmann would give to the question raised in the Preparatory Discussion, namely, how does a person experience God? Give evidence from the text to support your answer..

3 There appear to be contradictory ideas in this text.
   For example, in Lines 2-3 we read, *"We are conscious that the Spirit is something apart from secular life, and sense our own remoteness from God."*
   In Lines 11-12 we read about the *"unity between the experience of God and the experience of life"*.
   Is the writer contradicting himself? Explain the meaning of these two parts of the text.

4 What are the subjects of these verbs?
   　　　Line 3:　　.........　　*sense*
   　　　Line 6:　　.........　　*can talk*

5 On the basis of the ideas outlined in this text from the preface of Moltmann's book, which mode of discourse would you expect to predominate in the book?
   　　i)　　symbolic-analogical
   　　ii)　　existential
   　　iii)　　metaphysical　　　　　　　　　　..................................
   Give evidence from the text for your answer.

6. Identify an image or metaphor used in this text.　　..................................

PART 3

Preparatory Discussion

Briefly refer back to the Reading text in Part 2 of this Unit. You will notice that the word *"grace"* is not mentioned at all in the text. Why do you think the text has been included in a Unit on *Grace*? Discuss in small groups. Then share with the whole class.

Listening

Read through the text below and try to predict the missing words/phrases. Now listen to the text and write in the missing words.

1 Grace signifies the presence of God in the world and in human beings. When God chooses to be
2 present, the sick are made well, the fallen are raised up, the sinners are made just, the dead come
3 back to life, the oppressed experience freedom, and the despairing feel consolation and warm
4 intimacy.
5 Grace also .... the openness of human beings to God. It is .... of human beings to relate to
6 the ...., to enter upon a .... that wins them .... day by day and rewards them with
7 ....
8 Grace is always .... between a God who gives [Godself] and a human being who does
9 likewise. By its very nature grace is the .... of realms or .... that are closed in upon
10 themselves. Grace is relationship, exodus, ..., ..., ... and dialogue. It is
11 the history of ...., the meeting of ....
12 For this reason grace signifies the .... of heaven and earth, of God and humans, of time and
13 eternity. Grace is something .... , more than history, more than .... It is
14 ever something *more* which happens with .... gratuitousness.   [Boff, 1984, p 3.]

Check your answers in Listening Text 17 in Appendix A.

Reading Comprehension

Read this text and then answer the questions.

Grace

1 Grace has many faces. Within the Christian community, grace is a familiar term for most Christians and a
2 household word for the theologian. For some persons, it is a living reality in their daily lives; for others it
3 is something they get when they pray or go to church; for professional theologians it is a technical term;
4 and for still others it is a term they <u>have heard</u>, but one devoid of significance. Upon further reflection,
5 one realises that the horizons of grace are limitless. Grace encompasses all of Christian experience and
6 theology—the mystery of God, the human community, the event of God incarnate in Jesus Christ, the
7 church, the entire cosmos created and held in being by God.
    .....
8 The study of grace deals with questions of the relationship between God and the world, between God
9 and persons. **It** examines our basic understanding of human existence and the ways in which we
10 relate to the transcendent. Our queries about **these issues** are never-ending, our responses never
11 complete. The study of grace is a perennial one, challenging us in every age to reflect on and speak
12 anew about the experience of God's presence in the world.

13 As history moves forward, new questions emerge, persons have new experiences and new insights that
14 must be brought to bear on religious experience. Further, language changes and the words describing
15 grace a century ago may no longer be appropriate. 'Actual', 'habitual', 'prevenient' and 'sanctifying' are
16 some of the terms once used to explain the different dimensions of grace. While some still use this
17 terminology, others prefer to use language that is more in tune with contemporary experience. This
18 book reaches for broader categories and new language as well as examines the ways of the past that
19 have contributed to our understanding of grace.   [* Reference at end of Unit.]

Now answer these questions:-

1 What does the writer mean by using the metaphor *many faces* to describe *grace?* How many 'faces' does the writer mention and what are they?..

   ....

2 What is the dominant pattern of organisation of ideas in this text (refer to Unit 4)?:-
       i   analysis   ii argument
       iii contrast/comparison   iv description   ....

3 What is the most likely position of this text within the book?
      a From a chapter within the main part of the book
      b From an introductory section
      c From a concluding section.   ....
   Give reasons for your opinion.

4 To what noun does the pronoun *it* refer (Line 9)?   ....

5 What are ***these issues*** (Line 10)?   ....

6 This author claims some particular qualities for her book on grace. What are they?
   ....

Speaking

"... *language changes and the words describing grace a century ago may no longer be appropriate.*" (Lines 14-15 of the above text) Perhaps people of faith in another hundred years, at the beginning of the 22nd century, may think that too about the way we describe grace. What ideas or words might they think are better than ours today? Use your imagination to come up with ideas and talk about them in small groups. Then share with the whole class.

PART 4

Preparatory Discussion

> *If grace is all that we have described . . .* (the same kinds of things outlined in texts in this Unit so far), *then it is ever threatened by what we can call dis-grace . . .*

[Boff, 1984, p 4.]

In small groups brainstorm ideas about the kinds of things which might come under the heading of "dis-grace". Share with the whole class.

Listening

Listen to a short text on 'Grace co-existing with Dis-grace. Listen for as many words and/or phrases as you can which describe obstacles to grace (ie dis-grace). List them here.

....
....
....

Check your answers in Listening Text 18 in Appendix A.

Reading Comprehension

Read this text and then answer the questions.

Grace and disgrace

1 It does not take the most astute powers of observation to note that something is terribly wrong with the
2 human condition. The world is torn by wars, famines, massive global poverty, sufferings which find
3 their origins not just in the fickleness of nature but in a hardness of heart, an inability, an unwillingness
4 to do little more than maintain the status quo. Yet it is this very status quo which gave rise to the
5 problems in the first place. The question which confronts us all is "How do we get out of this mess?
6 Where can we turn for help?"

7 In general one could say that there are two types of solution for this human condition, both sharing a
8 common premise that our present situation is the result of a massive misuse of human freedom. Evil
9 occurs when the human heart freely turns from its proper good and becomes perverted in its goals. Yet
10 the two solutions are vastly different. The first sees human freedom as the basic problem. The
11 solution then is to do away with freedom. Such an abolition of freedom is achieved through a total,
12 unquestioning, automatic obedience to a designated authority. People must simply do what they are
13 told to do, and if they fail they must be expelled from human society. The second solution recognises
14 that freedom is the cause of our problems but it also recognises that when freedom is drawn to evil, it
15 is freedom itself which suffers. The solution to this problem is not less freedom, but more freedom, the
16 freeing of a freedom which has become trapped, enslaved in patterns of unfreedom. While the first
17 solution despairs in the human condition, the second rejoices in what is essential to human dignity, the
18 full flowering of human freedom.
19 Sadly, we have seen too many attempts to implement the first solution. The totalitarian excesses of
20 Stalin and Hitler have given us ample evidence that this solution easily falls into the demonic. Yet there
21 are many who would still see it as viable, if only we could find the right person or group to obey. Some
22 even suggest the Church as the right group, that the solution to the human condition would lie in
23 absolute obedience to the authority of the Church. However, as the teaching of the Second Vatican
24 Council has made clear, not even the Church can undermine the dignity of human freedom. When it
25 attempts to do so, it too finds itself no longer the agent of God but of dark forces which destroy true
26 humanity . . .
27 While many have identified Christianity as offering a solution of the first type, this is a misreading of
28 the Christian tradition. In his letter to the Galatians Paul exclaimed, "For freedom Christ has set you
29 free . . . do not submit yourself to the yoke of slavery once more" (Gal 5:1) At the heart of the Christian
30 faith is a story of one man's remarkable freedom, a freedom which was willing to take on the powers of
31 darkness, of sin and death. It was a freedom which was not diminished by its closeness to the divine,
32 but was empowered in a way which no other human freedom has experienced. Such a freedom could
33 not be contained by the powers of darkness but bursts forth again in the resurrection, bringing the gift
34 of freedom to all who will travel with him.

35 In a sense, this is what this book is about. It is the human story of freedom and its empowering by
36 the mystery which Christians have called grace, and its enfeebling by the sadder mystery of sin. All of
37 us are caught up in these elements of the human condition, not just as individuals living our private
38 lives, but as societies, communities caught up in the historical sweep of grace and disgrace, struggling
39 to find meaning and direction in a world of conflict which still yearns for peace, a world of corruption
40 which still longs for justice, a world of environmental devastation which still aches for a renewed
41 creation.   [Ormerod, 1992, pp 3-4.]

Answer these questions:-

1 The first few lines of this text describe what is wrong with the human condition. What are the "two types of solution" to the problems (Line 7) seen by this author?

   1st solution   ……………………………

   2nd solution …………………………….

2 The text says that these two solutions share a common premise (underlying cause). What is that common premise? ………………………………………………………..

3 According to the text, what is the attitude or feeling towards the human condition generally shared by those who prefer the first of the two solutions? …………………

4 Within the Christian understanding as outlined in this text, what condition is required in order to receive the gift of freedom? ……………………………………….

5 Do these statements from the text reflect the opinion of the author?   YES nor NO?

   • the solution .. is to do away with freedom. (L10-11)   ………………
   • people must be expelled from society if they fail to do as they are
     told to (L12-13)   ……….………
   • the solution to the human condition . . . lie[s] in absolute obedience
     to .. the Church (L22-23).   ………………
   • not even the church can undermine the dignity of human freedom
                                                    (L24)   ………………

6 What is the <u>dominant</u> mode of discourse of this text (see Unit 4)?
      a symbolic
      b empirical
      c metaphysical
      d existential   …………………………….
   Give reasons for your opinion.

Writing

In your own words, write about one page on Grace. Use these questions to structure your writing:

   What is the Christian understanding of grace?
   How does grace usually come to us?
   What can make it difficult for us to receive and accept grace?

• Reference for Part 3 Reading Comprehension [Dreyer, 1990, pp. 3-4.]

UNIT 19 VOCABULARY

Add to this list any more new words that you want to learn.

Nouns	**Verbs**	**Adjectives**	**Other**
continuity	advance	improper	freely
complexity	translate	aesthetic	vastly
convergence	envisage	perennial	simply
interplay	signify	totalitarian	
poise			
awe			
gratuitousness			

UNIT 20 JUSTICE, DEVELOPMENT AND 'GOOD NEWS'

PART 1

Preparatory Discussion

What *is* social justice? What *is* development? What is their connection with the 'good news' of the Christian message? What things in your country or local society stand in the way of social justice and human development? Discuss in small groups and then with the whole class.

Listening

Listen to a text about a woman of Asia who has been doing church work among her people. Listen for the answers to the following questions.

1. What is the woman's full name? ....
2. When and where was she born? ....
3. How old was she when she began theological studies? ....
4. Where did she study theology? ....
5. When did she graduate from her studies? ....
6. Where did she begin her ministry with the people? ....

Check your answers in Listening Text 19 in Appendix A.

Reading Comprehension

Read this text which continues the story begun in the Listening text. Then answer the questions below.

"Let Justice Flow"

1. Tina grew up in a missionary family. Her father Ferdinand spent much of his life in
2. leadership and pastoral roles in the church, ministering to the people, preaching the
3. good news, and leading them in Sunday worship. Even in childhood, Tina was aware
4. of an aspiration to be like her father. In her late teens, that desire developed in her
5. heart in private prayer to find its own expression—to become a servant of God
6. herself in the church's ministry. She began five years of study at a
7. new theological college **so that she could prepare for ministry. While**
8. **she was studying there**, she was powerfully influenced by the words of the prophet
9. Amos:

   ... Let justice flow like a stream and truth like a river that never runs dry. (5:24)

10. Commitment to justice and truth was to become a hallmark of Tina's later ministry.
11. **After she graduated,** she was ordained in her church community. Then she
12. began her ministry among the people. Through years of turmoil and political unrest,
13. she served in various roles and through times of personal crisis she grew to spiritual
14. maturity.
15. **When national development became the catchcry of the 1970s**, Tina, together
16. with many Christians around the world, grew more aware of the intrinsic connection
17. between the "good news" and human advancement. "Development is God's
18. mandate," she would say. If the church's message was to be credible, it must meet
19. people in their human needs now. She believed that salvation was something we
20. should begin experiencing here and now. "We take hold of it by faith, but its
21. outworking is to be seen in human relationships and social responsibility." Thus,
22. Tina's ministry, in pastoral, administrative and leadership positions, became
23. increasingly involved in issues of truth, justice and human development among the
24. people she served. **Because she has worked in this way**, Tina has become
25. internationally known in church circles as a woman who works for the liberation of her
26. people.

[Based on information in Kirk, M 1997.]

Answer these questions on the text:-
1. What seems to have influenced the young Tina in her desire to work for God in the church's ministry?..
2. Tina's later ministry was strongly affected by an experience during her years of theological study. What was this experience?..
3. What were some of the difficulties and problems which Tina had to cope with in her early years of ministry? ....
4. What is Tina's understanding of the meaning of 'salvation'? ....
   ....
5. What is the dominant structure (organisation of ideas) of this text (refer to Unit 4)?
   a narrative   b analysis
   c critique   d argument   ....
6. Can you find examples of the *writer's* opinions in this text?

Speaking

Think of a (or another) well-known person in your country—woman or man—who works for the good of the people. Work in small groups to build up a short story about the person. Try to include information about where the person was born, where he or she went to school or studied, what sort of work is done, where she or he works, and so on. Prepare to give a short talk to the class about the person chosen.

Revision of Grammar: Adverbial Clauses

An adverbial clause, which begins with an adverbial subordinator (eg *when, whenever, where, wherever, anywhere, while, since, before, after, until, so that, in order to, although, even though, as, as if,* etc) is part of a complex sentence, that is, a sentence with more than one clause. An adverbial clause modifies the verb of the main clause (the independent clause) by telling us *when, where, why, what purpose, how, how long, how far*, and by indicating *concession* and *contrast.*

An adverbial clause consists of: subordinator + subject + verb (+ complement)

The Reading Comprehension text above contains a number of adverbial clauses which are highlighted in bold print. Identify which adverbial function each one represents (eg time, purpose, reason, etc)

Note:-
* The adverbial clause may come first in a sentence, or it may come after the main clause. The meaning is the same.
Eg *When we have graduated*, we will share our knowledge with others.
   = We will share our knowledge with others *when we have graduated*.
* In clauses of purpose the conditional or infinitive of the verb is used:-
Eg They travelled *so that they **could learn** more.*
   OR They travelled *in order **to learn** more*.

Examples:
- **Because she has worked for justice**, she has become internationally known. (Adverbial clause of reason)
- **After she was ordained**, she began her ministry among the people. (Adv. of time)
- She began study at a theological college **so that she could prepare for ministry**. (Adv. of purpose)
- **Although there was dangerous political unrest**, she continued her ministry. (Adv. of concession)

- **While some people opposed Tina's aspirations for ministry,** other people supported her. (Adv. of contrast)
- People naturally want to live **where they can make a decent living.** (Adv. of place)
- The villagers fled **as if their lives depended on it.** (Manner)

Note: Consult a comprehensive grammar book for more detail.

REVISION EXERCISE 20.1

Combine the ideas below into one complex sentence, including an adverbial clause as directed, and introduced by a suitable subordinator. Underline the subordinating word/s. In some cases you may need to change the words slightly.

E.g.

a   She travelled to other countries. She wanted to learn about other cultures.
(Purpose)

She travelled to other countries *so that she could learn* about other cultures.
　　　OR   *in order to learn* about other cultures.

b   He returned from study overseas. He has been teaching in the college.   (Time)
Since he returned from study overseas, he has been teaching in the college..

1   The world has become a more dangerous place. We must continue our efforts for justice. (Concession)

　　...

2   She finished the essay. She handed it in to the teacher.   (Time)

　　...

3   He spoke out in defence of the poor. He was attacked by gunmen. (Reason)

　　...

4   They prepared themselves through assiduous study. They wanted to teach well. (Purpose)

　　...

5   The peasants were protesting.   They had no means of living. (Reason)

　　...

6   Refugees want to live in a safe place. They can escape suffering and persecution. (Place)

　　...

7   It was a dangerous journey. The refugees were prepared to attempt it.
(Concession)

　　...

8   Population in Java is very dense. It is relatively sparse in West Papua.
(Contrast)

　　...

9   They ate their food very quickly.   They were starving. (Manner)

　　...

PART 2

Preparatory Discussion

Liberation theology has been mentioned in Unit 17. What *is* liberation theology? What are some of the special characteristics of liberation theology, that is, what makes it different from other theologies? Brainstorm ideas and share them with the whole class.

Listening

Read through the questions below. Now listen to a short text on the ideas of liberation theologian, Gustavo Gutiérrez. Listen for the information to answer these questions or complete the statements.

1   Gutiérrez considers two traditional understandings of theology:-
      i)   theology as ....
      ii)   theology as ....
2   Liberation theology is defined as "..."
3   Marx commented that the point of philosophy was not to interpret the world but to change it. Does Gutiérrez <u>agree or disagree</u> with this opinion? ....
    How do you know?..
4   Liberation theology is critical in three ways:-
      i)   in the .... sense of Kant
      ii)   in regard to the .... aspect of life
      iii)   in regard to the .... aspect of life.
5   This sort of theology seeks out ....

Check your answers in Listening Text 20 in Appendix A.

Reading Comprehension

Read this text and then answer the questions

Liberation Theology

1   The context of liberation theology is the recognition of the suffering of a particular
2   oppressed group. Every word here is important. While frequently intertwined,
3   oppressions differ—poverty, political disenfranchisement, patriarchy . . . etc—so that
4   not all liberation theology is the same. Again, individuals suffer, but liberation theology
5   is generated when community is formed. Coming together in faith, people become
6   conscious of their situation, pray, study the scriptures, and seek actions which will
7   begin to change things for the better . . . As part of these groups, theologians are
8   able to articulate these insights systematically, but it is basically a people's theology
9   coming from the grass roots . . .
10 The context of liberation theology, then, is different from other forms of theology. It is
11 shaped by the experience of oppression, within groups who become conscious of this
12 and come together to work and pray with the sense that the situation *must* change.
13 The reflection of liberation theology is intrinsically intertwined with what is called
14 praxis, or critical action done reflectively . . . Thought and action mutually feed each
15 other. A very practical engagement with forces of oppression, therefore, is intrinsic to
16 the doing of liberation theology. In fact, a convincing case can be made that if one is
17 not engaged in action on behalf of justice, then one simply cannot do liberation
18 theology . . .
19 Liberation theology is highly conscious of the social nature of human existence. An
20 essential aspect of each of us as individuals is our relatedness to one another, along
21 with the structures we have created to embody that relatedness. There simply is no
22 such creature as an individual person outside this network of relationships. Therefore
23 sin, as it affects the human heart and is utterly personal, is also social and shows up
24 in the way we structure ourselves as a community . . . There is a great
25 consciousness of this sociality of human existence in liberation theology . . .
26 Liberation theology makes extensive use of social analysis. Unlike classical and
27 transcendental theology, whose "handmaid" was philosophy, and unlike narrative
28 christology which makes a partner of historical and biblical studies, this approach

29 utilises social, political, economic, and anthropological studies which lay bare the
30 structures of the social situation. With the help of these disciplines, the situation is
31 analysed to identify the forces that are causing the suffering . . .
32 In addition to the goal of classical theology, which was to understand the faith, the
33 goal of liberation theology includes the purpose of changing the unjust situation. It is a
34 practical goal in addition to an intellectual one that is endorsed. Theology here is
35 seeking not just the gift of meaning from newly interpreted dogmas, but also the
36 release of captives . . .
37 The vision which impels liberation theology is that of the reign of God, already
38 arriving. We do not have to wait until the last day for God to wipe all tears away from
39 people's faces and for there to be an end to mourning.

[Johnson,1990, pp 84-87.]

Answer these questions on the text:-
1 Which of these statements most accurately reflects what is said in this text?
    i) *All liberation theologies are the same.*
    ii) *All liberation theologies have the same basis.*   ....
    Explain the reasons for your answer.

2 What is the dominant structure (organisation of ideas) of this text?
    a evaluation   **b** explanation   **c** argument   **d** exhortation   ....

3 List the characteristics of liberation theology mentioned in this text.
   ....

   ....

   ....
   Compare this list with the ideas you shared in the discussion session.

4 How does liberation theology differ from other theologies? ....
5 Can you find an opinion of the *writer* in this text?

Vocabulary Extension - Lexical Transformation
Complete this table as far as you can.

Infinitive	Simple Past	Noun	Adjective/Past Participle
recognise	....	....	....
utilise	....	....	....
analyse	....	....	....
endorse	....	....	....
oppress	....	....	....
liberate	....	....	....
articulate	....	....	....
reflect	....	....	....
structure	....	....	....

Writing

Write one to two pages on a liberation theologian well-known in your part of the world. Include information about the person's origins, and explain what may have led this person to become a liberation theologian. Describe briefly this person's theological writings.

PART 3

Preparatory Discussion

Read through this list and discuss which words/phrases fit in least well with the rest. Be prepared to explain the reasons for your opinion.

economic justice, evangelisation, peace, mysticism, illiteracy, canon law, human development, transubstantiation, chronic disease, infallibility, proclamation of the gospel, covenant.

Reading Comprehension

Read the text and answer the questions.

Renewing, developing and uniting the church

1   It is certainly appropriate that churches who pray "Thy Kingdom come" should realise
2   the importance of renewal, development and unification.
3   When we talk about this matter we cannot avoid asking who is the subject and who
4   is the object of the process. Who does the renewing and who is renewed? ... We
5   ourselves are the church who must be renewed and unified. But who is the subject
6   who performs the renewing, who develops and unites? Clearly it is the Spirit who is
7   concerned for and who brings about the renewal of the church.
        ....
8   It is important to ask about who does what in renewal ... From Luke's account in
9   Acts we learn that the Holy Spirit is given to all Christians. Consequently, every
10 believer must take a part in the task of renewing, developing and unifying the church.
11 But Acts also warns us that we can mistake or even confuse the respective roles of
12 the Holy Spirit and our church officials. According to Acts 8:14-25 Peter and John
13 were sent by the other apostles in Jerusalem to visit Samaria, because they had
14 heard that many people there had been baptised but had not received the Holy Spirit.
15 In Samaria, these two ministers prayed that the Holy Spirit would come on the
16 believers, and then they laid their hands upon them. Their actions fascinated a man
17 called Simon. He offered them a sum of money in return for the authority to lay hands
18 on people without apparently realising the need of faith and prayer and fear of the
19 Lord that lies behind that authority. Here I speak to all office holders in the church. If
20 Simon had succeeded in his ambitious schemes his leadership would have had at
21 least three characteristics: he would have claimed to bestow the Holy Spirit without
22 himself being controlled by the Spirit, his relationship with the Lord would have been
23 lacking ... and he and his money would have been eternally destroyed.
24 We know that God's Spirit works in the world through all Christian believers, for
25 Scripture says: *"The Spirit will teach you all things, and make you remember all that I*
26 *have said to you ..."* (Jn 14-26)
27 The consequence is that in the context of renewal, development and unification,
28 every church member ... is both subject and object. This process must happen in a
29 person before it can happen through a person ... The lesson of Acts is that we are
30 only allowed to direct renewal if we are at the same time objects of the holy Spirit's
31 indwelling and under the Spirit's rule and authority ...
32 When we try to soothe the restlessness of the world before we have experienced the
33 power of the Holy Spirit to deal with the restlessness in our own hearts, do we not
34 stand under the same condemnation (as Simon)? Any development we undertake
35 will not be accompanied by the signs of the Kingdom if we work without the power of
36 the Holy Spirit ...
37 Perhaps the biggest obstacle confronting the whole ecumenical movement is our
38 tendency to think of ourselves as Renewers, Developers and Unifiers before we have
39 allowed ourselves to be renewed, changed and brought into unity with God and each
40 other.

[From an address to the General Assembly of the Council of Churches in Indonesia. July 1980, Tomohon, North Sulawesi, by Pdt A Lumentut, in Appendix, M Kirk, 1997, pp 221-222.]

Answer these questions:-

1. This writer is speaking to church leaders and others who have responsibilities to work for renewal in their churches. What, in the writer's opinion, is the necessary qualification for such work?

   ....

2. In your opinion, which of these statements better reflects the writer's main purpose in Lines 8-26 of the text?
   - i) to offer a reflection on Scripture, ie Acts 8:14-25, John14:26
   - ii) to offer a reflection on aspects of current church communities?

   ....

3. What can you infer of the writer's opinion of some church office holders among those whom she is addressing? What is the evidence in the text?

   ....

4. What, in the writer's opinion, is the main problem in the whole ecumenical movement?

   ....

5. In Lines 32-34, the writer finishes her sentence with a question –"do we not stand under the same condemnation (as Simon)?" What is the writer's purpose in asking this question?

   ....

6. What is the writer's main purpose in this whole text?
   i) explanation ii) exhortation   iii) analysis iv) argument   ....

7. Compare this text with those in Parts 1 and 2 of this Unit. What is the major difference?

   ....

Speaking

What ecumenical activities take place in your country or your local area? Which groups are involved? Who organises activities? What events take place? What progress is being made? What is the effect in the community? Work in small groups and put together information for a short talk to the class.

PART 4

Preparatory Discussion

What do you know about *political theology*? What does it mean? What relationship does it have to liberation theology? Share your knowledge, or make some predictions about what you think it could mean.

Listening

Listen now to a text on 'political theology'. Listen for the answers to these questions.

i) What is political theology? ....
ii) How long has the term been used in theological circles? ....
iii) What theologies does it include? ....
iv) Is it limited to Christian theology? ....

Check your answers in Listening Text 21 in Appendix A.

Reading Comprehension

Read the text and answer the questions.

The social dimension, structures of sin and the church

1 In the past, Christian preaching emphasised personal sin . . . In Chapter 5 of (On
2 Social Concerns) *Sollicitudo Rei Socialis*, John Paul II argues that it is impossible to
3 understand the troubled world of today without the theological category of structural
   sin. ....
4 [there is] the question whether the concept of "structures of sin" applies to
5 the Catholic Church as a social organisation. There is no mention of this in the papal
6 encyclical. The issue is a delicate one. While official Catholic teaching always
7 recognised that the church was a community of sinners, it always denied that the
8 church itself was sinful. Thanks to the special presence of the Holy Spirit, the church
9 as such was believed to remain holy. For this reason, the church as such was not in
10 need of repentance.
11 The recognition of sinful structures throws new light on this important ecclesiological
12 issue. Catholic teaching regarding justice in society and its institutions also applies to
13 the Catholic Church. The church is an organisation ruled by human beings and
14 made up of men and women who must live up to the principles of justice applicable to
15 all social institutions. One could not argue that the church is exempt from these
16 norms because it was set up for a supernatural end, an end that transcended the
17 dimensions of this world. This is not a valid argument because the Catholic Church
18 regards itself as "the sign and sacrament of the unity of the human race" and hence
19 as the earthly community that has overcome the divisions impairing human unity in
20 the world. As a sacramental sign, the church must be the visible embodiment of what
21 it means to be a just society.
22 We saw that in his encyclicals Pope John Paul II greatly emphasised that human
23 beings are meant to be "subjects," responsible agents, and that society and its
24 institutions are just only if those in authority respect the "subjectivity" of their
25 members. The pope has never applied this principle to the church. And yet there is
26 no reason why this principle should not apply to the church . . . The papal-collegial
27 structure [of the church] can give rise to autocratic rule and bureaucratic
28 centralisation, but the same structure could also be open to dialogue, consultation,
29 and cooperation, and thus generate a truly participatory ecclesiastical organisation.
30 *Sollicitudo Rei Socialis* draws attention to bureaucratic oppression as a sinful
31 structure diminishing the subjectivity of the people. Addressing himself to the [former]
32 East European situation, the pope laments the suppression of the right of economic
33 initiative and the rigid control of all economic activity by the state bureaucracy:
34   Experience shows us that the denial of this right . . . diminishes, or in practice absolutely
35   destroys, the spirit of initiative, that is to say the subjectivity of the citizens . . . In the place of

```
36  creative initiative there appears passivity, dependence, and submission to the bureaucratic
37  apparatus which, as the only "ordering" and "decision-making" body . . . puts everyone in a
38  position of absolute dependence, which is similar to the traditional dependence of the
39  proletariat in capitalism. This provokes a sense of frustration or desperation and
40  predisposes people to opt out of national life, impelling many to emigrate and also
41  favouring forms of "psychological" emigration. [No 15]

42  A little further on, the encyclical defines a system that destroys the subjectivity of
43  society as "totalitarian": "In this situation the individual and the people become
44  'objects', in spite of all verbal assurances and declarations to the contrary."
45  It is impossible to avoid the question to what extent the religious, pastoral, and
46  theological initiatives of the Catholic people are diminished and controlled by a
47  bureaucratic apparatus that regards itself as the only ordering and decision-making
48  body in the church, and to what extent the passivity, dependence, and submission
49  consequent upon this provokes a sense of frustration or desperation, and
50  predisposes many Catholics to opt out of ecclesiastical life, impelling them to leave
51  altogether or turn to psychological withdrawal, despite all verbal assurances and
52  declarations to the contrary offered by the bureaucratic apparatus.
53  There has emerged in the Catholic Church a sense that the recent social teaching,
54  with its ethical critique of institutional life and the denunciation of "structural sin,"
55  questions and challenges the church's own self-organisation. An autocratic exercise
56  of papal or episcopal authority introduces a contradiction in the church's life between
57  its official social teaching and its actual practice. The 1971 Synod of Bishops was very
58  conscious of this. If the church wants to summon society to social justice, the church
59  must appear just itself. The synod called upon the church to make a critical analysis
60  of its own institutional life.
```
[Baum, 1989, pp 110, 112, 123-125.]

What is the writer's main purpose in this text?
        i)   analysis   ii) contrast
        iii)   argument   iv) description   ....

2   In Lines 4-5, the writer asks the question whether "structures of sin" apply to the Catholic Church as a social organisation or not. The writer then explains reasons for a "no" answer before going on to explain reasons for a "yes" answer.
Summarise in point form the reasons given under these two headings:-

Reasons for "no" answer	Reasons for "yes" answer
....	....
....	....
....	....

3   What stance does the writer himself take on this question? Give evidence from the text to support your opinion.

....

4   Find an example of metaphorical or symbolic words/phrases in this text.

....

Writing

In your own words, and in not more than a page, write a brief account of what the writer is saying in this text. Begin with a statement of the writer's thesis. Describe his supporting points, other important information and his conclusion.

UNIT 20 VOCABULARY

Add to this list any more new words that you want to learn.

Nouns	Verbs	Adjectives	Other
aspiration	graduate	intrinsic	mutually
hallmark	ordain	anthropological	consequently
turmoil	oppress	respective	
catchcry	intertwine	structural	
mandate	utilise	ecclesiological	
disenfranchisement	endorse	autocratic	
patriarchy	fascinate	bureaucratic	
subjectivity	opt		
……………	……………	……………	…………….
……………	……………	……………	…………….

UNIT 21   UNDERSTANDING SCRIPTURE

PART 1

Preparatory Discussion

To be able to understand the gospels today, a scholar must first of all be able to read. What are some other areas of knowledge and skill necessary to the scripture scholar? What areas of academic enquiry have been particularly useful to scripture scholars in the past century? Share your ideas with the whole class.

Listening

Listen to a text on *'Form Criticism'*. Complete the blank spaces according to what you hear.

```
1    After World War I an important new development in New Testament scholarship took
2    place in Germany with the publication of Martin Dibelius' From Tradition to Gospel
3    (1919), KL Schmidt's The Framework of the Story of Jesus (1919) and Rudolf
4    Bultmann's The History of the Synoptic Tradition (1921). The method they employed
5    came to be known as "form criticism". Form criticism ………………… parts of the
6    …………………….. into literary forms or ……………… (in much the same way
7    that we might classify …………………………………………… according to their
8    literary forms: editorial, reports, letters to the editor, advertisements, etc). It is
9    ………………… which goes behind the ………………………….. (a parable
10   or …………………, for example) to …………………………… back
11   to the period of …………………………… about Jesus.
12   Having …………………… and classified the ……………………….,
13   the form critic asks how ……………………………………….was passed on or
14   modified in oral  and written …………………….. until it reached its final form.  What
15   was the function of the story in the ……………………………………….? He/she
16   is not trying to get to the earliest version but is looking at the Sitz im Leben  – …….
17   ………………… – in which the story or saying was told, and which ………….
18   **the telling** and the order of the story. For the form critic holds that the ………………
19   ………………, the ……………………………… of the early
20   Christian community had a direct bearing on the ………………………………
21   and **the……………… fashioning** of the written material.
                                              [Goosen  & Tomlinson, M, 1994, p 53.]
```

Check your completed text with Listening Text 22 in Appendix A.

Reading Comprehension

Read the text and answer the questions.

..................?..................

```
1    The word 'gospel' has a long history. The equivalent Greek word euangelion (good
2    news) acquired religious significance in the Roman Empire in the cult of the Emperor,
3    in which public appearances of the Emperor, his accession to the throne, and his
4    decrees were known as good news or gospels. It has been suggested that the New
5    Testament usage derives partly from the "good news" of freedom from captivity which
6    Isaiah proclaimed to the Israelites emerging from the Babylonian Exile (Spivey,
7    1982:61.)  In the New Testament, "gospel" also signifies the good news of salvation
8    (eg Mt 11:5, Mk 1:1). Early usage of "euangelion" in the Christian community
9    referred to the oral nature of the news;  however, with Mark, Matthew, Luke and John,
10   the Gospel became a specific literary category.
11   Until the [nineteenth] century, the Gospels were generally regarded as four
12   biographical accounts of the life of Jesus, written in much the same way as any
13   modern biography. So it could be imagined that one day Mark, for example, decided
```

14 that it was time that he wrote a biography of Jesus for the Christian community. He
15 looked around for any letters, reports or other documents. But there were none;
16 Jesus wasn't a letter-writer, and no enterprising journalist was there to interview him,
17 nor did anyone, apparently, keep any records. So Mark contacted as many
18 eyewitnesses of the events as he could (including Peter, who knew Jesus better than
19 most people), and made notes of their impressions. Eventually, he put it all together
20 in chronological order and wrote a small book: "Jesus Christ. A biography by John
21 Mark." This popular impression of the Gospels as biography presupposed a direct link
22 between the events as they were witnessed, and the first written accounts of them.
23 However, biblical scholarship in the last hundred years or so has radically challenged
24 this view.
25 The roots of modern biblical scholarship can perhaps best be located in the
26 eighteenth century Enlightenment, with the development of new scientific and
27 philosophical systems, and, early in the nineteenth century, new views on the nature
28 and methods of historical enquiry . . . [These came] to be applied to the Bible.*

[Goosen, & Tomlinson, 1994, pp 45-46.]

*Note: This excerpt is continued in the text in Unit 10 on page 58.

Answer the questions:-
1   Which of the following would be the most appropriate heading for this text?
    i)   Understanding the linguistic origins of 'gospel'
    ii)   Understanding the nature and meaning of gospels
    iii)   Modern scholarship challenges the understanding of gospels

    ....

    Support your opinion with evidence from the text.

2   Summarise three meanings of gospel referred to in the text.
    i)   ……………………………………………………..
    ii) ……………………………………………………..
    iii) ……………………………………………………..

3   Are these statements TRUE or FALSE according to the text?
                                                                                T/F?
    i)   The gospels were originally a verbal telling of news.   ....

    ii)   People who actually witnessed the events of Jesus' life
            were able to write a first-hand account of them.   ....

    iii)   The gospels are largely life stories of Jesus.   ....

Revision of Grammar: Gerunds and gerund phrases

A gerund has the same form as a present participle, that is *verb + ing*, but it always functions as a noun. Gerunds may also occur within a phrase. Note the examples of gerunds in bold print in the Listening text above: ***the telling** (of the story)*; ***the …… fashioning** (of the written material)*.

A gerund or gerund phrase functions in the same way as a noun or noun phrase, for example, as the subject or the object of the main verb, or as the object of a preposition or adjective. Study the following examples of some uses of gerunds or gerund phrases.

<u>As subjects</u>
Reading *delights many people.*
Suffering *often causes profound changes in people.*

English for Theology

Object of a verb.
*You should practise **speaking** daily.*
*He doesn't like **eating** vegetables.*

Object of preposition.
*He was advised to think about **enrolling.***
*It was raining but they insisted on **playing**.*

Object of adjective
*The refugees were happy **reaching** land.*
*The teachers were busy **preparing** the examinations.*

For a more detailed account of gerunds and gerund phrases, consult a comprehensive grammar book.

REVISION EXERCISE 21.1

Complete the following sentences with a gerund (sometimes this will form a gerund phrase). Choose the most suitable verb from the list below. Indicate whether the gerund (or gerund phrase) is subject, object, or object of a preposition or adjective. The first two sentences are completed as examples.

understand	*achieve*	*ask*	*translate*	*examine*	*watch*
learn	*fail*	*keep*	*revise*	*enrol*	

1 For the scholar of ancient texts, *translating* is an essential skill. (*subject*)

2 The student was concerned about *failing*. (*object of preposition*)

3 …………………… continues for the whole of life, if we are open to the possibilities. (………………………)

4 Many people like ……………………… TV (……………………….)

5 i………………….. competency includes ii…………………….. new words.
(i ……………………..)   (ii ……………………………)

6 Prolonged study is likely to bring increased ………………….. (……………..)

7 ………………… the peace challenges everybody's goodwill. (……………..)

8 The archaeologists were busy ……………….the ancient scrolls. (…………….)

9 The poor of the world are tired of ……………… for bread. (………………..)

10 The teacher said she should think about ……………………. (…………………)

REVISION EXERCISE 21.2

Identify some gerunds or gerund phrases in the books you are reading at present.
Write here the sentences in which they occur and say whether the gerunds are subject or object and so on as in the previous exercise.

………………………………………………………………………………………………………
………………………………………………………………………………………………………
………………………………………………………………………………………………………
………………………………………………………………………………………………………
………………………………………………………………………………………………………

PART 2

Preparatory Discussion

Have you ever, together with friends or colleagues, watched a TV documentary or film, or witnessed an accident or some public event? Have you and your friends ever tried reporting what you saw to others at a later time? Have you noticed variations in the story as told by different people? (You might like to try setting up a simple experiment along these lines.) Discuss with members of the class why these variations in reporting the event might occur. How can this sort of experience from everyday life enlighten our understanding of the gospels? Share your ideas with others in the class.

Listening

In Part 1 you listened to a text about *Form Criticism*. Listen now to the description of another method of scriptural enquiry. Make brief notes about the main ideas as you listen. Do not try to write down every word. Work in groups of three or four students and share your notes to reconstruct your version of the text you have heard. Compare your text with that of other groups in the class. Finally check your texts against Listening Text 23 in Appendix A.

Reading Comprehension

Read the text and answer the questions.

Background to the Gospel of Mark

1 The Gospel of Mark is anonymous. We have no certain knowledge about the text, the
2   author, the time or place of writing, or the intended audience, except what we can
3 infer from the text itself. According to one tradition, the Gospel was associated with
4 John Mark (Acts 12:12, 25; 15:37, 39), who may have met Peter and who travelled
5 with Paul. According to another, Mark translated and wrote down the teachings of
6 Peter in Rome. These are suppositions, however, not reliable traditions.
7 The author of the Gospel was probably a "Mark" otherwise unknown to us. It was a
8 common name, but no Mark was either a disciple of Jesus or an important missionary
9 after Easter. The identification with John Mark and the association with Peter were
10 probably second-century attempts to give the Gospel apostolic authority. It is not
11 clear whether or not the author was a Jew; his native language was probably Greek.
12 On the basis of its content, the Gospel appears to have been composed about forty
13 years after Jesus' death and resurrection at the end of the Roman-Jewish war,
14 around 70 CE. Its place of origin was probably somewhere in the eastern
15 Mediterranean directly affected by the war, perhaps Galilee. The intended audience
16 probably included both Jews and Gentiles: in some instances common Jewish
17 customs are explained; in others, knowledge about the Jewish tradition seems to be
18 assumed. The narrative is in simple Greek, with an oral storytelling style, which
19 suggests that the Gospel was neither written by nor intended for the small literate elite
20 of the Roman Empire. It is composed from a peasant perspective for a peasant
21 audience.
22 The Gospel of Mark, our first written Gospel, was composed in a world in which
23 only about 10 percent of the population was able to read or write. For the rest,
24 however, illiteracy was neither an economic nor a social handicap. For most, all
25 knowledge, learning, teaching, memory, entertainment, and business were oral.
26 Jesus was an oral teacher; he left no writings. After Easter, Christianity was an oral
27 phenomenon, spreading by word of mouth. This was the normal way for any popular
28 philosophical or religious movement to spread.

[Dewey, 1994, pp 471-472.]

Answer these questions:-
Indicate whether the following statements are True, Probably True, Possibly True/Possibly not true, or False according to information in the text. Record your answer by placing a tick in the appropriate column. The first two are completed as examples.

		TRUE	PROBABLY TRUE	POSSIBLY TRUE /POSSIBLY NOT	FALSE
1	The Gospel of Mark is anonymous.	✔			
2	Mark wrote down Peter's teaching in Rome.			✔	
3	Mark was an important missionary after Easter.				
4	Linking the gospel with Mark and Peter was a way for later Christians to give authority to it.				
5	The author of this gospel was a Jew.				
6	The author was a Greek-speaking person.				
7	Illiteracy was a social handicap for people in Jesus' time.				
8	The gospel narrative is written in Greek.				
9	The gospel was first written for people who could read it.				

Writing

Imagine you are describing in a letter some aspects of your study to a friend who has not studied theology. Write a simple explanation, in your own words, of the two approaches to studying the gospels mentioned in the Listening texts in Parts 1 and 2 of this unit, namely, *form criticism* and *redaction criticism*.

PART 3

Preparatory Discussion

Recall the story of Moses and the 'burning bush' in Exodus 3:1-6. The story says that Moses was puzzled by a bush on fire which was not being burnt up. Do you think that this is an empirical (factual) description of what Moses 'saw'? Does it matter one way or the other?

What do you think the writer of that story was trying to tell the people who first heard it in ancient times? How might a writer today describe the sort of experience which Moses seems to have had on that occasion? Share your ideas with the class. (For later discussion, find a modern day description of someone's experience of being 'called' by God.)

Reading Comprehension

Read the text and answer the questions.

Critical scholarship and the Bible

1. Let the interpreter therefore use every care, and take advantage of every indication
2. provided by the most recent research, in an endeavour to discern the distinctive
3. genius of the sacred writer, his condition of life, the age in which he lived, the written
4. or oral sources he may have used, and the literary forms he employed. He will thus
5. be able better to discover who the sacred writer was and what he meant by what he
6. wrote. For it is evident that the chief law of interpretation is that which enables us to
7. discover and determine what the writer meant to say . . .
8. But frequently the literal sense is not so obvious in the words and writings of ancient
9. oriental authors as it is with the writers of today. For what they intended to signify by
10. their words is not determined only by the laws of grammar or philology, nor merely by
11. the context; it is absolutely necessary for the interpreter to go back in spirit to those
12. remote centuries of the East, and make proper use of the aids afforded by history,
13. archaeology, ethnology, and other sciences, in order to discover what literary forms
14. the writers of that early age intended to use, and did in fact employ. For to express
15. what they had in mind the ancients of the East did not always use the same forms
16. and expressions as we use today; they used those which were current among the
17. people of their own time and place; and what these were the exegete cannot
18. determine a priori, but only from a careful study of ancient oriental literature ...
19. At the same time, no one who has a just conception of biblical inspiration will be
20. surprised to find that the sacred writers, like the other ancients, employ certain arts of
21. exposition and narrative, certain idioms especially characteristic of the Semitic
22. languages, and certain hyperbolical and even paradoxical expressions designed for
23. the sake of emphasis. "In the divine Scripture," observes St Thomas, with
24. characteristic shrewdness, "divine things are conveyed to us in the manner to which
25. men [sic] are accustomed."

[Pius XII, 1943, No 38, 39.]

1. What is the main purpose of this text?
   i explanation   ii analysis   iii exhortation   iv critique   ……………..
   What is the evidence in the text?
2. Summarise the most important ideas in each paragraph of this text.

Speaking

If you have found a description of someone's experience of being 'called' by God, share it with others in the class. Is the experience described as a one-off or single event, a gradual experience over time, or a combination of both? Consider some of the New Testament characters and the descriptions of their 'call' by Jesus. Do you think the descriptions are literal accounts of what happened? Discuss with others in the class.

PART 4

Preparatory Discussion

Prepare two columns in your note book. i) Take about sixty seconds to write in the first column as many ideas as you can that come into your mind when you hear the noun *home*.
ii) Now take the same time to write in the second column the ideas that come to your mind in connection with the noun *dog*.
Which column was easier to fill? Why? Talk about the differences between univocal and connotative words (refer to Unit 1 or the Glossary).

Reading Comprehension

Read the text and answer the questions.

What does it mean to call Scripture the Word of God?

1 Language, as contemporary linguistic and philosophical studies **attest**, is a much
2 more complex phenomenon than is often thought. Words, which might be naively
3 assumed to be a system of labels **designating** in relatively **unambiguous** fashion
4 the concrete realities of everyday experience, are in fact often used in nonunivocal
5 and nonliteral ways. This means that in order to understand language one must
6 recognise the kind of language being used and understand how such language
7 functions.
8 *The linguistic character of "word of God": Metaphor*. The term *word of God* is not
9 univocal or literal when it is used to speak of the Bible. First, *word of God* designates
10 not only, or even primarily, Scripture. It denotes first of all the second "person" of the
11 Trinity and that person made flesh in Jesus of Nazareth. From this it is immediately
12 apparent that *word of God* is not a literal designation, for Jesus is obviously not a unit
13 of language in bodily form but a human being. Second, theological reflection
14 supports the observation that word of God is not a literal designation for the Bible.
15 God is spirit and therefore does not have the physical apparatus of speech, does not
16 think discursively, and is not limited in self-communication by the vocabulary,
17 grammar, and syntax of language. In short, nothing about language, which is a
18 human phenomenon, is literally **pertinent** to divine self-disclosure.
19 The foregoing leads to the realisation that the term *word of God*, whether applied to
20 Jesus or to the Bible, is linguistically a metaphor. Sallie McFague, with other modern
21 theorists of language, insists that genuine metaphor is not primarily a rhetorical
22 decoration or an abbreviated comparison. It is a **proposition** (explicit or implied)
23 constituted by an irresolvable tension between what it affirms (which is somehow
24 true) and what it necessarily denies (namely, the literal truth of the assertion) . . .
25 The metaphor is, at the literal level, **absurd**, but obviously it intends serious meaning.
26 It forces the mind to reach toward meaning that exceeds or escapes effective literal
27 expression.
28 Effectively used, metaphor is one of the most powerful forms of human language.
29 It carries more meaning and generates deeper and more holistic response than literal
30 language because it appeals not only to the mind but also to the imagination.
31 Because true metaphor is not a stand-in for literal language but the only way to
32 express some complexes of meaning that defy adequate literal expression, effective
33 metaphors cannot be translated into univocal, literal language.
34 The linguistic tension that constitutes metaphor destabilises the literalistic mind.
35 This is its purpose and power. But because that destabilisation is uncomfortable,
36 keeping the mind "in motion" when it would like to "land" in literalistic concreteness,
37 there is an inveterate temptation when confronted with metaphor to literalise it. A
38 powerful example of how the literalisation of a metaphor can wreak intellectual and
39 affective havoc in the religious imagination is the metaphorical proposition "God is our
40 Father". Obviously, God is not literally a father because God is not a male sexual
41 being who copulates with a female sexual being to beget offspring. God does not
42 literally beget, generate, or father. But so imaginatively entrenched is the
43 literalisation of *father*, a necessarily masculine metaphor for God, that most

44 Christians are genuinely shocked by the use of feminine metaphors, such as *mother*,
45 for God. The idolatrous result of this literalisation can be traced through church
46 history in the patriarchalisation of Christian faith.

[Schneiders, 1993, pp 37-39.]

Answer these questions on the text.

1 Word matching:- Without using a dictionary if possible, match each of the words in bold print in the text with one of similar meaning from this list:-

relevant ……………………………   *indicating*………………………
silly   ……………………………   *witness* ………………………
clear   ……………………………   *statement* ………………………

2 What is the writer's main purpose in this text?   Choose one of the following.

   i)   description   ii) argument
   iii) analysis   iv) exhortation   ………………

   Point to evidence in the text to support your opinion.

3 Say whether these statements are TRUE or FALSE according to the text.
   Refer to evidence in the text to support your answer.   **T/F?**

   i   Words are a system of labels designating in relatively
        unambiguous fashion the concrete realities of everyday
        experience.   ………

   ii   The term *word of God* refers to Jesus.   ………

   iii The medium of language is the clearest way for God to
        self-disclose (reveal) to humans.   ………

   iv   The writer thinks that using metaphor these days in
        theological text is absurd.   ………

   v   It is better to translate metaphors into literal language. ………

Writing

Write one to two pages on "Understanding the Gospels". Include paragraphs on what a gospel is, how the gospels came to be written and some of the knowledge which a scripture scholar needs these days to understand what the gospel writer intended to say.

UNIT 21   VOCABULARY

Add to this list any new words that you want to learn.

Nouns	Verbs	Adjectives	Other
accession	modify	biographical	eventually
impression	derive	anonymous	discursively
supposition	presuppose	distinctive	
phenomenon	infer	hyperbolical	
philology	wreak	pertinent	
ethnology		holistic	
havoc		inveterate	

UNIT 22 ECOLOGICAL THEOLOGY

PART 1

Preparatory Discussion

"The Philippines is now at a critical point in its history . . . a . . . deep-seated crisis . . . we believe, lies at the root of many of our economic and political problems. To put it simply: our country is in peril. All the living systems on land and in the seas around us are being ruthlessly exploited. The damage to date is extensive and, sad to say, it is often irreversible."

[From A pastoral letter on ecology, Catholic bishops of the Philippines, 1988.]

Is there ecological damage in the country or region where you live?

Work in small groups to make a list of examples of damage to the environment in the country or region where you live. Share your lists with the whole class.

Listening

Listen to a short text on ecological damage in the Philippines. What *damage* has been caused and what *consequences* or *results* are mentioned in the text? As far as possible, complete the table below *according to what you hear*.

Damage done to the environment	Consequences/results
……………………………...	………………………………
……………………………..	………………………………
……………………………..	………………………………

Check your answers in Listening Text 24 in Appendix A.

Reading Comprehension

Read the text and answer the questions below. Note that this text follows on from the Listening text you have just heard.

"What is happening to Our Beautiful Land?"

1   As we reflect on what is happening in the light of the Gospel we are convinced that
2   this assault on creation is sinful and contrary to the teachings of our faith . . .
3   We will not be successful in our efforts to develop a new attitude towards the natural
4   world **unless we are sustained and nourished by a new vision**. This vision must
5   blossom forth from our understanding of the world as God intends it to be . . .
6   This vision is also grounded in our Faith. The Bible tells us that God created this
7   beautiful and fruitful world for all [God's] creatures to live in (Gen 1:1-2:40) and that
8   [God] has given us the task of being stewards of . . . creation (Gen 2:19-20).
9   The relationship which links God, human beings and all the community of the living
10 together is emphasised in the covenant which God made with Noah after the flood.
11 The rainbow which we still see in the sky is a constant reminder of this bond and
12 challenge (Gen 9:12). This covenant recognises the very close bonds which bind
13 living forms together in what are called ecosystems. The implications of this
14 covenant for us today are clear. As people of the covenant we are called to protect
15 endangered ecosystems, like our forests, mangroves and coral reefs and to establish
16 just human communities in our land. More and more we must recognise that the
17 commitment to work for justice and to preserve the integrity of creation are two
18 inseparable dimensions of our Christian vocation to work for the coming of the
19 kingdom of God in our times.
20 As Christians we also draw our vision from Christ. We have much to learn from the
21 attitude of respect which Jesus displayed towards the natural world . . . The
22 destruction of any part of creation, especially the extinction of species, defaces the
23 image of Christ which is etched in creation.

[From A Pastoral letter on ecology, Catholic bishops of the Philippines, "What is Happening to Our Beautiful Land?" in McDonagh, 1990, p 213.]

Answer these questions on the text:-

1   Line 2 refers to 'this assault on creation'. What does 'this assault' refer to?

....

2   What condition is necessary if there is to be success in developing a new attitude towards the environment?

....

3   What is 'this covenant' (Lines 12, 13-14)?

....

4   What is the dominant pattern of organisation of ideas in this text?
    a description   b analysis   c exhortation   d critique

                  ....

5   Find some examples of metaphorical or symbolic language in the text and write them here:-

      ....

      ....

6   Which particular 'endangered ecosystems' are mentioned in the text?

      ....

Revision of Grammar: Conditional clauses

Since theology, and especially developing theology, is by its nature largely speculative and exploratory, it makes much use of various kinds of conditional clauses.
For a detailed study of the ways of expressing condition in English, consult a comprehensive grammar book.
For our purposes here, we revise two main kinds of conditional clause introduced by *if*: open conditions and hypothetical conditions.

Open conditions

An open condition is one where the situation being considered may or may not be the actual state of affairs.
In the main clause of a sentence with an open condition, we often use the future tense of the verb.

Example: ***If*** *tankers spill oil on coral reefs, they **will cause** great damage.*
          If *dialogue is undertaken, social harmony **will improve**.*

A negative open condition is introduced by *'unless'*:

     Unless *we are sustained by a new vision, we **will not be successful** in our efforts. (ie If we are not sustained . . .)*

Unit 22 Ecological Theology

Note that the *'if'* or *'unless'* clause may be placed after the main clause. In this case there is no comma between clauses.
  Eg *Tankers will cause great damage if they spill oil on coral reefs.*

We may also use the present tense in the main clause if this is appropriate for the meaning intended.
Example*:* ***If** the earth is polluted and damaged, poor people **suffer** as well as plants and animals.*

  ***If** we accept the universal significance of Christianity, we **are faced** with a paradox.**

  ***If** we emphasise understanding, does theology **become** simply theoretical study?*

Hypothetical conditions

i) When we are talking about unreal or hypothetical conditions in the present, we use the past tense in the *'if'* clause and the modal auxiliary *'would'* in the main clause.
Example:
  ***If** all cars **were banned** tomorrow, atmospheric pollution **would** still **continue** for some years.*

  ***If** people **understood** the danger to health, they **would not smoke** tobacco.*

  ***If** I **were** you, I **would spend** an hour every day on practice.*

(In this type of conditional clause, we use the subjunctive form *were* instead of simple past *was*.)

ii) When we are talking about unreal conditions in past time, we use the past perfect tense in the *'if'* clause and the modal *'would'* + present perfect in the main clause.
Example:
  If** the Three Gorges Dam project in China **had not been approved**, millions of peasants **would not have been displaced.

  ***If** the Qumran scrolls **had not been found**, important information **would not have been** available to biblical scholars.*

iii) When we are talking about hypothetical or tentative conditions referring to future time, we use *were to + the infinitive* or *should + the infinitive* in the *'if'* clause and the modal auxiliary *'would'* in the main clause.

Example:
  If** I **were to write down** everything that Jesus did, the whole world **would not hold** all the books that **would have to be written (Jn 21-25).

  ***If** archaeologists **should find** the body of Jesus tomorrow, **would** that **change** the essence of your faith?*

Note: These conditional clauses may also be expressed this way:

  ***Were** I **to write down** . . .*
  ***Should** archaeologists **find** . . .*

After consulting a comprehensive grammar to review several other ways of expressing condition, build up a summary of examples in the space below as you encounter the various forms in your reading.

Summary of some further Conditional Expressions

Eg   ***On condition that*** *you take extra classes in Hebrew, you may enrol now.*
     In case *you cannot understand, have a dictionary with you.*

………………………………………   ………………………………………….

………………………………………   ………………………………………….

………………………………………   ………………………………………….

………………………………………   ………………………………………….

REVISION EXERCISE 22.1

Complete the following conditional sentences using the appropriate tense of the verb in brackets.

1   If more people truly followed the precepts of their religions, justice and peace……………. (*is*) more widespread around the world.

2   If we knew the answer to the question (of who the evangelist really was), we …………better ………………..(*understand*) what the evangelist has written.

3   If you consult several commentaries, you …………………….(*find*) a variety of different opinions on the issue.

4   They ………………………..……… (*take*) more precautions if they had been warned about the coming storm.

5   If evolutionary theory is a correct interpretation of origins, then many questions about traditional theology ………………………..(*follow*).

6   Many lives would be saved if they ……………… (*discover*) a cure for AIDS.

7   If you were to ask for help, you ………………… (*receive*) it.

8   I ………………………(*not ask*) her to help if I had known that she was sick.

9   The international community ………….. (*help*) if a tidal wave should cause damage.

10 If they ……………………..(*know*) that the boat would sink, they would not have travelled on it.

* Note: If you want to read more about this 'paradox', refer to Schillebeeckx, E, 1979, *Jesus An Experiment in Christology*, Collins, London, p 575.

PART 2

Preparatory Discussion

In the discussion in Part 1 you made lists of damage to the environment in the country or region where you live.

What steps are being taken to repair or stop the damage? What are the obstacles in your region – social, political, religious – which make that difficult? Work in small groups and then with the whole class.

Reading Comprehension

Read the text and answer the questions

The World Council of Churches – A new liberating theology

1 The WCC points out that throughout the world communities of people, land, animals,
2 and plants have been neglected and destroyed . . .
3 The WCC calls for a new theology that liberates life and moves beyond arrogant
4 human-centred views. It searches for a theology that will promote respect for all
5 communities of life in their diversity and advance connectedness among all things and
6 with God. This should be a "listening" theology, which hears the voices of the
7 oppressed. It should seek to liberate those who are oppressed and also the
8 privileged, who often live in complacent isolation. The WCC calls for a theology of
9 peace, justice, and respect for the integrity of creation . . .
10 The authors (of the Report*) turn to biblical witness in attempting to develop such a
11 theology. They admit that Christians have often been shaped by interpretations of
12 the creation story that have been human-centred, occupied with dominion, and
13 concerned about salvation from a sinful and fallen world. They admit that too often
14 this perspective has been used for the exploitation and destruction of the earth.
15 The WCC points out the need for a new reading of the creation story, one that sees
16 a cosmic world that is good and that engenders a loving care of the world. It calls for
17 a rediscovery of the Noahic covenant, which God made with all things. Here all things
18 in creation have intrinsic value, are interconnected, and are included in God's
19 salvation . . .
20 The World Council of Churches signals some innovative directions in theology. New
21 readings of scripture have revealed an interrelatedness of all creatures to each other
22 and with their Creator . . . In addition, alternate images of God are being retrieved
23 that are more appropriate to ecology than some past images. For example, the more
24 dominative images of lord and king are being replaced with the images of potter and
25 mother. The image of *church* has also been broadened to include all things, and
26 there is a renewed awareness that everything "lives and moves and has its very
27 being in God" (Acts 17:28).

[Hill, 1998, p 180, 181-2.]
*The Report referred to is "Liberating Life: A Report to the World Council of Churches".

Answer these questions on the text.

1 Lines 4-5 refer to "all communities of life". What does this mean?

   ....

2 According to the World Council of Churches, there is "need for a new reading of the creation story" (Line 15).
   i) Explain what is meant by "a new reading". ……………………………..

   ii) Why does the WCC think there is a "need for a new reading"?

   ....

To help you to answer this second question, make brief notes on the chief characteristics of both the 'old' and the 'new reading' of the creation story, according to the opinions of the WCC as outlined in the text. Use words from the text and give Line reference numbers in answering.

Take into account both 'old' and 'new' attitudes towards or the place/role of human beings, other communities of life, the earth itself and images of God.

Use a table like this to record your answers.

Ideas about	"New reading" of Creation Story	Old/traditional understanding
Human beings	Eg 'connectedness among all" (L 5) "interrelatedness of all creatures (L21) …………………………………	'arrogant human-centred views' (Lines 3-4, 12) …………………………………
Other communities of life	………………………………… …………………………………	………………………………… …………………………………
Earth itself	………………………………… …………………………………	To be 'exploited' (L14); humans to have 'dominion' over it (L12). …………………………………
Images of God	…………………………………	…………………………………

Writing

Using information and ideas from the readings and discussions so far in this Unit, write about one page on the topic: *Responding to the environment in.... (your own country or region).* Include an outline of damage already done and the causes, and refer briefly to the social, political and religious approaches being taken—or which could be taken—in efforts to repair or improve the situation.

PART 3

Preparatory Discussion

Indigenous people around the world have often demonstrated attitudes towards the environment markedly different from those of developed societies. What indigenous traditions exist in your country or region? Are there still indigenous communities living in your region? Share your knowledge of how they relate—or used to relate in times past—to the environment.

Listening

Listen to a story told by a woman in India. The woman begins her story by telling us that Gitanjali, her small child, is quite ill. Listen for the answer to these questions:-

1   What do they think has caused the child to be ill? ……………… …………..
2   What do the women do each morning at sunrise?
    ……………………………………………………………………… …………....
3   In the past, what did the river give to the people?
    i) …………………….. ii)……………………… iii)……………… ……

4   How does the woman describe the river now? ………………………………….
5   What do they have to do now to get 'decent water'? …………………………..
6   What has caused the river to be ruined?……………………………………..
7   What happens if the women try to protest about the situation?
    ……………...…………………………………………………… ……..

Check your answers in Listening Text 25 in Appendix A.

Reading Comprehension

Read the text and answer the questions.

Jurgen Moltmann – Creation as the home of God

'Jurgen Moltmann is one of today's most important theologians –[his] importance takes on increased significance with respect to a Christian ecological theology...'

1 Like many people today, Moltmann acknowledges that the "environmental crisis" puts
2 before us novel and profound questions. Especially in the context of both the
3 Christian faith and the current crisis, Moltmann asks: "Faced as we are with the
4 progressive industrial exploitation of nature and its irreparable destruction, what
5 does it mean to say that we believe in God the Creator, and in this world as [God's]
6 creation?" And given certain deleterious effects in history due to the Christian belief in
7 creation, Moltmann poses the question: "How must the Christian belief in creation be
8 interpreted and reformulated, if it is no longer to be itself one factor in the ecological
9 crisis and the destruction of nature, but is instead to become a ferment working
10 towards the peace with nature which we seek?" In response to these and other
11 questions, in the very first paragraph of the very first chapter of his work *God in*
12 *Creation* Moltmann clearly states that his intention with respect to the doctrine of
13 creation is to develop an "ecological doctrine of creation." . . .
14   *An ecological doctrine of creation implies a new kind of thinking about God.*
15   *The centre of this thinking is no longer the distinction between God and the*
16   *world. The centre is the recognition of the presence of God in the world and the*
17   *presence of the world in God . . .*
18 Moltmann's motivation for thinking of God and creation in this way lies, in part, in
19 what he perceives to be the deleterious consequences of an overemphasis on divine
20 transcendence. For example, he argues that "the ruthless conquest and exploitation
21 of nature which fascinated Europe during this period (modernity) found its appropriate
22 religious legitimation in that ancient distinction between God and the world." In short,

English for Theology

23 too much stress on divine transcendence vis-à-vis creation too easily leads to severe
24 ecological degradation ... Therefore, while the distinction between God and the
25 world "is a truth that must not be surrendered," it is also true that "an ecological
26 doctrine of creation today must perceive and teach God's immanence in the world" –
27 an approach which "does not mean departing from the biblical traditions."

[Bouma-Prediger, 1995, pp 103, 109-110, 115-116.]

Answer the questions below. Use information in the text and give Line references to support your answers.

1 What is meant by 'certain deleterious effects in history' (L6) and why are they 'due to the Christian belief in creation'? Use any information from the earlier readings in this Unit to explain your answer to these questions.

   ....

   ....

2 Moltmann's ecological theology implies "a new kind of thinking about God" (Line 14). What must this 'new' dimension be and how is it different from the old thinking?..

3 Moltmann is motivated to think in this new way (Line 18 ff) because of the "deleterious consequences of an overemphasis on divine transcendence (Lines 19-20). How does Moltmann explain the link between an 'over-emphasis on divine transcendence' and damage to the environment?

4 Answer these grammatical questions on the text:
   i) Find an example of a conditional clause. Lines ....
   ii) Line 18 refers to *"in this way"*. What is *'this* way'?

      ....
   iii) Line 27 refers to *"an approach"*. What idea/s are covered by this alternative form of reference? ....
   iv) Find at least three discourse markers in the text and say what logical function they indicate.
       (i) Line .... (ii) Line.................. (iii) Line................
       Logical function................... ....

Speaking

In your country or region are there ecological theologians at work? They may be Christian or representative of other world faiths. If there are none in your particular area, choose two or three who are prominent in the world generally. Work in groups of three our four students to compile information on
i) who is doing this work; ii) what motivated them to pursue this subject (ecological theology); iii) what approach characterises their work; and iv) what articles or books have they published, if any. Prepare to give a short talk to the class at a later session.

PART 4

Preparatory Discussion

Imagine this scenario: Developers have marked out a unique area of tropical forest for clearing in your region. They have just discovered that the forest is home for a community of village people, a colony of rare monkeys and a stand of a unique species of tree. The developers want to be ethical. In fact, they give some of their profits to the alleviation of poverty in your region, and they provide employment for some local people. They have come to you for guidance. They would be prepared to relocate the villagers to another place. Biologists have confirmed that neither the monkeys nor the trees are likely to be successfully relocated or transplanted.

On what criteria would you base your advice to the developers: that is, whose interests would you take into account—the poor in your region who would be helped, the colony of monkeys, the villagers to be relocated; the local people who would otherwise be unemployed, the unique species of tree? Discuss.

Reading Comprehension

Read the text and answer the questions.

..................?.....................

1   Any world view that places human beings at the centre of the universe, whether
2   physically, spiritually or ethically, can be called an anthropocentric view. In the
3   context of ecological discussions, anthropocentrism is usually understood to refer to
4   the view that human beings have ethical value in themselves ("intrinsic value"), while
5   other creatures are not seen as having value in themselves. In an anthropocentric
6   ethics the value of nonhuman creatures comes only from their relationship and
7   usefulness to human beings ("instrumental value").
8   It would be anthropocentric to argue that a rain forest should be cleared because of
9   the economic benefits that clearing would bring to a logging company or to potential
10 farmers. It would also be anthropocentric (and legitimate) to argue against clearing a
11 rain forest because of future benefits the retained rain forest would have for the
12 human community.
13 It is another thing altogether to argue that a rain forest has value in itself (intrinsic
14 value), and that this value must be taken into account in any decision about logging.
15 The argument of this book is that a Christian trinitarian theology leads to an
16 ecological ethics of intrinsic value. It is not an ethical view in which everything is
17 centred on human beings (anthropocentrism). Nor is it simply the alternative view,
18 which would see everything centred on living creatures (biocentrism). It is not even
19 simply a view which would see the whole Earth or the universe as the centre of
20 ethical discussion (geocentrism or cosmocentrism).
21 Rather, the argument here is that all things have value in themselves because of
22 their relationship with God. I am in agreement with the position articulated by James
23 Gustafson, who writes that we must "relate to all things in a manner appropriate to
24 their relations with God" . . .
25 Things have value in themselves because they are the self-expression of God.
26 They are the created articulation of the eternal Word, divine Wisdom, the Art of God.
27 Modern science has shown us *how* this articulation has occurred. It explains the
28 process – the interaction of chance and lawfulness, the expanding universe, and
29 biological evolution on Earth . . .
30 The contemporary Christian, faced with this extraordinary evolutionary story and with
31 the wonder of a tropical rain forest, cannot but see this diversity and vitality as the
32 Book of God, the ecstatic self-expression of divine fruitfulness. Wanton destruction of
33 this divine self-expression is deadly sin, unparalleled in human history.

[Edwards, 1995, pp 154-155.]

Answer these questions:-
1 Which of the following is the most suitable title for this extract:-
   i) An ecological world view
   ii) Intrinsic value of all creatures
   iii) Ethical dimensions of anthropocentrism
   iv) Trinitarian theology and ecology
   v) Beyond cosmocentrism   …………………………..
Give reasons for your answer.

2 What is the writer's main purpose in this text:
   i) to explain ii) to argue iii) to evaluate iv) to describe   ……………………

3 Re-read all the Reading texts in this Unit and summarise the similarities and the central idea or distinguishing emphases—if there are any—of each writer/s? Give Line reference numbers in your answers. Use a table like this to organise your ideas:-

Writer	Ideas common to all four texts	Central idea/distinct emphasis
Philippine bishops	……………………....	……………………………
	……………………....	……………………………
World Council of Churches	………………………	……………………………
	………………………	……………………………
Moltmann	………………………	……………………………
	………………………	……………………………
Edwards	………………………	……………………………
	………………………	……………………………

Writing

Using the information collated in the table above, write a short essay of about a page and half describing the ideas which are shared by these writers and explaining any special approach or emphasis made by each one.

OR

Write a summary of the advice you would give to the developers (see Preparatory Discussion) in the scenario outlined above and the reasons underlying your recommendations.

UNIT 22 VOCABULARY

Nouns	**Verbs**	**Adjectives**	**Other**
steward	nourish	complacent	rather
bond	fashion	arrogant	allegedly
ecosystems	lay	cosmic	
connectedness	deface	intrinsic	
diversity	etch	innovative	
dominion	engender	dominative	
legitimation	articulate	novel	
degradation		deleterious	
immanence		ecstatic	
anthropocentrism		wanton	
biocentrism			

UNIT 23   GENES, ETHICS AND THEOLOGY

PART 1

Preparatory Discussion

What words come into your mind when you think of *original sin*? Write down some of them and discuss in small groups why they are associated with the idea of *original sin*. What are your questions about the concept of *original sin*?

Listening

Listen to a text on Charles Darwin

1   Listen for the answers to these questions:-
    i)   What did he believe in his early years? ………………………………….

    ii) When did he begin to doubt? ……………………………………………

    iii) Why did he begin to doubt? …………………………………………..

    iv) What theory did he develop? …………………………………………..

2   Now listen to the text again. Take additional brief notes. Using these notes and your answers to the questions above, work in groups of three or four to write a reconstruction of the text in your own words.

Check your answers in Listening Text 26 in Appendix A.

Reading Comprehension

Read the text and answer the questions.

........?........

1   What does it mean to live in a state of sin? . . . Could it mean that we enter this life with
2   a genetic predisposition towards self-expression that contradicts our spiritual goals
3   and ethical values? . . . Sociobiology explains everything in human culture according to
4   one simple scheme: the drive for reproductive advantage by the selfish gene . . . The
5   phrase, "selfish gene", coined by Richard Dawkins, attempts to provide a biological
6   account of selfishness and altruism in human culture . . . Every aspect of our social
7   lives—our loving and hating, our fighting and cooperating, [and so on]—are but
8   transactions within the broader evolutionary economy . . . We are selfish because
9   the genes are selfish.
10 Sociobiologists, curiously enough, argue that even when we are altruistic to the
11 extent of self-sacrifice our behaviour is still explainable by the selfishness of the gene.
12 Why? Because what appears to be genuine altruism is, when genetically understood,
13 only an apparent or pseudo-altruism. The selfish gene allegedly uses altruism in the
14 form of cooperation . . . to perpetuate its own survival through the hereditary process.
15 Sociobiologists like to emphasise that altruism is tied to kinship. We as individuals
16 are willing to sacrifice ourselves for a brother or sister or someone to whom we feel
17 loyal; and the strength of feeling of loyalty is in direct proportion to the number of
18 genes we hold in common. Loyalty helps ensure the survival of someone belonging to
19 our own group, our own family, our own race, our own nation; and in this way loyalty
20 ensures the survival of our own genes. This explains how territorialism, xenophobia,
21 and war are expressions of altruism. This explains why we consider a soldier dying
22 bravely in battle as one who sacrificed for others, the others being those belonging to
23 our own nation or group and not our enemies. What theologians take to be the
24 highest human virtue—namely, self-sacrificial love on behalf of another—is,
25 according to sociobiologists, blind sacrifice in service to the perpetuation of privileged
26 genes. Altruism, just like selfishness, can be reduced to biological determinants.

[Peters, 2003, pp 93-95.]

Answer these questions.
1   Why are genes described as "selfish" (Line 5)? ………………………….
2   How is altruism explained by the 'selfish gene'? …………………….....
    ……………………………………………………………………………

3   What is the writer's main purpose in this text?
    i) to argue a position   ii) to evaluate a point of view
    iii) to explain a position   iv) to outline cause and effect   ………………..

4   Which of these headings most accurately reflects the main idea of this text?
    i) Selfish genes
    ii) Sociobiology and human culture
    iii) Altruism
    iv) Sociobiology and sin   ………………………………

5   The text above concludes with the statement (Line 26): *"Altruism, just like selfishness, can be reduced to biological determinants."* What is the functional meaning of this statement within the text? (Refer to Unit 11 if necessary.) Does this statement reflect the writer's opinion? Write down any words or phrases in the text which indicate the writer's personal attitude or opinion on the subject.

    …………………   …………………   …………………………

Revision of Grammar: Participles and participial phrases

Participles are formed from verbs. They may be used instead of a relative clause in two ways: as an adjective or in a participial phrase as a reduced relative clause.

Adjectival use
The present or past participle may be used as an adjective.
Examples:
Present participle: *a compelling theory; a willing candidate; challenging ethical questions.*
Past participle: *established law; revealed text; restricted circulation.*

Reduced relative clause
Present or past participles are used to form participial phrases in reduced relative clauses.
Examples:
The books located in the main library are all in English.
(= *The books which are located in the main library are all in English.*)
The students arriving next week will miss important information.
(= *The students who arrive next week will miss important information.*)

REVISION EXERCISE 23.1

Identify the participles in the following sentences by underlining and say whether they function as: i) adjective or ii) as participial phrase in a reduced relative clause. If they are part of a participial phrase, underline the whole phrase.

English for Theology

The first two are completed as examples.

1 One of the <u>enduring</u> issues is the question about human nature.
   (Adjective)

2 New techniques <u>discovered in the twentieth century</u> have enabled much progress. (Participial phrase, ie reduced from *which were discovered...*)

3 The phrase, "survival of the fittest", actually coined by Herbert Spencer, has become associated in the popular mind with Darwin.
   (……………………………..)

4 Essential information located in the revelation of Scripture will be consistent with human reason.
   (……………………………..)

5 Many people question whether unaided reason can correctly perceive all moral laws.
   (……………………………..)

6 Those persons accepted into the university will spend several years in study.
   (……………………………..)

7 It seems possible that eventually humans will be able to make directed changes in human evolution.
   (……………………………..)

8 There are so many competing views on the issues that it is hard to decide what is the best option.
   (……………………………..)

9 The students left their completed assignments in the office.
   (……………………………..)

10 The increasing technical capabilities of the human race lead into an unknown future.   (……………………..)   (……………………………..)

REVISION EXERCISE 23.2

Find examples in your reading of participles used as adjectives and in participial phrases in reduced relative clauses. Note them in the space below.

Participles used as adjectives		Participial phrases: reduced relative clauses
Present	Past	
………………	………………	………………………………………………
………………	………………	………………………………………………
………………	………………	………………………………………………
………………	………………	………………………………………………
………………	………………	………………………………………………

Speaking

As we have seen in the Reading text, sociobiologists suggest that the roots of human evil are to be found in the evolutionary processes of natural selection (the 'survival of the fittest'). Is this to be called *original sin*? Is this a better explanation of evil than the usual theological one? Or are they one and the same? Share your thoughts with the class.

PART 2

Preparatory Discussion

New developments in the medical field have raised many ethical questions in recent decades. The ability to clone (ie make an identical copy of a living creature—animal or human—through laboratory processes) is one of these developments? Work in small groups to make a short list of possible positive and negative outcomes of this development. Share your ideas with the whole class.

Listening

You will hear a short text on the Human Genome Project (HGP). Listen for the answers to these questions.

1 Why is there a sense of urgency about the ethical questions of HGP?

   ....

2 The Human Genome Project is sometimes referred to as the

   ....

3 When was this Project begun? ....

4 The Project involves i) many countries in the world,
       OR   ii) the project is limited to North America.
   ....

5 The annual cost of this project is around $US ....

6 The total cost of the project is estimated to be approximately $US
   ....

7 What is the goal of scientists involved in this project?..........................
   ....

Check your answers in Listening Text 27 in Appendix A.

Reading Comprehension

Read the text and answer the questions

........................?...........................

1 Catholic moral theology typically believes it has a universal ethic in the natural law.
2 Adherence to a natural law perspective gives one the ability to equate Christian
3 ethics with human ethics, for Catholic moralists adhering to the Thomistic tradition
4 believe it is possible for any human being to discern "right and wrong" by reason
5 alone. Of course, that which reason discovers will never violate the information and
6 precepts located in the special revelation of Scripture.
7 Many Protestants, on the other hand, have questioned the ability of unaided reason
8 to correctly apprehend morality. For these Protestant thinkers, the fallenness of
9 human beings affects their reason in such a way that they cannot adequately discern
10 the prescriptions of morality. Thus human beings must look to the revelation of God
11 for direction in moral matters. Obviously, this can be accomplished in a variety of
12 ways. The two Protestant ethicists that this chapter has examined (Ramsey and
13 Gustafson) develop an ethical position by extracting what they believe to be a central
14 emphasis of Scripture—covenant fidelity and theocentric perspective, respectively—
15 and apply these ideas to specific ethical decisions for adjudication.
16 Jewish ethics in general and Jewish bioethics in particular choose a different path

17 from both their Catholic and Protestant counterparts. Jewish ethics is typically
18 established by divine law in the revealed text of the Old Testament. The
19 methodology utilised for ethical decision making is as follows:
20   The basic scriptural norm is located, its rabbinic elaborations are traced through
21   the Talmud and related literature, its authoritative structure is determined, relevant
22   precedents (if there are any) are culled from the vast literature of legal *responsa* by
23   individual rabbinic authorities, and finally the person accepted by a community of Jews as
24   their legal authority frequently seeks the counsel of learned colleagues.*
25 Thus Jewish ethics in general and Jewish bioethics in particular are usually quite
26 concerned with explicitly following the detailed divine mandates of God revealed in
27 Scripture

[Rae & Cox, 1999, pp 36-37.]

*Novak, D, "Judaism" in *Encyclopedia of Bioethics*, edited by W.T. Reich, rev ed, vol 3, New York, Macmillan, 1995, p 1302.

Answer these questions on the text:

1. Choose the most appropriate title for this text from the following options:-
   i) Importance of a universal bioethics
   ii) Representative religious approaches to bioethics
   iii) Revelation is central to bioethics

   ………………………………………

2. Find the discourse markers in the text and say what logical function they indicate.

Discourse marker	Logical function
………………………	………………………
………………………	………………………
………………………	………………………
………………………	………………………

Writing

Under the appropriate heading (check the answer to the first question above in Appendix B), and using your own words, describe in 8-10 lines the essential points of the reading text above.

PART 3

Preparatory Discussion

Many bioethical problems face the world today. Issues of cloning, stem cell research, abortion, euthanasia and the sale of body organs for profit are just a few of them. What bioethical problems are current issues in the country or region where you live? Choose one such issue and talk about the circumstances which have led to the problem.

Reading Comprehension

Read the text and answer the questions

What is human nature?

1 [In discussions about genetic engineering] One of the more enduring and
2 recalcitrant issues is the nature of human nature. Books, journals, and databases are
3 filled with competing models and claims about human nature. In this section I want to
4 make two claims.
5   First, continuing my emphasis on the fact of evolution, we cannot claim that human
6 nature is static or fixed. What our nature is now is not what it was nor is it necessarily
7 what it will be. Given the fact of evolution, we cannot claim a human nature that was
8 created distinctly and apart from the animal kingdom.
9   To say that does not mean that one cannot speak of human nature. Rather, what it
10 means is that we must recognise that our claims are provisional and are time bound.
11 In the past such claims may have seemed less provisional because evolution typically
12 proceeded slowly. Now, however, given our knowledge of genetics and our
13 increasing capacities, there is the distinct possibility for a speedup in the rate and
14 direction of evolution. The map of the human genome will open vast possibilities
15 before us, and though the rate of actually achieving specific changes will typically be
16 slower than the development of our aspirations and plans, nonetheless the genetic
17 map offers a dramatic possibility for directing evolution.
18   A second theme is whether human nature is the sum of its parts or whether there is
19 a transcendent dimension to the human self. This issue is a key one, for on it hinges
20 the validity of various strategies for intervention in human nature. If one assumes, for
21 example, that human nature is the sum of its parts only, then one will have to argue
22 that all human activity at root is genetically caused. The implication is that human
23 nature and human actions and capacities can be changed exclusively or primarily
24 through genetic interventions. For a change in human nature to occur under our own
25 direction, all that is required is more knowledge, more skill, and more time. But
26 eventually, the genome will reveal its secrets, and we will be able to make purposeful
27 and directed changes in human nature as a consequence of altering the genetic
28 structure of the individual.
29   If, however, human nature is more than the sum of its parts, genetic knowledge will
30 continue to be important, but it will not hold a place of primacy. Other dimensions —
31 the environment, culture, and the person as a self — will have to be included in any
32 strategy for change. In this model, although change is possible and a good, specific
33 changes will be more difficult to achieve and less targetable.

[Shannon, 1998, pp 170-171.]

Answer these questions on the text:
1 Identify the main idea/s in each of the five paragraphs of the text. Clue: Find the topic sentences in each and underline or highlight them.
2 Summarise the main ideas:
      i)..
      ii)...
      iii)..
        iv)   a)..
              b)..

v)..

3   Now predict the most likely topic of the sixth (i.e. the next) paragraph in this text:-
vi)..

Writing

Write one to two pages on the topic, "A bioethical issue in ……. " (Name the country or region where you live.) Include a description of what the issue is, how widely it occurs, what conditions have led to the problem, and how the problem might be alleviated or reduced.

PART 4

Preparatory Discussion

Advances in biotechnology have now enabled human beings not only to create a human embryo in the laboratory but even to change the genetic structure of the embryo. This could mean that human beings will be able to choose the direction of evolution. Many people raise serious questions about these possibilities, asking "Are we playing God?" *Should* we be intervening in human nature in this way or not? What are some of the ethical values which might guide the human race in the face of such serious choices? Discuss briefly with three or four students and then share with the whole class.

Reading Comprehension

Read the text and answer the questions.

........................?..........................

1   New knowledge gained from genetics research is raising a host of challenging
2   ethical questions, and these ethical questions are prompting theological reflection.
3   The dramatic scale of the biomedical challenges throws us back upon first principles,
4   back to questions about the nature of human nature, about our relationship to
5   ourselves and to our divine source, God. In the popular press the issue is formulated
6   this way: Are we playing God? A more serious approach seeks to ferret out the
7   implications of the ethical issues and asks, How might theological insights guide and
8   direct ethical deliberation . . .
9   Virtually all Roman Catholics and Protestants who take up the challenge of the new
10 genetic knowledge seem to agree on a handful of theological axioms. First, they affirm
11 that God is the creator of the world and, further, that God's creative work is ongoing.
12 God continues to create in and through natural genetic selection and even through
13 human intervention in the natural processes. Second, the human race is created in
14 God's image. In this context, the divine image in humanity is tied to creativity. God
15 creates. So do we. With surprising frequency, we humans are described by
16 theologians as "co-creators" with God, making our contribution to the evolutionary
17 process. To avoid the arrogance of thinking that we humans are equal to the God
18 who created us in the first place, we must add the term "created" to make the phrase
19 "created co-creators". This emphasises our dependency upon God while pointing to
20 our human opportunity and responsibility. Third, these religious axioms place a high
21 value on human dignity.
22   By "dignity" I mean what philosopher Immanuel Kant meant, that we treat each
23 human being as an end, not merely as a means to some further end. Although this
24 may be a minimal definition, Christian churches mean this and more by human
25 dignity. The United Church of Canada eloquently voices the dominant view: "In non-
26 theological terms it [dignity] means that every human being is a person of ultimate
27 worth, to be treated always as an end and not as a means to someone else's ends.
28 When we acknowledge and live by that principle our relationship to all others
29 changes. Pope John Paul II begins to appropriate the dignity principle in an
30 elocution where he condemns "in the most explicit and formal way experimental
31 manipulations of the human embryo, since the human being, from conception to
32 death, cannot be exploited for any purpose whatsoever". As church leaders respond
33 responsibly to new developments in HGP, we can confidently forecast one thing: this
34 affirmation of dignity will become decisive for thinking through the ethical implications
35 of genetic engineering. Promoting dignity is a way of drawing an ethical implication
36 from what the theologian can safely say, namely, that God loves each human being
37 regardless of our genetic makeup and, therefore, we should love one another
38 according to this model.
39   Yet there is more. The theology of co-creation leads Ronald Cole-Turner to a
40 beneficent vision: "For the church, it is not enough to avoid the risks. Genetic
41 engineering must contribute in a positive way to make the world more just and more
42 ecologically sustainable, and it must contribute to the health and nutrition of all
43 humanity".

[Peters, 1998, pp 1, 33-34.]

English for Theology

Answer these questions on the text.

1. The popular press raises the question of whether medical scientists, with their new capabilities in genetic engineering, are "playing God" (Line 6). What answer do you think would be given to this question by the Christian theologians referred to in Line 9? Give evidence from the text to support your answer.

   ....

   ....

   ....

2. Select the most appropriate title for this text from the following:-
   i) *Common basic principles for Christian ethics*
   ii) *Roman Catholics and Protestants in agreement on ethical issues*
   iii) *Centrality of human dignity in ethical questions*

   ....

3. Make a summary of the main points of each paragraph of this text. Use an outline like the one below.

   Para 1   ....

             ....

             ....

   Para 2   ....

             ....

             ....

             ....

   Para 3   ....

             ....

             ....

             ....

   Para 4   ....

             ....

             ....

             ....

UNIT 23 VOCABULARY

Add to this list any new words that you want to learn.

Nouns	Verbs	Adjectives	Other
predisposition	emphasise	genetic	curiously
sociobiology	perpetuate	altruistic	obviously
territorialism	extract	hereditary	eloquently
precept	cull	theocentric	
adjudication	ferret	minimal	
axiom			

UNIT 24 CHRISTIANITY AND RELIGIOUS PLURALISM

PART 1

Preparatory Discussion

Jesus Christ—yesterday, today and forever! What does this mean? Is this true? Is there a difference between *truth* and *salvation*? Discuss these questions in small groups and then share with the whole class.

Listening

Listen to a text on the difference between the *theology of religion* and the *theology of religions*. Take notes as you listen to complete this table:-

In the light of Christian theology

Theology of religion asks.....?	Theology of religions studies.....?
....	....
....	....
....	....
....	....

Check your answers with Listening Text 28 in Appendix A.

Reading Comprehension

Read the text and answer the questions.

The Christological crisis and its presuppositions

1   We said [in an earlier part of the book] that our relation to 'the present ever new' must
2 be one of the factors that determine how we put into words the substance or content
3 of belief in Jesus as the Christ. This insight has far-reaching consequences. In fact if
4 Christianity really does have universal significance, we are faced with a paradox: on
5 the one hand Christianity will then transcend every historical definition of what one
6 may call the essence of the Christian faith; on the other, this essence will only be
7 found in specific historical embodiments of it. Identifying the essence of Christianity
8 exclusively with one historical form and manifestation of it or with one particular
9 definition of Christian belief then becomes impossible. That is the unavoidable
10 consequence of the 'universal significance' of Jesus Christ.
11   It follows that Christianity only stays alive and real if each successive period, from
12 out of its relationship to Jesus Christ, declares anew for Jesus of Nazareth. Then it is
13 impossible to determine 'first' the essence of the Christian faith in order subsequently
14 —'in the second instance', as it were—to interpret it as accommodated to our own
15 time. Anyone who, with the Christian churches, affirms the universal significance of
16 belief in Jesus must have the humility loyally to shoulder, along with that, the
17 difficulties accruing to it—or else must surrender the claim to universality. Only those
18 two possibilities are genuine and consistent. To accept the universality while at the
19 same time denying the hermeneutical problem—thereby positing one exclusive
20 definition, *ne varietur*,* of essential Christianity—is neither an accessible road nor an

21 authentic possibility. It is to disregard and evacuate of all substance the true
22 universality of the Christian faith.
23   All the same, we cannot make of Christianity just what we fancy ...

[Schillebeeckx, 1979, p 575.]

*May not be changed.

Answer these questions on the text.

1   What is the dominant pattern of organisation of ideas in this text? Choose one
    of the following:-
    i)   narrative   ii) explanation
    iii) analysis   iv) argument   ....

2   What is "this insight" (Line 3)? ....

3   *"We are faced with a paradox ..."* (Line 4). Who does "we" refer to in this text?
    ....

4   Complete this sentence according to the writer's point of view as expressed in the text:-
    Christianity will not stay alive and real unless ....
    ....

5   Whose 'voice' do we hear in this text - that of the writer, or that of others
    whose viewpoint is reported by the writer?   ....

Revision of Grammar: Apposition

Apposition describes the grammatical structure where two or more noun phrases of equivalent status occur next to each other in a sentence.
The noun phrases in question refer to the same person, thing or idea.

Example: ***Christology, the theological study of Jesus Christ**, has undergone
           many developments over the centuries.*

In this sentence, 'Christology' is the equivalent of '*the theological study of Jesus Christ*'.

Explicit apposition occurs when the second noun phrase exemplifies the first or is included in it. In these cases, the second noun phrase is usually preceded by an adverbial phrase such as *for instance, specially, mainly* and so on.

Examples: ***A number of 20th century theologians, notably Schillebeeckx,
           Balasuriya and Moltmann**, have had considerable influence on their
           societies.*

           ***New theological issues, for example, questions of ethics and
           technology**, are a challenge for theologians these days.*

Appositive clauses are nominal clauses and are similar in function to appositive noun phrases. Appositive clauses are often *that*-clauses or *to*-infinitive clauses, though there are some other variations.

English for Theology

Examples: ***The report (that the volcano had erupted)** caused great distress.*
'That the volcano had erupted' is in apposition to *'the report'*.

**It was her intention (to study theology overseas)*.
'To study theology overseas' is in apposition to *'her intention'*.

He made sustained efforts (to overcome his disadvantage).

'To overcome his disadvantage' is in apposition to *'sustained efforts'*.

For more detail on appositional phrases and clauses, consult a comprehensive grammar book.

REVISION EXERCISE 24.1

Identify the noun phrases and their appositive noun phrases or clauses in the sentences below by underlining both elements and by bracketing the appositive phrase or clause. The first one is completed as an example.

1. *Orthopraxis, (a right course of action), is possible only through understanding the issues correctly.*

2. *In earlier centuries, the language of metaphysics, the philosophy of being, underpinned much theological writing.*

3. *Developments in ecclesiology, the theology of the church, have been greatly assisted by the growth of basic Christian communities.*

4. *Another writer, Miriam Nguyen, argues similarly in her latest book.*

5. *Reconciliation, the overcoming of barriers between people and groups, is fundamental to building a wholesome society.*

6. *Muslims fast during the holy month of Ramadan, the ninth month of the lunar year.*

7. *Christians fast and do penance during the forty days of Lent which precede Easter, the Sunday following the first full moon after the March equinox.*

8. *The poorer countries of Asia, especially Bangladesh, Laos and Cambodia, have big development problems facing them.*

9. *The fact that cloning of embryos has already occurred is well known.*

10. *Many developing nations have made great efforts to overcome their poverty.*

11. *Another kind of theological reading, one intended to defend the existing social system, would see grace instead of dis-grace.*

12. *Some forms of suffering in life are inevitable. However, other kinds of suffering, such as that caused by human injustice, are totally unacceptable.*

Read the above sentences again. What do you notice about the punctuation of appositive phrases and clauses? (First check your answers in Appendix B.)

REVISION EXERCISE 24.2

Take notice of appositional phrases and clauses in your study reading.

PART 2

Preparatory Discussion

"... Which religion is the true religion? Are all religions true religions? Are they true in different ways? Is this even possible or conceivable? Christianity understands itself to be the true religion and for this reason, at least since the time of German Idealism, has spoken of its 'absoluteness'. Its claim is both absolute and universal. What should one understand by the truth of religion?"

[Bettscheider, 1999, p 25.] (See Reading Comprehension text below.)

Discuss these questions in small groups and then share with the whole class.

Reading Comprehension

Read the text and answer the questions.

Truth in interreligious dialogue

1 .... pluralism in religion has become a new, very important topic of discussion. This is
2 not just an old theological theme in a new disguise, but rather an existential, political
3 and hermeneutical problem concerning truth ...
4 ... can the question of the truth claim of a religion be totally ignored by emphasising
5 the meaning of religion as a way to salvation ...? Can the burden of joining the
6 difficult struggle to discover the truth be so easily sloughed off? Given that there are
7 many unavoidable differences between questions of truth and salvation, it is still
8 necessary to reflect on their precise relationship and how they permeate each other.
9 If this is not done, interreligious dialogue becomes nothing but empty chatter. What
10 then is truth? Can there be several truths, which are relative one to the other?
11 Catholic theology has responded differently in different contexts to the problem of
12 the multiplicity of religions. Essentially three positions can be identified, each of
13 which, with different emphasis, still has its proponents. They are: exclusivism,
14 inclusivism, and pluralism.
15 The position of exclusivism maintains that Christianity alone is the true religion and
16 salvation comes only through belief in Jesus Christ. Adherents of this position appeal
17 for proof to various New Testament statements about Jesus that stress exclusivity.
18 Jesus, for example, is seen as the "one mediator" between God and [humanity] (1
19 Tim 2:5). Again in the Acts of the Apostles it is stated that "there is no other name
20 under heaven given to the human race by which we are to be saved" (Acts 4:12) ...
21 The position of inclusivism is exemplified by Karl Rahner when he talks about
22 anonymous Christians and of many others who base their position on the Second
23 Vatican Council. This position holds that Christianity is the only true religion and
24 makes an absolute claim to validity. Salvation, moreover, comes only in and through
25 Christ. God in [God's] absolute freedom, however, can bring about salvation through
26 Christ in other religions. Even so, salvation always comes about in and through
27 Christ ...
28 For some 30 years, beginning with English-speaking writers, a third position has
29 been developing, namely that of pluralism or, better, a pluralistic theology of religions
30 which is now being debated vigorously. It begins from the stance that the **Absolute**
31 can only reveal itself in a contingent world. As a consequence, religions are
32 contingent responses to the revelation of the **Absolute**, dependent as they are on
33 circumstances of time and place. Basically, therefore, religions are all of equal value.
34 Any **absolute** claims of a religion are rejected. I would like to pursue the issue of
35 truth in interreligious dialogue in the light of the discussions regarding a pluralistic
36 theology of religions (henceforth PTR).

[Bettscheider, 1999, pp 26-27.]

Answer these questions on the text.

1   Lines 4-6 contain two sentences in the *grammatical form* of questions. What is the writer's *functional meaning* here? That is, is the writer asking a question or does the question have another meaning?

    ……………………………………………………………………………..

2   The two paragraphs beginning at Lines 15 and 21 explain the meaning of *exclusivism* and *inclusivism*.
    In the first we read (Line 15): *'the position of exclusivism maintains that Christianity alone is the true religion . . .'*
    In the second we read (Lines 21, 23): *'the position of inclusivism . . . holds that Christianity is the only true religion . . .'*
    Are these not the same? What is the key sentence in the second paragraph (Lines 21-27) which defines the difference between *exclusivism* and *inclusivism*?

    …………………………………………………………………………………

    ………………………………………………………………………………..

3   In Lines 30 and 32, why does 'Absolute' have a capital A, whereas in Line 34 it does not have a capital? What is the difference in meaning?

    …………………………………………………………………………………

4   What does the writer mean by a 'contingent world' (Line 31)?

    …………………………………………………………………………………

Writing

After reading again the text above, put away this book and write in your own words a brief explanation of exclusivism, inclusivism and plurality (in relation to the question about world religions).

PART 3

Preparatory Discussion

What are the main religious beliefs other than Christian in your society? Do you know what these other believers think about their own religion in relation to the issue of religious pluralism? Do you know what they think about Christianity? Share your knowledge with the whole class.

Listening

Listen to the introduction to an article on pluralism, relativism and subjectivism in Asian theologising (see also text below). Complete the blank spaces according to what you hear.

```
1   Ever since the Federation of Asian Bishops' Conferences (FABC) was founded in
2   .........., the bishops of Asia have officially encouraged and promoted the efforts of
3   ............................... to theologise in the context of Asia with her diverse
4   ...................., ...................... and .......................... One of the major
5   objections to some of these ................................................. has been the
6   ...................................... regarding the tendency of some of them to fall into
7   .............................. and .......................... This short essay is an effort to situate
8   the concepts of ............................., ....................................... and
9   .................................. in the context of theologising in Asia and then to show that
10  pluralism in theology is a ..................................................................
```
[Tirimanna, 2000, p 57.]

Check your answers with Listening Text 29 in Appendix A.

Reading Comprehension

Read the text and answer the questions.

Theologising in Asia: Pluralism, relativism and subjectivism

```
1       The world, as it was created by God, is plural; in fact, our own experiences
2   convince us that reality is manifold. Variety is the hallmark of the universe. No two
3   planets are the same . . . and no two human beings are the same. Consequently, the
4   way we perceive things differs not merely because the basic elements of reality are
5   diverse, but also because we, the perceiving subjects, also differ from one another.
6   As such, cultures and religions differ, and they have different worldviews. We, who
7   are born to a rich diversity of cultures and religions in Asia, are fortunate to
8   experience a rich diversity in our very day-to-day living . . . Pluralism generally
9   refers to a situation in which a variety of viewpoints, explanations or perspectives are
10  offered as accounting for the same reality . . .
11      Any discussion on pluralism always has to take care not to canonise relativism. A
12  pluralism which claims that all points of view of reality are of equal value, surely ends
13  up in relativism. When a point of view lacks a common reference to reality, it
14  amounts to the mere opinion of the subject who holds that opinion. When each and
15  every such point of view that cut off from a common reference to reality is assigned
16  an equal value, then each and every such point of view is automatically assigned a
17  relative, true representation of reality. Consequently, each and every point of view
18  ends up as equally true. This is relativism . . . In other words relativism holds that
19  there are many truths according to the subjects who hold different opinions of reality.
20  Such relativism distorts the rich meaning of pluralism.
21      It is true that as human beings, as perceiving agents, we come to know reality
22  around us as individual subjects. In this sense, our perceptions as individual subjects
23  are unique. But we also believe that God has created us not only as unique subjects,
24  but also as unique subjects who are related to other subjects. We are inter-related-
25  beings. Even in salvation history, God has revealed [Godself] not to isolated
26  individuals, but to persons in community, to inter-related-beings. It is in this sense
27  that our subjective perceptions of reality need a common reference point with regard
```

28 to that reality, in any type of acquiring knowledge, but especially in theological
29 knowledge. Otherwise, our perceptions and the knowledge which ensues end up in
30 what one may call an "exclusive subjectivism" which has nothing to do with reality in
31 an objective sense. But we, as inter-related-beings, need a common point of
32 reference, in our perceptions and knowledge of reality, which we may call an
33 "inclusive subjectivism". While such "inclusive subjectivism" in the perception of
34 reality may be helpful in enhancing pluralism, "exclusive subjectivism" is certainly
35 destructive in the sense it inevitably leads to relativism.

[Tirimanna, 2000, pp 58-59.]

Answer the questions on the text.

1   Note the structure of the first paragraph of this text (Lines 1-10). The topic sentence, the first one, introduces the main idea of the paragraph.
    Using the list of possible sentence functions which follows, identify for each of the 7 sentences its function within the paragraph, either in relation to the topic sentence or to the sentence which precedes it.
    Note that you will not need to use all of the possible sentence functions listed and that some functions may apply to more than one sentence.

    A list of possible sentence functions:-
    i)   example or illustration of a general idea
    ii)   contrasting information
    iii) repetition of an idea in different words
    iv)   expression of purpose
    v)   summary or definition
    vi)   local experience of the key idea
    vii) result or outcome

Sentence number and beginning	Function within the paragraph
1 'The world as it was created ...'	Topic sentence
2 'Variety is...'	....
3 'No two ...'	....
4 'Consequently, ...'	....
5 'As such, cultures ...'	....
6 'We who are born ...'	....
7 'Pluralism generally ...'	....

2   This text is largely an explanation by the writer of widely accepted academic meanings of *pluralism, relativism* and *subjectivism*. Can you find any clues—words—in the text which reveal the writer's more personal attitudes or feelings towards the ideas he writes about? Write them here.

    ....
    ....

PART 4

Preparatory Discussion

Do you know the names of any theologians who have made or are making a special study of religious pluralism in relation to Christianity? (Do some brief research before beginning Part 4 of this unit.) Share your knowledge in a short class discussion about who the theologians are, where they come from and why they have taken a special interest in this question of religious pluralism.

Reading Comprehension

Read the text and answer the questions.

Theology of religious pluralism

1   Our title is "Toward a Christian Theology of Religious Pluralism," not simply " ... of
2   Religions." Why? Reference has been made above to the new awareness that has
3   been dawning upon theologians of the reality of "religious pluralism," characteristic of
4   today's world. The term "religious pluralism," though coined only recently, is now
5   widely used in the context of the "theology of religions"; today the new expression
6   tends gradually to replace the former one. The change in terminology indicates a
7   change in theological perspective. The new perspective is no longer limited to the
8   problem of "salvation" for members of the other religious traditions or even to the role
9   of those traditions in the salvation of their members. It searches more deeply, in the
10 light of Christian faith, for the meaning in God's design for humankind of the plurality
11 of living faiths and religious traditions with which we are surrounded. Are all the
12 religious traditions of the world destined, in God's plan, to converge? Where, when
13 and how?
14   "Pluralism" and "plurality" seem, as a matter of fact, to be used indifferently in this
15 context. The renewed problematic is expressed as follows in the statement published
16 by the thirteenth Annual Meeting (December 1989) of the Indian Theological
17 Association, entitled "Towards an Indian Christian Theology of Religious Pluralism:
18 Our Ongoing Search":

19   We want to express what the plurality of the religions we meet everyday of our lives in
20   India means to us as believers, as people who experience themselves as touched and
21   strengthened by the ineffable mystery of existence. As we perceive the signs of the
22   Absolute Presence also in the lives of our sisters and brothers around us professing
23   various religions, we ask in the light of the Divine Truth revealing itself, what we should
24   affirm about these religions, and how we [should] understand the purpose and meaning of
25   the wonderful religious variety around us and its role and function in the attainment of
26   salvation ... As Christians, we approach these questions from our faith perspective.

27   This goes to show that the current theology of religions means to look at religious
28 pluralism not merely as a matter of course and a fact of history (pluralism de facto)
29 but as having a raison d'etre in its own right (pluralism de jure or "in principle"). The
30 question no longer simply consists of asking what role Christianity can
31 assign to the other historical religious traditions but in searching for the root-cause of
32 pluralism itself, for its significance in God's own plan for humankind, for the
33 possibility of a mutual convergence of the various traditions in full respect of their
34 differences, and for their mutual enrichment and cross-fertilisation.

[Dupuis, 1997, pp 10-11.]

Answer these questions.

English for Theology

1. In Lines 5 and 6 reference is made to *'the new expression'* and *'the former one'*.
   What is the *'new expression'* referred to? ....
   What is the *'former one"*? ....

2. Why has there been this change in terminology relating to world religions?
   ....

3. To what noun or noun phrase does the pronoun *it* (searches) in Line 9 refer?
   ....

4. Whose 'voices' do we hear in this text"? Give Line references.
   ....
   ....
   ....

5. Find two sentences in this text which each encapsulate, in slightly different ways, the essence of what the *theology of religious pluralism* is about.

   ....

   ....

   ....

Speaking

"There is as much fear, and reluctance, to participate in inter-faith dialogue as there is a need for it. The fear may or may not be well-founded, yet it is there."

Is this statement accurate in relation to people in your society? What reasons might there be for the fear and reluctance to participate in inter-faith dialogue? Talk about the questions in small groups and then report back to the whole class.

---

* Kamar Oniah Kamaruzzaman, 2001, "Interfaith dialogue: moving forward; setting premises and paradigms" in Camilleri, J, editor, *Religion and Culture in the Asia Pacific: Violence or Healing?*, Vista Publications, Melbourne, p 114.
  Dr Kamaruzzaman is a lecturer in the Department of Usul'ad-din and Comparative Religion, International Islamic University of Malaysia.

UNIT 24 VOCABULARY

Add to this list any new words that you want to learn.

Nouns	Verbs	Adjectives	Other
manifestation	determine	accessible	exclusively
pluralism	accommodate	precise	automatically
multiplicity	accrue	contingent	
	posit	ineffable	
	ensue		
	slough		
	coin		
	assign		
....	....	....	....
....	....	....	....

LINGUISTIC GLOSSARY

Analogical: Based on analogy, where one thing is affirmed as having some likeness to another. In theological language, such an affirmation relating to God must be accompanied by negation, that is, God is like . . . and <u>not</u> like . . .

Connotative: Having a number of meanings suggested by association; having more than one meaning, that is, non-univocal (see univocal below). Usually referring to a noun.

Denotative: Referring to a noun which has one specific and clear meaning, ie univocal.

Dialectical: Proceeding by bringing two opposing views or realities into dialogue.

Discourse (modes of): The characteristic way/s in which writers use language to convey meaning in particular academic discipline communities.

Existential: Referring to a philosophical approach which emphasises the importance of human existence, with its experience of freedom and responsibility.

Genre: A particular type of text with its own characteristic structure, including a beginning, a middle and an end.

Matrix: That from which something takes its origin or form; that in which something is embedded.

Metaphorical: Figurative language which suggests resemblance, but is not to be taken literally or empirically.

Mythical: Pertaining to a traditional story, usually from long ages in the past, which attempts to explain the origins of things.

Referent: The word or object to which a term refers; in grammar, the noun to which a pronoun refers.

Syntax: The manner in which words are ordered or arranged to convey meaning and argument in sentences.

Text Structure: Within a text, the way ideas are organised in various patterns, eg explanation, cause-effect, evaluation, and so on.

Univocal: Having only one possible meaning. (See denotative)

THEOLOGICAL GLOSSARY

Reproduced with permission from the *Handbook of Readings: Diploma in Theological Studies XTHS 105* University of Otago, Dunedin New Zealand, 1991.

A posteriori:	Latin phrase referring to thought or knowledge based on, or arising consequent to, experience.
A priori:	Latin phrase referring to thought or knowledge which arises from a concept or principle, or which precedes empirical verification, or which occurs independently of experience.
Arian:	Relating to the teachings of Arius (c 250 c 336), who believed that Jesus Christ was not of one being with God, and whose views were condemned at the Council of Nicea (AD 325).
Christocentrism:	Thought or theology which makes Jesus Christ central.
Christology:	Branch of theology concerned with the doctrine and the person and work of Jesus Christ.
Christomonism:	A theological system in which Jesus Christ is used as the overriding regulative principle.
Cosmology:	Study or comprehensive understanding of the cosmos or universe.
Demythologising:	A process of interpreting traditional texts considered mythological (in the sense that they express their meaning in terms of outmoded or mythological worldviews), with the aim of showing that their continuing existential or practical relevance can be grasped despite their mythological expression. Rudolph Bultmann is the best known advocate of this process.
Dichotomy:	Split or division into two, eg, mind and body, fact and value, sacred and secular.
Docetism:	The view that Jesus Christ was not a real man, but simply appeared so. This undermines not only the incarnation, but also the atonement and the resurrection.
Dogmatics:	A coherent presentation of Christian faith through its doctrines.
Dualism:	A view of the world which holds that there are two ultimately distinct principles, or spheres, such as good and evil, or matter and spirit.
Ecclesiology:	Understanding or doctrine of the church.
Economic Trinity:	Trinity in relation to creation, and the revealing of God through history.
Empirical:	An approach to knowledge based on what can be arrived at through sense experience.
Epistemology:	The study of human knowing, regarding its bases, forms, and criteria.
Eschatology:	Understanding or doctrine of the *eschaton*, or ultimate destiny of the world.

Exegesis:	Detailed and methodological interpretation of a text.
Existentialism:	A movement of thought, most influential in philosophy, theology, literature, and psychotherapy, which focuses on individual existence and subjectivity.
Hermeneutics:	Study of interpretation and meaning.
Hypostatic union:	Definition of Christology agreed at the Council of Chalcedon (AD 451), which affirms the dynamic union of two natures, divine and human, in the one person or 'hypostasis' of Christ.
Idealism:	Philosophical tradition originating in Plato, which understands the mind, ideas, or spirit as fundamental to reality.
Immanent Trinity:	Trinity understood in itself through the interrelationship of three persons.
Incarnation:	Literally, becoming flesh, the event of God becoming a human being.
Isomorphic:	Something having the same form as another.
Justification:	Being pronounced or made righteous, the act of God, through the death and resurrection of Jesus Christ, bringing about reconciliation between God and human beings.
Kerygma:	From the Greek word for a herald's message, a term used for the proclamation of the New Testament church about Jesus.
Liberation theology:	Theology originating in Latin America in the 1960s, in contexts of political and economic oppression, which seeks to apply the Christian faith from the standpoint of the needs of the poor and exploited.
Logos:	Greek for 'word', used more widely in Christology to refer to Jesus Christ as the Word of God, God's self-disclosure.
Magisterium:	The teaching authority of the Roman Catholic Church.
Methodology:	Reflection on the systematic approach to a topic or field.
Monarchianist:	Referring to the 2nd or 3rd century heresy of monarchianism, which stressed the unity of the Trinity at the expense of the distinction between its members, and which understood Jesus as divine in a secondary sense.
Mythology:	The projection of human images into the infinite unknown; or, the expression of religious meaning through stories and symbols.
Natural theology:	Theology attempting to know God, and God's relationship to the world, through nature and human reasoning without divine revelation.
Noetic:	Referring to the mind or intellect, or to understanding gained through human rational processes.
Nominalism:	An understanding of universal categories as class names which have no reality outside the individual particulars which make them up (in contrast with *realism*).
Objectivity:	State of being detached from, and external to, whatever is being perceived or affirmed, often previously seen as aiding neutrality and therefore accuracy in judgment, but now seen as impossible or inappropriate in both science and theology.

Ontic:	Referring to existing reality.
Ontology:	Branch of philosophy concerned with the study of being, of reality in its most fundamental and comprehensive forms.
Orthodoxy:	Right belief in, and adherence to, the essential doctrines of a faith as officially defined; or, conventional or traditional belief.
Orthopraxis:	Right belief combined with right practice, with the emphasis being on the latter, a term specially used in Latin American liberation theology, often in contrast with an orthodoxy seen as insufficiently interested in the practical and political content of faith.
Panentheism:	An understanding of all creation as existing in God, yet without negating the transcendence of God; often also holding that the world and God are mutually dependent upon one another for their fulfilment.
Pantheism:	An understanding which identifies God and the world as one; either without qualification, or with the world as a divine emanation.
Passibility:	Capability of undergoing suffering or pain, or of being changed by an external power.
Perichoresis:	Greek term for the mutual indwelling or co-inherence of the three persons of the Trinity.
Polytheism:	Belief in many gods.
Pneumatology:	Branch of theology dealing with the doctrine of the Holy Spirit.
Proleptic:	Anticipating; holding forth in the present what is realised in the future.
Protestant:	A name for those Christians and churches which separated from the Roman Catholic Church at the Reformation, and for other churches and groups descended from them.
Putative:	Reputed; supposed.
Rationality:	That which is characterised by conformity with reason, adhering to qualities of thought such as intelligibility, coherence, consistency, order, logical structure, testability, and simplicity.
Tritheism:	Belief in three gods, often referring to doctrines of the Trinity in which the unity of God is seen as compromised.
Unitarianism:	An understanding and religious movement associated with the rejection of the doctrine of the Trinity, denying a differentiated understanding of the Godhead and the divinity of Jesus Christ and of the Holy Spirit.
Universalism:	An understanding of the all-encompassing nature of salvation including the believe that ultimately all will be saved.
Vicarious:	Relating to a state of being or an action which is undertaken on behalf of others, usually referring to the humanity or the death of Jesus Christ.

APPENDIX A – TEXTS FOR LISTENING EXERCISES

[Note: Texts without reference are written by the author.]
Listening Texts may be heard at the corresponding track number on the accompanying CD.

Unit 12 Focus on Asia

1   The face of Asia

Asia is big and young. It occupies 30 percent of the world's land area and hosts three fifths of the world's nearly 6 billion population. Over 60 percent of Asians are young people. Thus, though ancient, Asia is also a continent of the young.

Asia is multi-religious. It is home to major religions of the world: Buddhism, Hinduism, Judaism, Christianity, and Islam. Taoism, Sikhism, Shintoism, Jainism, and numerous primal or traditional religions also thrive in the region. Christianity is but a minor religion in Asia. The only countries where Christians are a majority are the Philippines and East Timor. Due to the strong influence of religions on culture, Asians are very religious.

[Pedregosa et al, pp 1-2.]

2   Pacific religion

Before we embark on a description of some features of Pacific religion, it is worth noting that it is from its vocabulary that have been drawn two highly important words which have been prominent in the comparative study of religion—*mana* and *tabu* (or taboo). The latter indeed has passed into the stock of ordinary English usage. The term *mana* came to prominence through one of the major theories of the origin of religion formulated by the anthropologist RR Marett (1866-1943) . . . He drew upon the reported finding by a fellow anthropologist . . . that the fundamental concept of their religion was *mana* or power: for instance the power residing in a chief, or a rock, or in some sacralised object. It came to be noticed that similar ideas were to be found in a variety of small-scale cultures across the world . . .

  Tabu reached the West through the account by the famous explorer Captain Cook (1728-1779) of his third voyage to the Pacific. He used the Tongan word *tabu* which is equivalent to the more general Polynesian *tapu* and Hawaiian *kapu*. The idea of *tabu* came to be important in writing on the nature of religion and society, referring to [prohibitions] on actions which had a sacred force. Sigmund Freud (1856-1939) of course gave the term a new psychological force in his famous [book], *Totem and Taboo*.

[Smart, 1989, pp 162-164.]

Unit 13 Theology and Spirituality

3   Spirituality

Spirituality can be described as the whole of our deepest religious beliefs, convictions, and patterns of thought, emotion and behaviour in respect to what is ultimate, to God. Spirituality is holistic, encompassing our relationships to all of creation—to others, to society and nature, to work and recreation—in a fundamentally religious orientation. Spirituality is larger than a theology or set of values precisely because it is all-encompassing and pervasive. Unlike theology as an explicit intellectual position, spirituality reaches into our unconscious or half-conscious depths.

[Carr, 1986, p 49.]

4   What is Christian spirituality?

Christian spirituality is essentially a following of the Will of God as revealed in Scriptures which culminates in the words, the deeds and the Person of Jesus Christ in the gospels. The history of Christian spirituality demonstrates the variety of ways in which the gospel teaching has been interpreted, adapted and applied to the needs of nations, cultures and individuals. Spirituality involves the twin elements of *contemplation* and *practice* where traditionally practice depends on the fruits of contemplation. Contemplation is a prayerful openness and reflection on God's revelation with the hope that God's will would become clearer for one's life and world. It is the understanding of God's will for one's life and world that generates differences in Christian spirituality. In essence, there should only be one Christian spirituality since there is only one wellspring who is Jesus Christ. The appellations *old* and *new* spirituality only point to the development and growth in the understanding of God's will revealed through Jesus Christ and its applicability to a constantly changing world which may be characterised by new realities.

[Ojoy, 1997, p 19-27.]

Unit 14 Language and Theology

5 Origins of language

We are profoundly ignorant about the origins of language, and have to content ourselves with more or less plausible speculations . . . We do not even know for certain when language arose, but it seems likely that it goes back to the earliest history of [the human race], perhaps over a million years. We have no direct evidence, but it seems probable that speech arose at the same time as tool-making and the earliest forms of specifically human cooperation . . .

How did language arise in the first place? There are many theories about this, based on various types of indirect evidence, such as the language of children, the language of primitive societies, the kinds of changes that have taken place in languages in the course of recorded history, the behaviour of higher animals like chimpanzees, and the behaviour of people suffering from speech defects. These types of evidence may provide us with useful pointers, but they all suffer from limitations . . .

[Barber, 1972, pp 23-24.]

6 Metaphorical theology

Christian theology is always an interpretation of the "Gospel" in a particular time and place. So [another] task is to show that a metaphorical theology is indigenous to Christianity, not just in the sense that it is permitted, but is called for. And this I believe is the case. The heart of the Gospel in the New Testament is widely accepted to be the "kingdom of God'; what the kingdom is or means is never expressed but indirectly suggested by the parables of the kingdom.

[McFague, 1982, p14.]

Unit 15 Religion and Culture

7 Indonesia: People and religions

Civilisation has flourished in Indonesia from ancient times. Because of several waves of migrating people throughout history, there is today great ethnic, linguistic, cultural and religious diversity in the country. In early times, Brahmin priests and traders from India settled along the coasts and influenced Indonesia. In the fifth century, both Hindu and Buddhist cultures were present. In the eighth century, Indian communities flourished throughout the islands, and around this time the Sailendra rulers built Borobudur, the great Buddhist monument. Over time, both Buddhist and Hindu elements blended with earlier animist beliefs to form a distinctively Javanese type of mysticism and religious practice. Muslim Arab traders were already in Indonesia by the eighth century but many more arrived in the fourteenth century. This began the period when the Islamic faith spread throughout Indonesia. It has become the dominant religion. In the sixteenth century, the Portuguese came to Indonesia. They brought with them the Christian faith, which developed strongly, especially in eastern Indonesia. The Dutch later also brought Christianity to the islands of Indonesia. Thus, today Indonesia is a mosaic of cultures and religions.

8 Culture and human life

It is a fact bearing on the very person of [human beings] that they can come to an authentic and full humanity only through culture, that is, through the cultivation of natural goods and values. Wherever human life is involved, therefore, nature and culture are quite intimately connected. The word "culture" in its general sense indicates all those factors by which [humans] refine and unfold [their] manifold spiritual and bodily qualities. It means [their] effort to bring the world itself under [their] control by . . . knowledge and . . . labour. It includes the fact that by improving customs and institutions they render social life more human both within the family and in the civic community. Finally, it is a feature of culture that throughout the course of time [humans] express, communicate and conserve in [their] works great spiritual experiences and desires, so that these may be of advantage to the progress of many, even of the whole human family. Hence it follows that human culture necessarily has a historical and social aspect and that the word "culture" often takes on a sociological and ethnological sense.

[Vatican II, Church in the Modern World, para 53.]

Unit 16 Revelation and Theologising

9 Revelation

Revelation is the self-communication of God. It is a process which God initiates and which we recognise and accept because of our radical capacity to be open to the presence and action of God in our history and in our personal lives. *God is disclosed always sacramentally*, mysteriously, symbolically. Revelation, or the "unveiling" of God, occurs in nature itself, in historical events, through the words and activities of special individuals (prophets, Apostles, et al), of special communities (the Church in particular), and supremely in and through Jesus Christ, who is at once God-revealing and God-revealed. All of history, and therefore all of revelation, is oriented toward the Christ-event as history's centre and core.

[McBrien, 1994, pp 264-65.]

10 Models of revelation – five types

Contemporary systems [of revelation] . . . may be divided into . . . five types . . . here set forth in summary fashion.

1. *Revelation as Doctrine.* According to this view revelation is principally found in clear propositional statements attributed to God as authoritative teacher. . . .
2. *Revelation as History.* This type of theory . . . maintains that God reveals [Godself] primarily in God's great deeds, especially those which form the major themes of biblical history . . .
3. *Revelation as Inner Experience.* For some modern theologians, both Protestant and Catholic, revelation is neither an impersonal body of objective truths nor a series of external, historical events. Rather it is a privileged interior experience of grace or communion with God . . .
4. *Revelation as Dialectical Presence.* A number of European theologians, especially in the years following World War I, repudiated the [first three types] . . . God, they insisted, could never be an object known either by inference from nature or history, by propositional teaching, or by direct perception of a mystical kind. Utterly transcendent, God encounters the human subject when it pleases [God] by means of a word in which faith recognises God to be present . . .
5. *Revelation as New Awareness.* Especially since the middle of the twentieth century, an increasing number of theologians . . . hold that revelation takes places as an expansion of consciousness or shift of perspective when people join in the movements of secular history. God, for them, is not a direct object of experience but is mysteriously present as the transcendent dimension of human engagement in creative tasks.

[Dulles, 1983, pp 27-28.]

Unit 17 Christology

11 Some questions about Jesus

[John the Baptist asked] "Are you the one who is to come, or should we expect someone else?"
[The Magi asked] "Where is he?"
[Greek worshippers at Jerusalem asked] "Sir, we wish to see Jesus."

These three statements from the gospels broadly encapsulate the anxiety, mood, and expectations of Asian Christians about Jesus. The first one expresses the misgivings and the ambivalence Asian Christians feel about the images of Jesus that were first introduced to them by foreign missionaries and still dominate their thinking. The other two epitomise the urge and the desire of Asian Christians to discover for themselves the evidence of his presence in their midst and his place among other saviour figures of the region.

[Sugirtharajah, 1993, p viii]

12 Liberation Christology

The realisation that concern for justice is an intrinsic part of christology receives a sharper and more critical focus when it is articulated by people who are actually suffering from injustice. The major Catholic theologians who developed transcendental christology in the 1960s, recovering the genuine humanity of Jesus, and narrative christology in the 1970s, recovering the history of Jesus, have a great deal in common: they are all white, well-fed, well-educated, prosperous, privileged, European males. They all theologise, however compassionately, out of an experience of political, economic, and social privilege. Starting in the 1970s and moving into the 1980s, a third wave of renewal in Catholic christology has developed as the poor and dispossessed in the world have begun to find their voice. On virtually every continent, reflection on faith from the "underside of history" has resulted in forms of theology collectively known as liberation theology. It is a new way of doing theology, one which draws on the experience of systematically oppressed and suffering peoples. [. . .]

Liberation theology originated in Latin America after the Second Vatican Council, although its roots reach back into the base-community movement begun decades earlier.

[Johnson, 1990, p 83.]

13 Christian experience in China

From 1966 to 1976 there was in China a ten-year period of anarchy and disorder, the Cultural Revolution . . . Christian churches all over China were closed down and put to other uses if not dismantled. Our seminary in Nanjing became the headquarters of the red guards of the city and we were all driven out of it. Many of our colleagues in the church had to suffer in all sorts of ways . . .

Even in those early days Christians did not forget the teaching in the Epistle to the Hebrews that Christians should not cease to meet. We met in homes. We got together once a week, or once in two weeks, or still less often, ten or fifteen or twenty or more of us. We would have a tea together, say our prayers together, study the Bible together, and talk over together what we each got out of the passage. Nobody was the minister; we ministered unto each other. Ministers should not insist on their being ministers and be teachy, as they were just members of the group. There was sharing in depth, called "communication," and that was spiritually fulfilling. We all had our Bibles taken away from us, but many Christians could recite various passages from memory and we all put them down in our notebooks. We developed simple ways to celebrate the Eucharist: the name given to it was simply thanksgiving, or breaking bread.

All that I want to say is that, although we have church buildings such as this one which is historic and helps us greatly to worship God in the beauty of holiness, the church of Jesus Christ can exist in all sorts of places wherever Jesus Christ himself is with his disciples, particularly as he breaks bread with us. As the New Testament shows, Christians had been meeting in homes long before there were church buildings.

[Ting, 1999, pp 158-159.]

Unit 18 The Problem of Suffering

14 Why suffering?

While suffering in all of its forms is present in the human condition, the real anguish of suffering is found in its perceived meaninglessness. More than twenty-five hundred years ago, a man named Job stood under the curse of meaninglessness. He could not find a reason or a purpose for his suffering. The suffering of children is a particularly painful expression of meaninglessness. Humanity cries out for its elimination. There is so much innocent and meaningless suffering that no easy interpretation of suffering is possible. History presents itself to us as a mixture of meaning and meaninglessness, of sorrow and happiness. Such a mixture raises the question whether in the last resort we can trust life at all. The quest to find meaning in our life is our primary motivational force.

[Richards, 1992, p 1.]

15 Suffering and theology

Schillebeeckx, Rahner and Kung are only a few examples of theologians whose objectives [since Vatican II] have sometimes been misunderstood. Nevertheless we are entering into a new way of doing theology for many audiences that we must learn from and whose primary characteristic is a deeper insertion of the believer into the modern world. Schillebeeckx founds his theology on the experience of suffering humanity. While suffering can be a salutary act . . . there exists useless suffering . . . While the former can be humanising the latter is dehumanising and bears no apparent salvific quality. Salvation of humanity in Jesus cannot reconcile dehumanisation. It must be resisted, rejected, and refused. No matter what religious or non-religious belief one has chosen, atheist, Buddhist, Christian, etc, all agree on the dehumanising character of suffering and the need to eradicate it.

[Mueller, 1984, p 58.]

Unit 19 Grace

16 What is grace?

If we see God as creator and sustainer of the cosmos, and if we subscribe to an open-ended notion of grace, we realise that nothing, [a priori] need be excluded from it. [Grace is universal.] Every person, every reality has the potential to be touched by God's love. Grace is relational. It always involves relationships. The word "grace" initially points to the relationship between God and the world. Within this larger sphere, grace functions in a distinctive way in the God-human relationship. Of course, relationships with each other and with the world cannot be separated from the God-human relationship, and, in fact, are deeply affected by it. Initially, God is discovered in and through relationships among humans. One hears the Good News from the community into which one is born. Some persons experience God most tangibly in their relationships with others. Others find God in prayer and then make connections with their human relationships. Still others find God in the beauty of nature. While emphases differ, grace is a dialectical experience.

[Dreyer, 1990, p. 21.]

17 Grace

Grace signifies the presence of God in the world and in human beings. When God chooses to be present, the sick are made well, the fallen are raised up, the sinners are made just, the dead come back to life, the oppressed experience freedom, and the despairing feel consolation and warm intimacy.

Grace also signifies the openness of human beings to God. It is the ability of human beings to relate to the Infinite, to enter upon a dialogue that wins them their humanity day by day and rewards them with deification.

Grace is always an encounter between a God who gives [Godself] and a human being who does likewise. By its very nature grace is the breaking down of realms or worlds that are closed in upon themselves. Grace is relationship, exodus, communion, encounter, openness, and dialogue. It is the history of two freedoms, the meeting of two loves.

For this reason grace signifies the reconciliation of heaven and earth, of God and humans, of time and eternity. Grace is something more than time, more than history, more than humanity. It is ever something *more* which happens with unexpected gratuitousness.

[Boff, 1984, p 3.]

18 Grace and disgrace

If grace is all that we have described above, then it is ever threatened by what we can call dis-grace, that is, lack of encounter, refusal to dialogue, and closing in upon oneself. Grace and dis-grace are two possibilities of freedom. This is the mystery of creation, an absolute mystery to which reason does not have access.

Grace is the absolute meaning that brings fulfilment to everything. It is a light that illumines everything and makes all comprehensible. Dis-grace is . . . sheer darkness without a trace of light.

For a created being grace is grace amid the possibility of dis-grace. The human being is always a threatened being who can be dis-graced. As a history of evil, violence, destruction and cruel inhumanity, history itself is a history of dis-grace in the world; and it is fleshed out in the closing up of beings in themselves.

[Boff, 1984, p 4.]

Unit 20 Justice, Development and "Good News"

19 A woman of Asia

Agustina (Tina for short) Lumentut was born on February 10, 1937 in the valley of Rampi high in the jungle-covered mountains of Central Celebes (later called Sulawesi). Her parents, Eliseba and Ferdinand Lumentut, committed Christians, came from Minahasa in the north-eastern part of Celebes. Dutch missionaries had already begun educational and missionary work among the people of Celebes when they chose Ferdinand Lumentut, one of their graduates, to pioneer an educational outreach program in the isolated area of Central Celebes. He was later ordained by his church community and spent much of his life in leadership and pastoral positions, ministering to the people, preaching the good news, and leading them in Sunday worship. It was in this context that their daughter, Tina, grew up. At the age of 17 she began five years of study at a new theological college in Macassar (later called Ujung Pandang) so that she could prepare for ministry in the church. She graduated in June 1959. After ordination, Tina began her ministry among the people in Sulawesi, where she continued working for many years.

[Based on information in M. Kirk, 1997.]

20 Gutiérrez on liberation theology

[Gutiérrez, in his book, *A Theology of Liberation*,] considers two traditional understandings of theology, theology as wisdom and theology as rational knowledge, and compares them with an understanding which is prevalent in Liberation Theology. Liberation Theology defines theology as critical reflection on praxis. Praxis is a central concept of Liberation Theology. It refers to committed action in the social, political sphere. Gutiérrez traces the Christian understanding of praxis from a central focus on charity, through Ignatian spirituality, to recent talk about reading the signs of the times. Praxis is also central to Marxist philosophy, indeed, to many modern philosophies. Gutiérrez notes with approval Marx's comment that the point of philosophy is not to interpret the world but to change it! . . .

One should note also that theology is defined as a critical reflection on praxis. It is critical not just in the epistemological sense of Kant, but also critical with regard to the economic and socio-cultural aspects of life. It critically analyses the economic and cultural presuppositions which a theologian brings to his/her work, seeking out hidden ideological assumptions. Such a theology is not naïve about its own political implications.

[Ormerod, 1990, pp 130-131.]

21 Political theology

Political theology has grown up in societies where some minority groups suffer significant oppression. Such groups may be marginalised because of poverty, ethnicity, class, gender or religion. The term 'political theology' has been used in church circles since around the 1960s. It broadly refers to a range of theologies which critique the unjust structures of society through applying biblical principles to social analysis and political action. While political theology originated in societies where Christianity was dominant, it is certainly not limited to that faith, since other major religions also find liberating principles within their own traditions. Political theology would include the, by now, well-known approaches of liberation theology, feminist theology and black theology.

Unit 21 Understanding Scripture

22 Form criticism

After World War I an important new development in New Testament scholarship took place in Germany with the publication of Martin Dibelius' *From Tradition to Gospel* (1919), KL Schmidt's *The Framework of the Story of Jesus* (1919) and Rudolf Bultmann's *The History of the Synoptic Tradition* (1921). The method they employed came to be known as "form criticism". Form criticism classifies parts of the biblical text into literary forms or genres in much the same way that we might classify parts of a newspaper according to their literary forms: editorial, reports, letters to the editor, advertisements etc. It is a method which goes behind the written unit (a parable or a miracle, for example) to trace its history back to the period of oral tradition about Jesus.

Having examined and classified the form of the text, the form critic asks how this story or saying was passed on or modified in oral and written stages until it reached its final form. What was the function of the story in the Christian community? He/she is not trying to get to the earliest version but is looking at the *Sitz im Leben*—the setting in life—in which the story or saying was told, and which shaped the telling and the order of the story. For the form critic holds that the needs and interests, the circumstances and beliefs of the early Christian community had a direct bearing on the oral transmission and the eventual fashioning of the written material.

[Goosen & Tomlinson, 1994, p 53.]

23 Redaction criticism

The earliest form critics regarded the Synoptic writers as editors (redactors) rather than authors—editors who systematically strung together or arranged the pericopes with which they were familiar. But after World War II another method of enquiry developed—[namely,] the analysis of the editorial work of the writers in relation to their sources, or redaction criticism. Attention was focused on the way that the writers handled the material; they were not simply stringing the pericopes together, but were arranging their material in creative ways. In the selection and omission of material, in the arrangement and editing, in the alteration of the pericopes, in the connecting links constructed between pericopes, they revealed their particular theological perspective.

Redaction criticism assumes that the work of form criticism on the material and its history has already been done, and goes on to enquire into the use of the material by the final author of the text and what it reveals about the author's particular theological stance. The final writer was in fact an author, engaged in a much more creative task than merely stringing together bits of material.

[Goosen & Tomlinson, 1994, pp 56-57.]

Unit 22 Ecological Theology

24 The Philippines

One does not need to be an expert to see what is happening [to the environment] and to be profoundly troubled by it. Within a few short years brown, eroded hills have replaced luxuriant forests in many parts of the country. We see dried up river beds where, not so long ago, streams flowed throughout the year. Farmers tell us that, because of erosion and chemical poisoning, the yield from the croplands has fallen substantially. Fishermen and experts on marine life have a similar message. Their fish catches are shrinking in the wake of the extensive destruction of coral reefs and mangrove forests. The picture which is emerging in every province of the country is clear and bleak. The attack on the natural world which benefits very few Filipinos is rapidly whittling away at the very base of our living world and endangering its fruitfulness for future generations.

[From the Philippine bishops, Pastoral letter, 1988.]

25 Story from India

"My heart is heavy these days. My little one, Gitanjali, is quite ill and we have no way to get medicine or care for him. We think it is the water in this area that has made him feverish and weak.
Each morning at sunrise I go with the other women with our brass pots balanced on our heads to try to get water from the Nandira River. It used to be a beautiful river and gave us fresh water and fish each day and a place to wash our clothes. Now the river is gray, covered with a thick coat of ash. We have to dig holes in the beach and hope to get some decent water. There are no longer fish in the river. All this comes from the new coal-fired power plant upstream. It has ruined our river and our lives with its toxic waste. We have tried to protest but the police beat us with canes and drive us away. We are not sure where to turn."

[Calemba Sivarramurti, Orissa, India, in Hill, 1998, p 155.]

Unit 23 Genes, Ethics and Theology

26 Darwin

Charles Darwin [who died in 1882] was a biologist who, in his early years, was at the same time a believing Christian. He accepted the fixity of species and their special creation as depicted in the book of Genesis. But doubts began to emerge in 1835 when he visited the Galapagos Archipelago, where he noticed that very small differences were present in the so-called species inhabiting separate islands. His original doubts were only reinforced by additional observations of flora, fauna, and geological formations at widely separated points of the globe. All living things, he tentatively concluded, have developed from a few extremely simple forms, through a gradual process of descent with modification. He developed a theory of natural selection to account for the process, and especially for the adaptations of living things to their often hostile environments. His findings were published in *The Origin of Species* in 1859.

[McBrien, 1994, p. 103.]

27 Genes and theology

The ethical questions emerging from the field of genetics are creating a sense of urgency due to the enormous scale of research associated with the Human Genome Project (HGP), sometimes referred to as the Human Genome Initiative (HGI). Begun in 1988, HGP is a "big science" project, international in scope, involving numerous laboratories and associations of scientists strewn across the landscape, having a current annual U.S. budget of $200 million with a fifteen-year time line and a $3 billion total price tag. The scientific goal is to map and sequence the human DNA.

[Peters, editor, 1998, p. 1.]

Unit 24 Christianity and Religious Pluralism

28 Theology of religion and theology of religions

A distinction has been made earlier between a theology of religion and a theology of religions; they differ, though being organically related and indeed inseparable. The theology of religion asks what religion is and seeks, in the light of Christian faith, to interpret the universal religious experience of humankind; it further studies the relationship between revelation and faith, faith and religion, and faith and salvation. However, since, owing to the nature of the human being as spirit incarnate and a person in society, religious experience is naturally embodied in a religious tradition—made up of creed, cult and moral code—the theology of religion becomes in turn a theology of religions. Christian theology of religions studies the various traditions in the context of the history of salvation and in their relationship to the mystery of Jesus Christ and the Christian Church.

[Dupuis, 1997, pp 7-8.]

29 Asian bishops and religious pluralism

Ever since the Federation of Asian Bishops' Conferences (FABC) was founded in 1970, the bishops of Asia have officially encouraged and promoted the efforts of Asian theologians to theologise in the context of Asia with her diverse cultures, religions and peoples. One of the major objections to some of these theological efforts has been the valid concern regarding the tendency of some of them to fall into subjectivism and relativism. This short essay is an effort to situate the concepts of pluralism, subjectivism and relativism in the context of theologising in Asia and then to show that pluralism in theology is a must in the Asian context . . .

[Tirimanna, 2000, p 57.]

APPENDIX B   ANSWERS

SECTION 1 ANSWERS TO TASKS
UNIT 2

Task 1:   1 book   2 encyclical letter   3 journal article
          4 pastoral letter   5 church newspaper

Task 2:   Check your responses with your teacher/others in the class.

Task 3:   1 unpublished thesis   2 letter   3 book
          4 pastoral/synod statements   5 journal   6 scriptures
          7 magazine   8 conference papers/proceedings
          9 encyclical   10 newspaper   11 journal article   12 report

Task 4:   cover page   publication data   title page   contents
          back cover/dust jacket blurb   foreword/preface/introduction
          acknowledgments   bibliography/references
          chapters   index   notes
          [11 items are listed here.]

Task 5:   1 reference/bibliog.   2 contents   3 chapters   4 index
          5 foreword/intro/pref. 6 public. data   7 cover page   8 notes
          9 acknowledgments   10 back cover/dust jacket blurb.

Task 6:   a references   b back cover/dust jacket   c notes   d foreword/preface
          e contents   f acknowledgments   g cover or title page

Task 7:   Check your responses with your teacher/class members.

Task 8:   Share your responses with your teacher/class members.

UNIT 3

Task 1: Dramatic language (lang. of action) – action of encounter, wrestling and struggle, confronting exchange, limping away.

Supernat. agency   -   the one who appeared to him (Line 4).

Evocative lang. (with several levels of meaning/connotations)
          -    eg 'wrestled' with him; 'touched' the thigh which 'withered'; 'your name shall no longer be . . .'; 'have seen God face-to-face and survived'.

Alogicality   mysterious persons do not normally appear in
Remoteness   the night and wrestle till daybreak; the content of exchange—not an everyday conversation; Israelites obviously looking back to a distant past (Line 14).

Task 2: | Item/thing | Examples - symbolic/metaph. words/phrases |
         | L 5-6 human search for truth | 'insatiable' (need); 'hunger' (for freedom); 'beats', 'pulsates' |
         | L 7 conscience | 'voice' of conscience |
         | L 7-8 church's pastoral responsibility | seeking to 'see humans with the eyes of Christ' |
         | L 19-22 needs/prayers of humanity | heal wounds, pour down dew on dryness, wash away stains of guilt, bend hearts, melt the frozen, etc. |

[Note: These are some obvious examples of metaphorical words/phrases. You may find more.]

Task 3: Examples of metaphysical language
  L 7-8 the unity of God   L9 infinity of God
  L 12 God as first cause   L13 first in a sequence of causes
  L 16-17 God's independence flows from existence—but not God's unity, infinity or omnipotence.

Task 4: Examples of existential language
  L 2-3 (the gift comes) through the words and deeds of others
  L4   meets us as we are—love and concern of others
  L6   invites a level of trust
  L8   dependency of the infant upon the mother
  L9   acceptance of child on part of the mother
  L12-13 experiences of human acceptance and trust (or rejection, distrust)

Task 5: Examples of empirical language
  L1, 3 loss/destruction of rain forests
  L8   around the world forests are being cleared . . . etc, burned, cut for lumber flooded for dams . . .
  L9   17 million hectares destroyed each year
  L14   Amazon Basin has the biggest part of world's rain forests.

UNIT 4

Tasks 1-4:   Share your responses with your teacher and others in the class.
Task 5: 1 c effect-cause   2 e explanation   3 d contrast
    4 a narrative   5 b argument

Task 6: **A**
   1 today (time/sequence)
   2 for instance (example)
   3 furthermore (additional information); also (additional information)
   4 likewise (comparison/similar case)
   5 thus (result/effect/consequence)
   Note: 'nowadays' (L 9) could also be considered a signpost word indicating time/when.
  B 1 thus   (effect)
    2 consequently (effect/result)
    3 also (additional point) [twice]
    4 moreover   (additional information)
    5 therefore (result/consequence)
    6 in fact (emphasis)

UNIT 5

Task 1:   Air pollution   Soil Erosion
 eg   carbon dioxide increase   too much clearing of vegetation
    increased temperature   bad agricultural practices
    ozone layer hole   over-grazing
    global climate change   loss of top-soil
    melting ice caps   too much irrigation-salinisation
    chlorofluorocarbons   etc.

Task 2: 1 *acid rain*—-and ——*smog* or *heavy concentrations of carbon dioxide*
    2 both *humans* and *animals*—or *vegetation*
    3 (any 3 of) eg *industrialisation, coal burning, motor transportation, pronounced urbanisation*

Task 3: Discuss your responses with your teacher and others in the class.

Task 4:   Political and social desires   Inward and personal desires
 eg   aspects of freedom – of speech,   to understand the interior life;
    of movement, of association,   levels of awareness, prayer;
    social justice – housing,   possibilities of transformation
     employment, etc.

Task 5:	Clues in the text	Probable content of next paragraph
	'powerful counterforces' (against ecumenism)	
	'within the Catholic church'	- description of the counterforces within the Catholic church
	'without the Catholic church'	- description of the counterforces in other churches.

Task 6: The next 3 paragraphs will probably be about
     i core experience   ii collective memory   iii interpretation
The chief clues are these 3 words/phrases in the text itself.

UNIT 6

Task 1: How quickly did you identify your language? Languages starting with F?

Task 2: No

Task 3: Nos 3, 9. Discuss with your teacher other likely titles in the list which might include references to Christology.

Task 4: Nos 6, 9, 12, 13.

Task 5:	Key words	Relevant section
eg i	science, solar system stardust, cosmos, salvation of the universe	p 139 'made from stardust' p 148 'science & theology on the future of the universe'
ii	women, feminist(ism) gender	p 61 feminist christology
iii	Jesus/non-Christian religions, other religions	p. 64 Jesus the Wisdom . . . and other religious traditions

Task 6: <u>Suffering</u> 1) suffering (pp 13, 84-85, etc) 2) the cross (p. 13, etc) 3) death of Jesus (p 57-59)

<u>Humanity of Jesus</u> 1) human nature (p 9 etc) 2) hypostatic union (p 29, 42)
    3) incarnation (pp 19-31 etc) 4) self-consciousness of Jesus (p 35-47)

Task 7: From Section 3 'Salvation outside the church' and following sections 4, 5, 6.

Task 8: "The living Spirit" p 1596 "The Power of Prayer" p 1597

Task 9: Liberation theology: Lines 10-11—voice of the poor, Jesus Christ as liberator.
       Jesus/other religions   Line 15—question of universal influence of Jesus

UNIT 7

Task 1:	News item	Most appropriate heading
	1.............................	14
	2.............................	1
	3.............................	7
	4.............................	11
	5.............................	2
	6.............................	12

Task 2: c. An adequate theology...
Task 3: c. Each generation...
Task 4: c. Action for justice...
Task 5 b. The term 'grace'...

UNIT 8

Task 1: A TS= Sentence 6 'In fact...' (last position)
       B TS= Sentence 2 'There is a host of . . .' (2nd position)

          C   TS=Sentence 1 'At the end . . .' (1st position)

Task 2: A   Topic – The study of theology today
                 CI   embraces many important areas

        B   T   Controversies around the topic of Christology
                 CI   . . . nowhere more evident than in . . . problem . . . approp language

        C   T   Planet earth's crisis
                 CI   there are several reasons for . . .

        D   T   Ethnic conflict a problem
                 CI   in many parts of the world

        E   T   Globalisation
                 CI   benefits and challenges of

        F   T   Different spiritual traditions in the church
                 CI   can be like springs of life-giving water

Task 3: Share your ideas in a class discussion.

Task 4: (Read sentences in order across the page)
       1   TS= c. In most countries . . .   e. There are first . . .
              b. elementary or primary   a. many students nowadays . . .
              d. a proportion of high school   f. in fact…

       2   TS= b. Human rights as they are now understood . . . e. first there are…
              f. these include such rights   c. next there are the social
              d. a 'third generation' . . .   a. these solidarity rights
              g. all these rights together

       3   TS= c. The conditions necessary   f. at the most basic level
              d. then there are the social requ.   b. as well as these
              a. ultimately, people also need   e. all of these conditions

       4   TS= c. The unfathomable   e. as the [story]
              a. tracing these changes   d. rather, words about God
              b. as cultures shift

       5   TS= d. As far as religion is concerned   c. however, the situation
              e. since then…   a. some of the violence
              f. but the rest has been   b. an example

UNIT 9

Task 1:   S= subject   V=verb   O=object   Ind/Dep
        1   The book (S) was published (V)   I
        2   Which (Obj.) he (S) had written (V)   D
        3   . . . you (S) had…written (V) the article (O)   D
        4   . . . they (S) discovered (V) the ancient scrolls (O)   D
        5   who (S) contributed (V)….   D
        6   He (S) spoke (V)   I
        7   The villagers (S) contributed (V) …   I
        8   . . . the players (S) trained (V) ….   D
        9   Words (S) have (V) different meanings (O) …   I
       10   . . . they (S) could not translate (V) the documents (O) D

Task 2:

Verb	F/NF	Verb	F/NF
were	F	is	F
given	NF	was accepted	F
saving	NF	recognises	F
helped	F	explaining	NF
understood	F	shared	F
saved	F	were redeemed	F
interpret	F	created	F
liberating	NF	accepts	F
broke	F	has been broken	F
had evaluated	F	written	NF

Task 3:

	Finite verbs	Past participles
1	is received	described
	is marked	
2	is	prized
	has been denied	
3	is understood	accepted
		inherited
4	has arrived	destroyed
5	are . . . promoting	committed
		desired

Task 4: Main clauses only
1. grace is received in a divine-human meeting
2. freedom of speech is undoubtedly a most prized human value
3. revelation... is understood in many different ways
4. the entire world community... must commit itself to comprehensive, decisive action
5. they are surely promoting peace...

Task 5: Main clauses
1. The problem of suffering ... concerns all people
2. The sun . . . is a religious symbol . . .
3. Poverty afflicts far too many of the world's people

Task 6: Main clauses
1. Modern and postmodern society is characterised by cultural and ideological pluralism
2. many contemporaries claim that Christianity . . . has run its course
3. The emergence of basic Christian communities and their praxis are of singular importance

Task 7: Main clauses
1. we must keep an open mind about the traditional presentation of the church
2. one theologian writes that the focus is not "who" is Jesus Christ but "where" is Jesus Christ for Asian women
3. liberation theologians hold a more present-oriented eschatology

Task 8: If you try this exercise, discuss your diagram with your teacher and other students.

Task 9: Main clauses in the text
Purity was political . . .   Purity systems are found in many cultures   . . . they are systems of classifications, lines and boundaries. A purity system is a cultural map . . . Things that are okay in one place are impure or dirty in another . . . a purity system is a social system . . . The polarities of pure and impure establish a spectrum or 'purity map' . . . These polarities apply to persons, places, things, times and social groups.
. . . We can see the sociopolitical significance of compassion . . . we see an alternative social vision, a community shaped by . . . compassion.

UNIT 10
Task 1: 1   that time = twentieth century

2 another ... **advance was**
3 'key ancient parchments' = 'Qumran scrolls', or 'these critical documents' or 'ancient texts'
4 the century = twentieth century
5 before that ... when radiocarbon dating enabled exegetes to date critical documents with precision.
6 they = exegetes, or biblical scholars
7 L 4 – consequently (result, effect)
   L5 – however   (contrasting/different idea)
   L 11 – for example   (illustration, example)

Task 2:
2 'their' refers to John the Baptist and Jesus
3 this effort = the effort to refute Reimarus' allegation that Jesus was a political revolutionary
4 these biographies = whole series of 'lives of Jesus'
5 those = circumstances
6 same saying = a saying of Jesus in circumstances different ...
7 it = 'the attempt at connecting sections of the four Gospels into a 'harmony'
8 the latter three, they, their ... refers to Matthew, Mark and Luke
9 so = It is ... simply ... a case of choosing between John or the Synoptics for an accurate biographical account
10 this effort = attempts to reconstruct Jesus' life and teaching from the sources available
11 these sources = the sources available (L26)
12 his = DF Strauss
13 this point = 'that John's concern was primarily theological was recognised early'.
14 this gospel = John's gospel, ie, the one referred to in L28, 'John's concern'.

UNIT 11

Task 1: Share your findings with other students in the class.
Task 2: Questions 2 and 5 require you to make inferences.
   1 They are promised employment (L6).
   2 Because rural families are usually very poor and desperate to earn a living.
   3 They are sold into prostitution (L7-8).
   4 Because of shame (L13).
   5 Probably not—because they are so desperately poor.

Task 3: Authorial voice—what the author thinks—is evident in the following:
L4 - *people seem ...*
L5-7 *They sense ... effective in their lives.* Note: The author here is apparently using what others think to convey what he too thinks. Note the emphasis—*are really symptoms*, and the obligation, *forgiveness must address*.
L8 ... *people have a sense*—this is the author's view of what people think.
L10 ... *for many people today is sin.* Note the finite verb—again, this is a view
        attributed to others but it stands for what the author also thinks.
Lines 11-19 tell us what the writer thinks Paul understands about sin.
L11, the verbs *fits, is*, and Line 14, *are*. Finite verbs here convey the writer's definite interpretation of what Paul thinks. Similarly, Lines 15-19 contain the verb *is* a number of times—the writer's considered view of what Paul thinks.

Lines 20-29 move from interpreting what Paul thinks to telling the reader what the writer himself thinks. This is evident particularly in the use of first person—*my sense, we now have the means to grasp imaginatively* (note use of emotive adverb here).

Task 4: The first part of this text outlines four common themes relating to trinitarian
        theology, as the writer understands them. Lines 14-17 contain an explanatory
        comment which gives us further insight into the writer's view.
        The next part of the text—Lines 18-35—outlines the work of a particular
        theologian in a given book. This is largely description, but the text contains a

number of evaluative words which indicate what the author feels and thinks about this book. Note the following: L23—*masterly* work; L24—*responsibly and wisely*; L29—*astonishing;* L31—*convergence* (this indicates an assessment of the line of enquiry taken by the scholars concerned).

You may wish to discuss other indicators in the text which you consider show authorial voice.

Task 5: This text is largely description of two approaches to theology. The author's voice is evident in several words/phrases. Eg

1. L4 – *unfortunately;* L15—*on the positive side*; L27-28—*However . . . various questions;* L 30-31—*I have never . . . asked this question*!; L32—*clearly*; L33-34—This final sentence gives us the author's evaluation of this theology.
2. Pragmatic meaning—where the author wants to communicate what he <u>feels</u> about something—occurs 3 times in this text, in the sentences ending with an exclamation mark, ie L14-15, L24-25, and L30-31.
3. On the whole, the author's attitude to the theologies which dominated the nineteenth century is negative. We know this, early in the text, because he says it was '*unfortunate'* (L4) that these theologies reached into the twentieth century as well.
4. In L15, the phrase 'on the positive side' suggests that the previous outline was mainly negative.
5. The author's evaluation of scholastic theology is in L27-30—'*However . . .*
6. This sentence is an explanation of the approach taken in classical theology, ie what is in the first sentence (topic sentence).
7. This sentence is also an explanation of the type of theology written by Thomas Aquinas.
8. This sentence registers disagreement/contrary evidence to the claim reported in the previous sentence.
9. This sentence represents the author's evaluation and conclusion on the topic of scholastic theology.

SECTION 2
Note: Answers to Listening exercises are found within the Listening texts in Appendix A.
UNIT 12
Part 1 Reading
1 Answer in Line 3.   2 The writer notes negative effects—L5.
3 Answer in L 15.   4 Answer in Lines 18-19.
5 Several reasons as listed in Lines 21-26. 6 L14–use of first person pronoun 'our Asian societies' suggests writer is Asian. Also the sentiments suggest an Asian identity.

Revision Exercise 12.1
1 has	2 have	3 attract	4 rises	5 flies
6 live	7 includes	8 speak	9 does not speak/speaks	
10 catches	11 causes	12 watches	13 goes	14 do not go/walk

Revision Exercise 12.2
1 are causing   2 are building   3 are(they) standing
4 are waiting   5 are rising

Part 2 Reading
1 i the spiritual/invisible ii the world we can see/experience
2 the places where humans live
3 mainly to attempt some control of the gods (L7)
4 . . . visit us
5 for the people about whom the author is writing, ie traditional Polynesians
6 fear of weakening chief's power by lower-caste marriages
7 mainly i (description), but some elements of iii (explan.)
8 comment in L14-15 in brackets; also L 18
Part 3 Reading
1 c politics and economics (Discuss your reasons in class)

2 L3-4 – features listed
3 4 – physical, cultural, religious, social.
4 the 'worship' of money is like a religion for some
5 example (of the great range of differences in the region)
6 The purpose of these 2 rhetorical questions is to introduce the following description of the differences. The writer is inclined to a 'yes' answer: L13 'However (=contrary to the differences) . . . there are common themes . . .' and following lines.

Part 4 Reading
1 Australian Aborigines   2 Because they believe they are sacred/holy places where people may access divine power/healing etc.
3 False (see L10-11, 15-16, 17). 4 *such* is a cohesive device referring back to 'places associated with the lives of great religious leaders' (L11-12)
5 d

UNIT 13
Part 1 Reading
1 Theology involves faith, religious studies does not necessarily require faith (L4-5).
2 It is never finished, a continuing search (L6)
3 Because new questions are being generated all the time (L7)
4 Intelligence and reason are essential for theology, but not for the others.
5 Lines 12-16 – questions listed.
6 Explain
7 Must be faced, in spite of difficulties (L16-17.)

Revision Exercise 13.2
1 Unfolding history generates new questions.
2 What criteria determine faith?
3 Theology involves the use of intelligence and reason.
4 Theology requires a faith stance.
5 The failure to examine difficult questions retards theological development.
6 The uncertainties of modern life disturb many people.
Passive forms
1 Theologians are often supported by ecclesial communities.
2 Our spirituality is expressed in everything we do.
3 Theology and spirituality are influenced by culture and history.
4 Misunderstanding is often resolved by careful discussion.
5 Revelation is systematically studied by the theologian.
6 Revelation is understood in different ways by different people.

Part 2 Reading
1 Text A—more like definition—because shorter, essential points only; Text B—explanation because longer, including some elaboration of ideas.
2 Here = the deepest centre of the person (L2-3)
3 'this movement' = movement towards the Other (the divine) within, self-transcendence; movement (outwards), self-expression
4 i false (Isaiah's description is base of spirituality *everywhere*—L2)
   ii false (L3-4).

Part 3 Reading
Answers to 1 and 2 may be found in the Listening text (4).
3 Author in favour – the world is constantly changing, bringing new realities.

Part 4 Reading
1 false (L3-4)   2 false (L7)   3 true (L10-11) 4 Lines 4-6; because it can be predominantly unconscious.

UNIT 14
Part 1 Reading
1. examines/explores   contain/encompass   basic/fundamental
   aspect/dimension   contradictory/paradoxical   multiform/polymorphic

2. Explanation in L2-3.
3. Because it explores realities which transcend the human mind.
4. i) great increase in primary materials on language, adding complexity, and ii) philosophical questions about whether it is meaningful to speak of God at all.
5. A

Revision Exercise 14.1
1 the	2 the	3 the	4 the	5 the
6 the	7 the	8 the	9 the	10 a
11 the	12 a	13 a	14 a	15 an
16 a	17 an	18 the		

Revision Exercise 14.2
1 unique	2 unique	3 unique	4 forward	5 unique

Revision Exercise 14.3
A
1 the	2 a	3 a	4 the	5 the
6 the	7 the	8 an		

B the-backward reference: No 1 – the academic; No 5 – the pastoral approach;
No. 7 – the reality (ie the reality of a particular social situation mentioned in L2-3 of the text.

Part 2 Reading
1. *this* tendency = religious conservatism (insisting on literal reference of language to God.
2. 1) fact, according to religious conservative movement.
   2) fact, according to the author. Note: It could be said also to be a strongly expressed opinion.
3. Reasons for relig. literalism (in addition to fear of relativism and plurality): i) the understanding that such language is 'true'; ii) many people have lost the practice of contemplation and prayer; iii) positivistic science has narrowed the view of what is true in our culture; iv) we do not think in symbols the way our forebears did.
   Inability to think in symbols is the most fundamental reason = the 'deeper reason' for religious literalism.

Part 3 Reading
1. a in all places/pervasive   b deepest/profoundest   c many/manifold
   d takes away/undermines   e top priority/unsurpassed   f works/functions
   g influences/molds   h very much/exceptionally   I group/corporate

2. Example – Lines 8-9.
3. The women's movement in civil society and the church.
4. It= 'this exclusive speech about God' L21.

Part 4 Reading
1. a. because he is convinced that 'this principle is continually overlooked . . .' L4-5
   b. he feels strongly concerned, ie 'alarmed' L 5.
2. 3 more expressions of author's reasons (in addition to L4-5):
   i L19-20   ii L24-25 .. 'time and again'.   iii L29-30.
   Note: Lines 38-39 also express the same basic reason.
3. a
4. 'this single formal proposition' L37 (ie we can only speak about God in analogy)

UNIT 15
Part 1 Reading
1 Mahavira the Jain, Gautama the Buddha, St Thomas the apostle.
2 After its origins in the seventh century.
3 False
4 False
5 b narration of facts

Revision Exercise 15.1

1 was	2 grew up	3 had	4 was	5 came
6 influenced	7 went	8 came	9 combined	10 had
11 practised	12 went	13 worked	14 worked out	15 used
16 took on	17 did	18 gave	19 taught	20 became

Revision Exercise 15.2
Compare your lists with others in the class. Check with your teacher, or a grammar book.

Revision Exercise 15.3
In constructing your sentences, note the difference in meaning between *when* and *while*.
2 Archbishop Romero was saying Mass when the soldiers shot him.
3 When the earthquake struck, most of the people were sleeping.
4 When relief supplies came, the villagers were already starving.
5 While she was completing her postgraduate studies, she taught at the university.
6 They were guarding their sheep when they discovered the ancient scrolls.
Check your sentences with your teacher and other students if they differ from these answers.

Revision Exercise 15.4

1 saw	2 threw	3 were	4 took	5 was
6 resulted	7 escaped	8 was	9 left	10 felt
11 could not	12 gave rise			

Revision Exercise 15.5
Irregular verbs (infinitive): see, throw, take, leave, feel, give rise

Part 2 Reading
1 contrastive, definitional
2 The writer prefers the empirical definition, because it is open to change and development (l2-16)
3 Negative attitude – L7 later generations can only stand in awe, ie have no participation. L7-8 – too rigid, no variations allowed, etc.

Part 3 Reading
1 iii
2 this process = the dynamic process of inculturation as explained in L5-7.
3 This sentence *explains* the previous sentence about the process being reciprocal.
4 i 'the literary history of the way the Christian message came to be written and edited
   ii 'the way (the message has been interpreted) through time even to the present day

Part 4 Reading
1 A iv   B vi   C ii   D viii   E iii
2 Consider the earlier effects of an 'imperialistic' approach to communicating Christianity.
3 This sentence illustrates or explains further the previous sentences.
4 b – a mixed blessing (notwithstanding mistakes and 'blunders', essential message of Christianity is worth further understanding, development.)

UNIT 16
Part 1 Reading
1 Lines 2-3: 'a process for the uncovering and transmission etc . . .of Jesus of Nazareth.'
2 Meanings and values of Jesus: i) the person of Jesus himself – ie how he lived;
   ii) the meanings and values he passed on to his disciples – by word and example;
   iii) recovering and transmitting those meanings (to others).
   Necessary condition: guidance/inspiration of the Holy Spirit.

3 False (L9-11)
4 'Peoples' (L10) is the plural of *a people*, which refers to a specific communal, ethnic or cultural grouping of humans, for example, the Hebrew people, the Chinese people, etc.
   People, in the ordinary sense, is the collective noun for persons in general.
5 *It* refers to Christian revelation.

Revision Exercise 16.1
1 to/towards   2 to
3 about   4 with
5 in/through; in   6 for

Revision Exercise 16.2
1 between   2 for   3 of   4 with
5 in   6 for   7 with   8 on
9 in   10 from   11 about   12 about
13 with   14 to

Part 2 Reading
1 Some metaphorical words used: L2, God was . . . *bound* with us; L3, *word becoming flesh;* L 4, *image*; L5, *hearer* (of God's word).
2 The revelation occurred within the historical limits of how things were in first century Palestine.
3 Existential: L10-11, 13-14, 15-16.
4 Jesus' rejection was a direct result of what he said and did among those around him – it was not simply incidental.

Part 3 Reading
1 i) inner illumination; ii) information in the form of propositions; iii) God's self-revelation.
2 This writer prefers the third model: Implicit in Lines 5-7 – *today . . . at least in most important theological reflection.* Explicit in Lines 7-8.
3 Gnostic idea = information . . . otherwise inaccessible to reason and ordinary experience (L10-11).
4 The writer believes iii) and iv) are most important – L 12-14. Curiosity is trivial compared to transformation and hope.
5 A person would need to have a sense of promise and hope generated by faith.

Part 4 Reading
1 ii) L 5-12
2 The first three are true, assuming that Christian tradition is *in conversation with* our experience. The fourth statement is true (L9-10).
3 ii) existential. Most of the text describes experience.

UNIT 17
Part 1 Reading
1 This is the forward-reference use of the definite article, used when the identity of the noun, i.e. Jesus, is made clear in what follows—that is, not just any description of Jesus, but specifically the one who is portrayed in Mark's opening chapters.
2 strong, vibrant, vulnerable, keenly aware (of his mission).
3 Reign of God—what is described in Lines 4-5, and elaborated in Lines 5-9.
4 The conditions formerly thought to be necessary or preferred to be worthy of God's love – i.e. good health, male gender, good family and wealth. They were swept away because Jesus showed that no such distinctions counted with God.
5 Relative pronouns. *which, that*
6 b Description

Revision Exercise 17.1
2 who calls him Son and beloved   R   Subj
3 whose status would normally permit them access to the channels of power   R   Poss.
4 who might have considered themselves excluded from those blessed by God   R   Subj.
5 who was worthy of the God of Israel   R   Subj
6 whom Jesus reveals   R   Obj

Revision Exercise 17.2
1 Mark's gospel tells the story of a woman who had been suffering for twelve years. R
2 The woman who touched Jesus was cured. R
3 Has anyone seen the book which I left on the table? R
4 The scriptures tell us that Judas, whose kiss had betrayed Jesus, committed suicide. NR
5 Gustavo Gutiérrez, who lived in South America, is one of the founders of liberation theology. NR
6 Ecological theology, which has developed because of the poor state of the environment, is gaining more attention. NR

Revision Exercise 17.3
1 which had declared the Christological dogma (L4) – Subj. R
2 that was incorporating concern for justice into its sense of mission (L6) Subj. R
3 who had long been left out of the conversation about Christ (L10) Subj. R

Part 2 Reading
1 c argument
2 Liberation christology – L1, L3-5. Because this christology is what is liberating for the writer (L3-5, L6-15)
3 Argument contained in Lines 6-15.
4 L9 – *it* = the word "lord" (L7)
5 Relative clauses: L8 – which in my own country . . . conflicts; L9 that exist there today; L10 which is still used in countries like Pakistan for those; who have taken their place;
   L11 which is opposite to what Jesus taught and exemplified; L13-14 who serves. (Six relative clauses.)
6 'This sinful situation' is the centuries-old 'lording over' women—ie the oppression
    of women.

Part 3 Reading
1 iv
2 This refers to the Jesus brought by the western 'missionary irruption' in the 15th century. The first 'visit' was Jesus own birth and life in Palestine.
3 The writer views presentation of Jesus during that period as generally distorted—he came as an 'alien', 'clannish god', 'sanctioning subjugation' (L11-13).
4 This refers to the resources which Asians have in their own traditions—literary, cultural and religious—for discovering, understanding and interpreting the meaning of Jesus for them.

Part 4 Reading
1 Work with your teacher and/or each other in making your notes about similarities and differences.
2 Not very important—as long as the task gets done. (L14-16.)
3 Braided cord, formed by plaiting strands of fibre.
4 i) Bread and wine are foreign elements—and expensive. The coconut is local and plentiful.
    ii) The drink and food of the coconut comes from one fruit—just as blood and flesh
       are part of one body—so therefore a more apt symbol.

UNIT 18
Part 1 Reading
1 iii) suffering because of perceived absence of God (L7); iv) unmerited suffering—for which no explanation (L 9-10); v) scandalous suffering (L12-14).
2 'Such' refers back to the 'scandalous suffering' mentioned in L13-15.
3 a mute   b deluded   c realise   d unreal   e unmerited
4 i Yes   ii No   iii No, not necessarily, but suffering is *likely* for a *great* cause (L6). iv No (L13-14).   v Yes

Revision Exercise 18.1
3 i Declarative ii Object
4 i Declarative ii Object
5 i Declarative ii Object
6 i Declarative ii Subject

7 i Interrogative ii Object
8 i Interrogative ii Subject

Part 2 Reading
1 Check in a dictionary.
2 This distinction is meant to raise awareness that the understanding of God revealed to us through Jesus is different from an understanding of 'God as directly or indirectly involved with . . . innocent suffering'.

3

	Schillebeeckx	Soelle
i	Yes. ….	L1 'There is a suffering from which we can learn …'
ii	Scandalous suffering.	Suffering of the innocent.
iii	Nil – no explanation	Same
iv	May contribute to maturity – or may lead to victimisation and dehumanisation	Same or similar
v		Discuss with other students and teacher.

Part 3 Reading
1 Religions tend to have two effects in relation to suffering. The two effects are explained in Lines 16-18
2 Class discussion with teacher.
3 In considering Schillebeeckx's views, take into account particularly Lines 16-21 (Part 1 Reading) and for Soelle, Lines 13, 19-21 (Part 2). Your discussion may draw out further implications from the two texts.

Part 4 Reading
1 Line 16 word omitted: *response*.
2 In general, Lines 15-25 suggest a contrasting approach to Schillebeeckx and Soelle. You can identify the lines which suggest a response opposite to the resistance stance emphasised by those two writers. (NB Distinguish between Beker's own ideas and the ideas contained in the book of Revelation.)
3 In the realm of 'suffering at the hands of human injustice', Paul would agree with Schillebeeckx and Soelle. In your discussion refer to evidence in the three texts.

UNIT 19
Part 1 Reading
1 From the Greek word *charis*.
2 ii–overlapping meanings.
3 The theological meaning has nothing to do with the idea of the 'grace' of a ballet dancer.
4 Because the Christian scriptures hardly ever make a link—draw a connection—between the word *charis* and an aesthetic quality (L8-9).
5 These three words have evolved in meaning quite separately from one another. The phrase has a metaphorical meaning.
6 Because this was the original term used in the Christian scriptures.

Revision Exercise 19.1
1 possibility   2 obligation   3 permission   4 obligation   5 ability
6 advice   7 probability 8 advice   9 possibility 10 not necessary
11 negative obligation

Revision Exercise 19.2
1 He *may/might/must* be sick.
2 She *can* read . . .
3 *Should/ought to* spend . . .
4 *Needn't* come...
5 ...we *can* work together . . .

Revision Exercise 19.3

1 has revealed	2 have developed	3 have lived	4 has taught
5 have contributed	6 has heard	7 have built up	8 have found
9 has spoken	10 have written		

Revision Exercise 19.4
1. Tom has finished . . . Question: Has Tom finished writing his essay?
2. You have read that book before. Question: Have you read that book before?
3. They have flown in aeroplanes before today. Question: Have they flown in aeroplanes before today?

Part 2 Reading
1. Because he assumes most of us would not presume to know what the workings of the Holy Spirit feel like.
2. He would probably say we can experience the Spirit in our own 'everyday experiences' (L6).
3. Spirit thought of only as 'something apart', that we are 'remote' from God: Moltmann wants to change that view so that we can come to recognise our experience of God as being *within* life.
4. Line 3: We (at beginning of sentence) . . . sense;   Line 6: Then we (at beginning)… can talk.
5. ii existential – The writer wants to open people to their own experiences of life (L12-13).
6. Eg L11 – 'great river' of eternal love.

Part 3 Reading
1. 'Many faces' is a metaphor to convey the idea that grace comes to us in many ways and forms. At least 4 'faces' are mentioned: L2-4 – living reality in daily life; something you get when you pray; a technical theological term; a term with no meaning.
2. iv Description
3. b From an introductory section, because the writer is setting out the scope of the study of grace (L9), which would be appropriate in an introduction, and she foreshadows what will be in 'this book' (L18).
4. L 9 – *it* refers to 'the study of grace' (L8).
5. L10 – *these issues* = the issues referred to in L8-10, ie relationship between God/world, between God/persons, our understanding of human existence, how we relate to the transcendent.
6. The author claims that her book examines grace in 'broader categories', in 'new language' and that it also examines how the past has contributed to our present understanding (L18-19).

Part 4 Reading
1. 1st solution: L10-13 – 'The first sees human freedom as the . . . problem . . .' etc.
   2nd solution: L13-16 – 'The second solution . . .' etc.
2. The common premise: 'massive misuse of human freedom' (L8) is cause of our condition.
3. Those who prefer the 1st solution usually feel 'despair' (L17) about the human condition.
4. The gift of freedom can come 'to all who will travel with him' (ie Christ) (L34).
   (What does it mean to 'travel with him'?)
5. L10-11 -   No, does not reflect author's opinion.
   L12-13 -   No
   L22-23 -   No
   L24   -   Yes
6. d existential

UNIT 20
Part 1 Reading
1. Tina wanted to be like her father (L3-4).
2. The words of the prophet Amos powerfully influenced her (L8-10).
3. There was much social turmoil and political unrest (L12-13).
4. L17-20 – we should begin experiencing 'salvation' here and now.
5. a narrative
6. Much of the text tells the facts of the story of Tina's life. L10 and L13 include the writer's evaluation of aspects of Tina's work or experience. L15-16 indicate the writer's assessment that 'many Christians around the world' were also growing aware of the justice-'good news' connection.

Revision Exercise 20.1
Note: The order of the clauses may be reversed.
1 <u>Although</u> the world has become a more dangerous place, we must continue our efforts for justice.
2 <u>After</u> she finished the essay; she handed it to the teacher.
3 <u>Because</u> he spoke out in defence of the poor, he was attacked by gunmen.
4 They prepared themselves through assiduous study <u>in order to</u> teach well.
5 The peasants were protesting <u>because</u> they had no means of living.
6 Refugees want to live in a safe place <u>where</u> they can escape suffering and persecution.
7 <u>Even though/although</u> it was a dangerous journey, the refugees were prepared to attempt it.
8 <u>While</u> population in Java is very dense, it is relatively sparse in West Papua.
9 They ate their food very quickly <u>as if</u> they were starving.

Part 2 Reading
1 ii liberation theologies have the same basis.
2 b explanation
3 Liberation theology is: i a people's theology; ii shaped by the experience of oppression; iii intrinsically linked with critical action done reflectively; iv highly conscious of the social nature of existence; v makes extensive use of social analysis; vi includes the purpose of changing the unjust situation.
4 In addition to the list above, where other theologies mainly sought to *understand the faith*, liberation theology wants to *change unjust aspects of society*.
5 L 2 – 'every word here is important (evaluation); L 16 – 'a convincing case . . .' (comment); L38 'We do not have to wait . . .' (author identifies with this vision).

Part 3 Reading
1 L5 – 'We ourselves . . . must be renewed and unified'.
2 ii) L 19 – 'Here I speak to all office holders . . .' – The implications of the text are to be brought to bear on the community. See also L27-31.
3 Perhaps the writer felt that some office holders were not fully renewed themselves (L19 , L28-31, L32-36,).
4 The main problem is outlined in Lines 37-40.
5 This is a rhetorical question – the writer means that 'we <u>do</u> stand under the same condemnation . . .' – if the stated condition is not met.
6 ii exhortation
7 This text is a face-to-face address to a group of people. The first two texts were written accounts.

Part 4 Reading
1 iii argument
2 <u>Reasons for 'no'</u>   <u>Reasons for 'yes'</u>
  - church itself not sinful (though individuals are) - church ruled by human beings who
  - church enjoyed presence of Holy Spirit   are capable of sin;
                                                                                 - supernatural end of church not an
                                                                                 argument against capability of sin.
3 Writer himself thinks church is capable of sin because it is ruled by human beings (L15-21).
4 L11 'throws new light'. Can you find any more examples?

UNIT 21
Part 1 Reading
1 iii (L23-28)
2 i Greek *evangelion* – good news; ii New Testament usage – good news of freedom from captivity; iii also in New Testament usage – good news of salvation.
3 i True (L9); ii False (L23-24); iii False (L23-24).

Revision Exercise 21.1
3 learning (subject); 4 watching (object); 5 i achieving (subject) ii revising (object);
6 understanding (object); 7 keeping (subject); 8 examining (object of adjective); 9 asking (object of preposition); 10 enrolling (object of preposition).

Revision Exercise 21.2
Compare your lists with those of other students and check with your teacher.

Part 2 Reading
1 True; 2 Possibly T/possibly not T; 3 Not true; 4 Probably true; 5 Possibly true/possibly not true; 6 True; 7 False; 8 True; 9 False.

Part 3 Reading
1 iii
2 L1-7: Interpreters should take advantage of all recent research in uncovering meaning intended; L8-18: Interpreters need to go beyond the literal sense to discover context, spirit of the times, literary forms in use in times past. L19-25: Sacred writers used various arts and idioms characteristic of their times.

Part 4 Reading
1 relevant/pertinent; silly/absurd; clear/unambiguous; indicating/designating; witness/attest; statement/proposition.
2 ii argument
3 i False (L2-5); ii True (L10-11); iii False (L17-18); iv False (only taking metaphors literally is absurd – L25-27). v False (L31-33).

UNIT 22
Part 1 Reading
1 'This assault' refers to the attack on the environment referred to in the listening text (No 24) you have just heard.
2 People need to be sustained and nourished by a new vision which comes from understanding the world as God intends it to be (L4-6).
3 The covenant which God made with Noah after the flood (L10).
4 c exhortation.
5 Metaphoric/symbolic language: 'assault' on creation (L 2); 'nourished' by vision, vision must 'blossom' forth (L4-5). Can you find some more?
6 Forests, mangroves, coral reefs.

Revision Exercise 22.1
1 would be; 2 would [better] understand; 3 will find; 4 would have taken;
5 will follow; 6 discovered; 7 would receive; 8 would not have asked;
9 would help; 10 had known.

Part 2 Reading
1 'All communities' refers to plants and animals as well as humans. (We need to move beyond merely 'human-centred' views (L4).
2 i 'New reading' means a new way of understanding. ii New understanding needed because old understanding led to exploitation and destruction (L12-14). Complete the table with detail from the text.

Part 3 Reading
1 'Deleterious effects' refers to the exploitation of nature and irreparable damage mentioned (L4). Due to the old Christian understanding that humans were to dominate the earth and its creatures.
2 The new dimension must be to think about God/God's presence as in the world, not separated from it (L14-17).
3 L20 ff – The ruthless damage to the environment found its 'legitimation' in the idea that God was quite distinct and apart from the world.
4 i L 8 – if it is no longer …; ii 'this way' refers to the way described in L14-17.
   iii 'an approach' – this is an appositional phrase which refers back to an ecological stance that perceives God's immanence in the world (L26).

   iv (i) L 20, for example (illustration/example); (ii) L22, in short (summing up);
       (iii) L24 therefore (consequence). Can you find any more?

Part 4 Reading
1. ii Intrinsic value of all creatures.
2. ii to argue.
3. Do this exercise together with a partner or small group of students. Discuss your ideas with others and with your teacher.

UNIT 23
Part 1 Reading
1. Because the gene reproduces for its own advantage.
2. Even what appears to be altruism is really the genes (group, family, clan etc) looking after their own interests (L12-14).
3. iii to explain a position.
4. iv Sociobiology and sin.
5. This statement is a summary, or concluding sentence, of the explanation which has been outlined earlier in the text. This does not necessarily reflect what the writer thinks. Indicators of writer's thinking: L 1 – *could it mean…?*; L10 – *curiously enough* – the writer thinks this argument is curious; also L13 – *allegedly* (writer does not think this is certain); L 25 – *according to sociobiologists* (ie not necessarily what the writer thinks).

Revision Exercise 23.1
3. Actually <u>coined by Herbert Spencer</u> (reduced relative)
4. <u>Located in the revelation of scripture</u> (reduced relative)
5. <u>Unaided</u> reason (adjective)
6. <u>Accepted into the university</u> (reduced relative)
7. <u>Directed</u> changes (Adjective)
8. <u>Competing</u> views (Adjective)
9. <u>Completed</u> assignments (Adjective)
10. <u>Increasing</u> technical capabilities . . . (Adjective); <u>unknown</u> future (Adjective)

Revision Exercise 23.2
Share your lists with other students and check with your teacher.

Part 2 Reading
1. ii Representative religious approaches to bioethics.
2.

Discourse marker	Function
Of course (L 5)	emphasis
On the other hand (L7)	contrast
Thus (L10)	consequence
Obviously (L11)	writer's view
Thus (L25)	consequence

Part 3 Reading
2. i) Nature of human nature – an enduring issue.
   ii) Human nature not static or fixed, and not created distinctly apart from animal kingdom.
   iii) Human nature does have its own reality, but we need to recognise that our claims are provisional, time-bound. But now we may be able to direct evolution ourselves because of the human genome project.
   iv) a. Is human nature just the sum of its parts or is there a transcendent dimension?

   b. If just the sum of its parts, then humans can intervene to make genetic changes and direct evolution.

   v) If human nature is more than the sum of its parts, attitudes and approach to change will have to include the other—more intangible—dimensions, such as environment, culture, and the person as self.

3. vi) Probably the next paragraph will discuss the dimensions referred to in v) and the likely effect on change or the direction of change.

Part 4 Reading
1   These theologians would not necessarily think humans were playing God, because all agree that while God is the creator of the world and continues to create (L11-12), humans are already—and meant to be—'co-creators' (L16).
2   i) Common basic principles
3   After preparing your summary according to the plan, share your ideas with other students. Check with your teacher.

UNIT 24
Part 1 Reading
1   iv argument.
2   This insight = that the present is 'ever new'..
3   All of those, including the author, who grapple with the question of the universal significance of Christianity. The author 'speaks' from within this community of persons.
4   Christianity will not stay alive and real unless . . . if in each successive generation there are people who believe anew in Jesus Christ out of a real relationship with him (L11-12).
5   We hear the author's voice in this text. This is evident from his use of first person 'we'; note also the emotive tone in words such as impossible, unavoidable, must have the humility; sentence in L21 is a strong statement of position.

Revision Exercise 24.1
2   The language of metaphysics (the philosophy of being).
3   Ecclesiology (the theology of the church)
4   Another writer (Miriam Nguyen)
5   Reconciliation (the overcoming of barriers between people and groups)
6   The holy month of Ramadan (the ninth month of the lunar year).
7   Easter (the Sunday following the first full moon after the March equinox)
8   The poorer countries of Asia (especially Bangladesh, Laos and Cambodia)
9   The fact (that the cloning of embryos has already occurred)
10 Great efforts (to overcome poverty)
11 Another kind of theological reading (one intended to defend the existing social system)
12 Other kinds of suffering (such as that caused by human injustice)

Check your responses to Revision Exercise 24.2 with other students and your teacher.

Part 2 Reading
1   These are rhetorical questions. The writer is expressing the opinion that these claims cannot be ignored.
2   The key sentence is in Line 25. Discuss what this means.
3   In the first instance, 'the Absolute' acts as a noun, referring to the Supreme Being, God. In the second instance (L34), absolute is simply an adjective.
4   A contingent world is a dependent world, ever-changing. It is not its own cause.

Part 3 Reading
1 1 The world….   Topic sentence
   2 …   Repetition of idea in sentence one
   3 …   Example or illustration of general idea
   4 …   Result or outcome
   5 …   Repetition of idea in different words
   6 …   Local experience of the key idea
   7 …   Summary or definition

2 Words which reveal writer's more personal attitude: L7 'We who are born to a rich diversity . . . are fortunate' (note the adjectives – positive evaluation). L20 'rich meaning of pluralism' – again, positive evaluation of pluralism. L35 'destructive' – negative evaluation.

Part 4 Reading

1. New expression is 'religious pluralism'; old one – 'theology of religions'.
2. Change in perspective because of new understanding that it is not a matter of evaluating the different religions, but of attempting to understand God's purpose in the fact of the plurality of religions.
3. It = the new perspective referred to in L7-9.
4. We hear the author's voice – L1-13, L27-34; and we hear the voice of the Indian Theological Association (L19-26).
5.   i) L 9-11 'It searches more deeply . . . are surrounded.'
    ii) L29-34 'The question . . . and cross-fertilisation.'

APPENDIX C List of sources of published texts used.

Azyumardi Azra, A, 2001, "Islam and Christianity in Indonesia: the roots of conflict and hostility", in Camilleri, J, editor, *Religion and Culture in Asia Pacific: Violence or Healing?*, Vista Publications, Melbourne, pp 84-92.

Balasuriya, T, 1988, "Emerging Theologies of Asian Liberation" in Boff, L & Elizondo, V, editor, *Theologies of the Third World: Convergences and Differences*, T&T Clark, Edinburgh, pp 35-45.

Barber, CI, 1972, *The Story of Language*, Pan Books, London and Sydney.

Baum, G, 1989, "Structures of Sin", in Baum G & Ellsberg, R, editors, *The Logic of Solidarity*, Orbis, Maryknoll, New York, pp 110-126.

Beker, JC, 1994, *Suffering and Hope,* Eerdmans Publishing Co, Grand Rapids, Michigan, 2nd edition.

Bettscheider, H, 1999, "Truth in Interreligious Dialogue", in *Verbum SVD*, 40:1, Steyler Verlag, The Netherlands, pp 25-40.

Boff, L, 1984, *Liberating Grace*, Orbis Books, New York.

Borg, MJ, 1995, *Meeting Jesus Again for the First Time*, HarperCollins, New York.

Bouma-Prediger, S, 1995, *The Greening of Theology*, Scholars Press, Atlanta, Georgia.

Bourke, V, editor, 1962, *The Pocket Aquinas*, Washington Square Press, New York.

Byrne, B, 1990, *Inheriting the Earth*, St Paul's, Homebush, New South Wales.

Calemba Sivarramurti, Orissa, India, in Hill, BR, 1998, *Christian Faith and the Environment*, Orbis Books, Maryknoll, New York.

Caritas Australia Newsletter, No 89, 2002, North Sydney.

Carr, A, 1986, "On Feminist Spirituality", in Wolski Conn, J, editor, *Women's Spirituality: Resources for Christian Development*, Paulist, New York, pp 49-50.

Catholic Bishops of the Philippines, "What is happening to our beautiful land?", Pastoral Letter on Ecology, in McDonagh, S, 1990, *The Greening of the Church*, Canterbury Press, Scoresby, Victoria, Appendix 2.

Dancy, J, 1985, *Contemporary Epistemology*, Blackwell, Oxford.

Dewey, J, 1994, "The Gospel of Mark", in Schussler-Fiorenza, E, editor, *Searching the Scriptures*, Crossroad, New York, pp 470-509.

Dobbs-Higginson, MS, 1993, *Asia Pacific: Its Role in the New World Disorder,* Heinneman, Australia.

Dreyer, E, 1990, *Manifestations of Grace*, Michael Glazier Inc., Delaware.

Duffy, S, 1993, *The Dynamics of Grace*, Liturgical Press, Collegeville, Minnesota.

Dulles, A, 1983, *Models of Revelation*, Gill & Macmillan Ltd, Dublin.

Dupuis, J, 1997, *Toward A Christian Theology of Religious Pluralism*, Orbis Books, Maryknoll, New York.

Edwards, D, 1995, *Jesus the Wisdom of God: An Ecological Theology*, St Paul's, Homebush, New South Wales.

Evans, CA, 1996, "The Historical Jesus and the Deified Christ: How Did the One Lead to the Other?", in Porter, SE, editor, *The Nature of Religious Language*, Roehampton Institute London Papers 1, Sheffield Academic Press, Sheffield, pp. 47-67.

Fabella, V, 1993, "Christology from an Asian Woman's Perspective", in Sugirtharajah, RS, editor, *Asian Faces of Jesus*, SCM Press, London, pp 211-222.

Geertz, C, 1973, *The Interpretation of Cultures*, Basic Books, New York.

Goosen, G & Tomlinson, M, 1994, *Studying the Gospels: An Introduction*, Dwyer, Sydney.

Haught, J, 1988, *The Revelation of God in History*, Michael Glazier, Wilmington, Delaware.

Havea, Sione 'Amanaki, 1987, "Christianity in the Pacific Context", in *South Pacific Theology*, Papers from the Consultation on Pacific Theology, Papua New Guinea, pp. 11-15.

Hellwig, M., 1993, *What Are the Theologians Saying Now?*, CollinsDove, North Blackburn, Victoria.

Hill, BR, 1998, *Christian Faith and the Environment*, Orbis, New York.

Holland, J & Henriot, P, 1986, *Social Analysis*, Dove & Orbis, Washington.

John Paul II, 1979, *Redemptor Hominis*, para 18, St. Paul Publication.
——— Message for World Day of Peace, 2000.
——— Message for World Day of Peace, 2001.

Johnson, E, 1990, *Consider Jesus*, Chapman, London.
——— 1994, *She Who Is*, Crossroad, New York.

Kelly, G, 1992, "Dominican Spirituality and Tradition", in *Dominican Ashram*, Vol 11 No 3, pp 99-107.

Kiley, B, 1995, *Jesus in Mark's Gospel*, St Paul's, Homebush, N.S.W.

Kirk, M, 1997, *Let Justice Flow: An Asian Woman Works Creatively for the Liberation of Her People*, ISPCK, Delhi.

Kung, H, 1978, *On Being a Christian*, Collins Fount Paperbacks, Glasgow.

Lonergan, B, 1971, *Method in Theology*, Darton, Longman & Todd, London.

Lumentut, A, 1980, Address to the General Assembly of the Council of Churches in Indonesia, Tomohon, North Sulawesi, in Appendix, Kirk, M., 1997, *Let Justice Flow*, ISPCK, Delhi, pp 221-222.

McBrien, RP, 1994, *Catholicism*, CollinsDove, North Blackburn, Victoria.

McDermott, B, 1984, *What are they saying about the grace of Christ?*, Paulist Press, NewYork.

McDonagh, S, 1986, *To Care for the Earth: A Call to a New Theology*, Chapman, London.

McFague, S, 1982, *Metaphorical Theology*, SCM Press, London.

McGinn, B & Meyendorff, J, editors, 1985, *Christian Spirituality Origins to the Twelfth Century*, SCM Press, London.

Moltmann, J, 1992, *The Spirit of Life*, SCM Press, London.

Moltmann-Wendel, E, 1994, "Is There a Feminist Theology of the Cross?", in Tesfai, Y, editor, *The Scandal of a Crucified World: Perspectives on the Cross and Suffering*, Orbis Books, Maryknoll, New York, pp 87-98.

Mueller, J, 1984, *What are they saying about theology?*, Paulist Press, New York.

O'Connell Killen, P & de Beer, J, 1995, *The Art of Theological Reflection*, Crossroad, New York.

Ojoy, VA, 1997, "The emerging spirituality in the Philippine Church: its projected impact on the economic and socio-political dimensions of society", in *Justitia*, Vol 4, Dominican Province of the Philippines, Manila, pp 19-27.

Ormerod, N, 1990, *Introducing Contemporary Theology*, EJ Dwyer, Sydney.
——— 1992, *Grace and Disgrace*, EJ Dwyer, Sydney.

Pannenberg, W, 1991, *Systematic Theology*, Vol 1, translated by G Bromiley, T&T Clark, Edinburgh.

Pedregosa, QT et al, 1998, "Asia: its challenges and opportunities to the Order of Preachers", in *Justitia*, Vol 5, Dominican Province of the Philippines, Manila, pp 1-14.

Peters, Ted, 1998, 'Genes, Theology and Social Ethics: Are We Playing God?' in Peters, Ted, editor, *Genetics Issues of Social Justice*, The Pilgrim Press, Cleveland.
——— 2003, "The Genesis and Genetics of Sin", in Reid, D, and Worthing, M, editors, *Sin and Salvation*, ATF Press, pp 89-112.

Piepke, JG, 1999, "Inculturation and Beyond", in *Verbum SVD*, Volume 40 No 1, Steyler Verlag, Netherlands, pp 43-53.

Pius XII, 1943, *Divino Afflante Spiritu.*

Porter, SE, editor, 1996, *The Nature of Religious Language*, Sheffield, UK. Press, New York.

Rae, SB & Cox, PM, 1999, *Bioethics A Christian Approach in a Pluralist Age*, Eerdmans, Grand Rapids, Michigan.

Rahner, K, 2000, "Experiences of a Catholic Theologian", in *Theological Studies 61*, Marquette University, Milwaukee, pp 3-15.

Richard, L, 1992, *What are they saying about the theology of suffering?*, Paulist Press, New York.

Riley, M, 1989, "Feminist Analysis: A Missing Perspective", in Baum & Ellsberg (editors), *The Logic of Solidarity,* Orbis, New York, pp 186-201.

Schillebeeckx, E, 1979, *Jesus, An Experiment in Christology*, Collins, London.
——— 1980, *Christ, the Experience of Jesus as Lord*, Crossroad, New York.

Schneiders, S, 1993, "The Bible and Feminism", in LaCugna, CM, editor, *Freeing Theology*, HarperSanFrancisco, pp 31-57.

Shannon, TA, 1998, "Genetics, Ethics and Theology: The Roman Catholic Discussion", in Peters, Ted, editor, *Genetics,* The Pilgrim Press, Cleveland, Ohio, pp 170-171.

Smart, N, 1989, *The World's Religions*, Cambridge University Press, Cambridge.

Smith, C, 1987, *The Way of Paradox*, Darton, Longman & Todd, London.

Sugirtharajah, RS, editor, 1993, *Asian Faces of Jesus*, SCM Press, London.

Synod of Bishops, 1971, *Justice in the World*, Rome.

The Tablet, London.

Ting, KH, "Address to the Lutheran World Federation", in Yeow Choo Lak, editor, 1999, *Doing Theology with Asian Resources, Mission and Human Ecology,* Vol 4, Association for Theological Education in South East Asia, Manila, pp 158-163.

Tirimanna, V, 2000, "Theologising in Asia: Pluralism, Relativism and Subjectivism', *The Asia Journal of Theology*, Vol 14, No 1, April, pp 57-67.

Tracy, D, Kung, H & Metz, JB, editors 1978, *Toward Vatican III*, Concilium, Seabury, New York.

Vatican II, Constitution on the Sacred Liturgy, para. 10.
——— Church in the Modern World, para. 53.

Yewangoe, AA, 1987, *Theologia Crucis in Asia*, Rodopi, Amsterdam.

Evaluation—Feedback *English for Theology*

Thank you for using the first volume of *English for Theology*. To assist us in possible future editions of this book and/or production of a further volume of English language resources for theology or religious studies students from non-English speaking backgrounds, we would be grateful for your evaluation and feedback.

In your response, it may be helpful to consider the following aspects as a guide:

    A. Overall focus of the book—ie major focus on reading skills
    B. Grammatical and linguistic features   **C.** Types of exercises
    D. Texts or topics selected   **E.** Format   **F.** Any other aspect

1. What would make this book more useful for your purposes?
    i) What would you like to see CHANGED?

    ii) What you like to see ADDED?

2. Would you be interested in a further volume of language development resources in theology (or related discipline, eg religious studies) for students from non-English speaking backgrounds?

    YES/NO (Please circle your answer)

3. If **YES** to question 2, what would you like to see included in a further volume?

4. Your overall comment on the usefulness of this book?

OPTIONAL INFORMATION

Your name: ....Teacher or student?: ....

Your country: ....

Name of institution where the book was used: ....

Place where you bought the book: ....
If you would like to be advised of future editions please supply your contact details:

Please remove this page from the book and send to:
    ATF Press, PO Box 504, Hindmarsh SA 5007
    AUSTRALIA
    or
    FAX + 61 8 8340 34 50

Ingram Content Group UK Ltd.
Milton Keynes UK
UKHW051808120723
425029UK00003B/7